Narwhal:
Revealing an Arctic Legend

Edited by
William W. Fitzhugh
and
Martin T. Nweeia

Published by
IPI Press & Arctic Studies Center,
National Museum of Natural History,
Smithsonian Institution

Distributed by
University Press of New England

This book is the companion to the exhibit
Narwhal: Revealing An Arctic Legend
at the Smithsonian Institution's National
Museum of Natural History opening
August, 2017.

Copyright © 2017
Arctic Studies Center/Smithsonian Institution

Library of Congress control number
9780996748018

ISBN 978-0-9967480-1-8

Design: Harp and Company Graphic Design

Post Office Box 212
Hanover, New Hampshire 03755

The Arctic Studies Center
Department of Anthropology
Natural History Building, MRC 112
The Smithsonian Institution
PO Box 37012
10th and Constitution, NW
Washington, DC 20013–7012

0.0 Seasons of the Inuit

This illustrations shows the seasons of the year as described by Inuit tradition and the animals and changes they experience during the course of a year. The illustration was painted by the Cape Dorset Inuit artist, Kenojuak Ashevak (1927–2013).

(credit: Dorset Fine Arts)

MAP KEY: *Nearly all the world's narwhals live in just a few places.*

Narwhal Population Range

Narwhal Population Range (rare sightings)

Summer Sea Ice Range

Winter Sea Ice Range

Map made using ArcGIS® software by Esri with Natural Earth
raster map data from naturalearthdata.com (2012)

CHINA

RUSSIA

West
Siberia

SEA of
OKHOTSK

East
Siberia

LAPTEV SEA

KARA SEA

Novaya Zemlya

BARENTS
SEA

FINLAND

SWEDE

NORW

Arctic Circle

ARCTIC OCEAN

NORWEGIAN
SEA

Spitsbergen

NORT
SEA

Chukotka
Peninsula

CHUKCHI
SEA

GREENLAND
SEA

ICELAN

*Ellesmere
Island*

Arctic Circle

Alaska
(U.S.)

BEAUFORT SEA

GREENLAND
(DENMARK)

GULF of
ALASKA

BAFFIN
BAY

• POND INLET

Baffin Island

Northwest
Territories

Nunavut

ATLANTIC

CANADA

LABRADOR
SEA

OCEAN

HUDSON
BAY

Quebec

Labrador

Newfoundlan

Table of Contents

xii   **Preface**
Kirk Johnson, Sant Director, National Museum of Natural History, Smithsonian Institution

xv   **A World of Questions**
Martin T. Nweeia, Harvard School of Dental Medicine, Case Western Reserve University School of Dental Medicine and Smithsonian Institution
William W. Fitzhugh, Smithsonian Institution and Dartmouth College

Part 1: The Narwhal World

3   **Chapter 1**
What is a Whale?
Joy S. Reidenberg, Mount Sinai School of Medicine

33   **Chapter 2**
The Universally Beloved Unicorn
Barbara Boehm, The Metropolitan Museum of Art

Part 2: Tooth to Tail

41   **Chapter 3**
Narwhal Biology: An Overview
Cortney A. Watt, Fisheries and Oceans Canada

54   **Listening to Narwhals**
Marianne Marcoux, Fisheries and Oceans Canada

55   **The Physics of Flukes**
Frank Fish, West Chester University

59   **Chapter 4**
The Extraordinary Narwhal Tooth
Frederick C. Eichmiller, Delta Dental of Wisconsin
David H. Pashley, School of Medicine, Georgia Health Sciences University

66   **Whale In the Net!**
Jack R. Orr, Fisheries and Oceans Canada
Sandra Black, University of Calgary

68   **Making Sense of the Tusk**
Martin T. Nweeia, Harvard School of Dental Medicine, Case Western Reserve University School of Dental Medicine and Smithsonian Institution

71   **Chapter 5**
Narwhal DNA
Winston P. Kuo, CloudHealth Genomics
John Wilkin, University of California, Santa Barbara
Alexander J. Trachtenberg, StART for Families, Inc.
Pedro A. F. Galante, Hospital Sirio-Libanes, Sao Paulo
Lucila Ohno-Machado, University of California San Diego
Baojun Beryl Gao, CloudHealth Genomics
Jason G. Jin, CloudHealth Genomics

80   **Why Sequence Whole Genomes?**
Daniel L. Distel, Northeastern University

82   **The Narwhal Genome Initiative: A Progress Report**
Martin T. Nweeia, Harvard School of Dental Medicine, Case Western Reserve University School of Dental Medicine and Smithsonian Institution
Jeremy Johnson, Broad Institute of MIT and Harvard
Elinor Karlsson, Broad Institute of MIT and Harvard

85   **Chapter 6**
Deep Time: the Narwhal and Beluga Fossil Record
Ryan Paterson, Canadian Museum of Nature
Natalia Rybczynski, Carleton University and Canadian Museum of Nature
David J. Bohaska, Smithsonian Institution
Vladimir V. Pitulko, Institute of Material Culture Studies, Russian Academy of Sciences

89   **Narwhals and Climate**
R. Ewan Fordyce, University of Otago

0.1 Arctic Regions Showing Summer Sea Ice and Narwhal Distribution (map: K. Moeller)

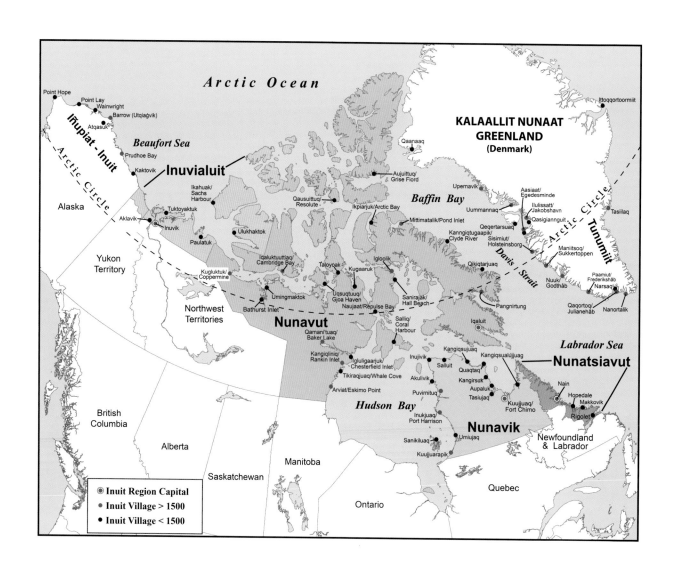

**0.2 North American Arctic showing Canadian territories
of Nunavut (pink), Nunavik (green), and Inuvialuit (tan),
and settlements in regions visited by narwhals.**
(map: D. Cole, K. Moeller)

Part 3: Narwhal and Inuit

93   Chapter 7
Qaujimajatuqangit: Inuit Knowledge
and Modern Life
Henry P. Huntington, Pew Charitable Trust
Kristin Westdal, Oceans North Canada

102   Nunavut Government Symbols
Nunavut Legislative Assemby, Canada

105   Chapter 8
Inuit and Narwhal
David S. Lee, Nunavut Tunngavik Incorporated
George W. Wenzel, McGill University

123   Chapter 9
Inuit Contributions to Narwhal Knowledge
Martin T. Nweeia, Harvard School of Dental Medicine,
*   Case Western Reserve University School of Dental*
*   Medicine and Smithsonian Institution*
David Angnatsiak, Hunter, Pond Inlet,
*   Nunavut, Canada*
Pavia Nielsen, Hunter, Uummannaq, Greenland
Cornelius Nutarak, Hunter (Deceased), Pond Inlet,
*   Nunavut, Canada*

PART 4: The Narwhal Future

135   Chapter 10
Climate and the Changing Arctic
Mark C. Serreze, Arctic Snow and Ice Data Center
*   and University of Colorado*

146   Narwhals and the Global Mercury Issue
Rune Dietz, Aarhus University
Christian Sonne, Aarhus University

148   As Goes the Arctic...
Luc Bas, International Union for the Conservation
*   of Nature*

150   Narwhal: An Uncertain Future
Steven H. Ferguson, Fisheries and Oceans Canada
David S. Lee, Nunavut Tunngavik Incorporated

154   The Last Ice Area
Clive Tesar, World Wildlife Fund

157   Chapter 11
Arctic Change, Resource Extraction, and
Inuit Communities in Nunavut
Noor Johnson, Smithsonian Institution

170   Drowning in Noise
Christopher W. Clark, Cornell University

173   Rethinking Human Development
Pamela Peeters, Institute for a Sustainable Planet

174   Now is the Time
Melanie Lancaster and Brandon LaForest,
*   World Wildlife Fund*

177   Chapter 12
Out of the Arctic, Into the Smithsonian:
Making the Narwhal Exhibition
Laura Donnelly-Smith, Smithsonian Institution

191   Contributors

202   Acknowledgments

207   References

228   Index

233   Credits

0.3 Hunting a "cheval marin" in the Barents Sea from Pierre Martin de La Martinière's Voyages de la Pais Septentrionaux. *(De le Martinière 1671: 140)*

In the summer of 1985, I was part of a paleontological survey of western Axel Heiberg Island in the Canadian High Arctic. Four of us were camped on Strand Fiord, mapping geology and searching for fossils. On our first morning we set out on a four-mile trek along the north shore. The fiord was not frozen but it was clogged with icebergs and smaller bergs were piled along the shoreline. This was polar bear habitat and the abundance of sea ice next to the beach spooked me, so I climbed up the slope until I was 400 yards from the water. My colleague, Cliff Morrow from the Carnegie Museum, was less fearful and stayed below. I kept a wary eye on Cliff as he hiked along the beach ridge below me. Suddenly he started jumping up and down and yelling. At first I thought he had seen a bear but then it became clear that he was happy, not scared. I rushed down to join him and discovered he had found a

narwhal skull, complete with a 7-foot long ivory tusk. Its location on the raised beach ridge suggested it was thousands of years old. This was a remarkably lucky bit of beachcombing for Cliff, and it was my fear, however reasonable, that prevented me from being the one to make the find. Thirty-two years later, the skull resides in the Canadian Museum of Nature in Ottawa, and my missed moment of discovery still nags me.

Since that day, I have been fascinated with these mysterious Arctic whales. I've searched in vain for them on cruises to east and west

0.4 Kirk Johnson and
Leo Hickey on the
Kanguk River, Strand Fiord,
Axel Heiberg Island,
Nunavut, Canada, 1985.
(credit: Kirk Johnson)

Greenland and Baffin Island. My timing has never been right, until
now. With the opening of the Narwhal exhibition at the National Museum
of Natural History in August, 2017, I need only to walk down two flights
of stairs to encounter a host of information about this curious cetacean, the
scientists that study it, and the Inuit people who have subsisted on it for
centuries.

Exhibit text is sparse for good reason but there is much to learn about
narwhals and this book provides a broad overview of an animal that most
people have never even considered. Without question, the tusk of the
narwhal is the origin of the unicorn misconception, but real narwhal are
far more fascinating than mythical tusked horses. This svelte book
provides a comprehensive view of the animal and the diverse array of
people who find themselves drawn to it and its icy world.

Kirk Johnson
Sant Director
National Museum of Natural History
Smithsonian Institution

A World of Questions

Martin T. Nweeia and William W. Fitzhugh

Narwhal. The word embodies so many images, real, imaginary, and mythical. Though narwhals have shared the planet with us for thousands of years, many people are not aware that the species is still alive today, let alone 180,000 strong.

The narwhal enters our daily lives in the most peculiar ways. Campaign operations during the 2012 Obama election were called "Project Narwhal." Tech start-ups in Canada valued at over one billion are referred to as "narwhals," a reference by venture capitalist Aileen Lee to their rarity. The movie "Elf", grossing a quarter of a billion dollars, and the ad campaign by telecom giant Sprint continued the entrée of this elusive Arctic whale into our conversations.

0.5 View of Qaarsut
Ubiquitous poppies frame this village on the Nuussuaq Peninsula that combines colorful Danish charm and a modern Inuit settlement amidst the grandeur of the glaciated Greenland Arctic landscape. (photo: W. Richard)

0.6 The Wondrous Narwhal
This sociable creature is the least known of all Arctic mammals. (photo: G. Williams)

The most prominent and noteworthy part of this Arctic denizen is its unusual tusk which inspired legends of the unicorn one thousand years ago. Two Flemish tapestry series, the *Hunt of the Unicorn* at The Met Cloisters Museum in New York, and the *Lady and the Unicorn* series at the Musée de Cluny Museum in Paris have captivated millions of art seekers whose curiosity stems from fascination with the mythology of the unicorn—the most popular mythological creature for children of all ages. The tusk protruding from the unicorn's head is depicted as a narwhal tusk with its unique spiral twist.

0.7 Lady and the Unicorn
One of six tapestries woven around 1500 from wool with silk embroidery, this one is titled À mon seul désir, of obscure meaning but thought to represent love or understanding. The tapestries were sponsored by a nobles connected with the French court and are often cited as among the finest art of the middle ages. (Musée National du Moyen Âge, formerly Cluny Museum, Paris)

The narwhal tusk was also highly prized by aristocracy, formed in royal scepters in at least three countries, a Danish royal throne, and even an entryway to a palace in Japan. Narwhal tusk ground into a fine powder was the most sought-after antidote to the potential poisoning of kings in the middle ages. Danish explorers brought back these prized tusks, one of which could buy a castle in the 17th century. Science has also been intrigued with the tusk since the writings of Albertus Magnus in 1450. Since then, biologists, physiologists, and marine mammal researchers have drawn conclusions that help piece together our understanding of the narwhal and its unique tusk. And still, unanswered questions arise.

The Mystery Unfolds

Narwhal: Revealing an Arctic Legend is a tale of curiosity, as modern day science unravels the spiraled tusk and examines this iconic whale of a tooth. Readers discover the narwhal, the Inuit who live among narwhals, and the changing Arctic ecosystem during a time of climate change that impacts the region at double the amount and rate of the planet. What we encounter is the fascination of discovery. Each new finding leads to a hundred more questions. And we are still uncovering many of those questions!

- How does a whale that dives to a depth of 4,500 feet adapt to such sudden pressure changes?

- How is this broad spectrum sound scale from 300 Hz to over 100 kHz used in the palate of communication? (Narwhals have signature vocalizations, so, yes, Uncle Joe likely knows Aunt Betty's voice!)
- How do we explain the most extraordinary tooth in nature? (The narwhal tusk is nature's only straight, spiraled, and unusually flexible and strong tusk.)
- How did the narwhal tusk form at the expense of twelve other teeth, whose growth is "silenced" at birth?
- How do narwhals catch their food, when most of the fish they eat swim faster than they do?
- How is the narwhal faring with rapidly melting ice and changing Arctic climate?
- How does this climate change affect the lives of Inuit communities living with and dependent on narwhals?

Answering the growing list of intriguing questions required teams of researchers from myriad backgrounds, armed with new approaches and cutting-edge science. The curious mind needed to expand. Even the senses of the investigators had to be challenged. We had to listen more carefully to the Inuit voices that give insights and observations that hundreds of years of scientific collection could not provide. We had to see with a new set of eyes equipped with visual images from CT, MRI, and electron microscopy. Scientists had to jump into the water with the whales, yes, even in 36° F waters, and touch the magnificent creatures that challenge their methods

and minds. All the senses would be needed, paralleling the Flemish tapestries of the unicorn, one for each sense. Like the tapestries, each thread of a discipline would help form a new vision and understanding of the narwhal.

In the pages that follow, the exploration begins, first with understanding what defines a whale. This is not such an easy task as descriptions include ways to differentiate them from other aquatic animals and from other marine mammals like walrus and seal. When the unusual tusked *Odobenocetops* was discovered off the coast of Peru, the debate began between those who thought it was a walrus and others who claimed it was a whale (see Chapter 6). The scientists finally settled it: it was a whale.

0.8 Narwhal Throne
This throne representing the power of the Danish Kingdom and the combined Danish and Norwegian Kingdom (1671–1814), was commissioned by King Frederick III (r. 1648–1670) and created between 1662 and 1671 by Bendix Grodtschilling. The narwhal tusk uprights drew of the magical power of the unicorn and Danish-Norwegian practical knowledge of the narwhal. Gilded elements were later additions. (Royal Danish Collection; photo: J. Meehan)

Who would imagine that whales are related to ungulates, cows, deer, and even camels (Chapter 5)? And why the division between baleen whales that filter feed and toothed whales that consume larger fish (Chapter 1)? We learn about a chambered stomach, a spine that moves up and down, so different from the side-to-side movements of fish. And hair? Yes, hair that forms whiskers, often sensory. Whales are smart by many measures and we establish a deeper understanding of their intelligence.

Next we learn how the narwhal has captured our imagination as the one-horned irrepressible unicorn and about 13th-century medicines using narwhal tusk to cure leprosy, epilepsy, and even constipation (Chapter 2). Ground tusk was a highly sought antidote for poisoning, the major threat to kings in the middle ages. We learn about Flemish tapestries that depict the narwhal, and their unusual origins and place in art history.

We explore the narwhal from tooth to tail, highlighting the biology that brings scientists together to better understand this Arctic cetacean. Teams of researchers attach satellite tags on narwhals to observe their movements, migration, distribution, and diving depths. Tags also record narwhal sounds, and their body movements even as they swim through variable gradients of salinity. Other researchers are examining fluke and fin movements to better understand narwhal locomotion. Laboratory analysis of body tissue like fatty acids gives scientists an indicator of the narwhal diet. And teams investigate the function of the narwhal tusk, an evolutionary mystery that has intrigued and baffled the scientific community.

One team investigates the narwhal tusk as a sensory organ system, and we follow them on a quest that reveals millions of sensory connections to the outside environment (Chapter 4). The tusk is capable of detecting changing salt gradients! We examine the unusual asymmetrical tusk expression, with one commonly erupted tusk on the left side approaching two to three meters and one embedded tusk on the right usually no longer than half a meter. We consider the great difference in the expression of teeth between males and females, as many females only express the embedded tusk.

Throughout the scientific quest, we begin to witness the passion, dedication, and persistence of scientists in the often harsh Arctic environment as they collect information and data that can produce one more piece of the puzzle in the understanding of narwhal biology. As much as we know, there is much more that we do not know. We hope to inspire a new generation of young scientists as they quest for new approaches and seek pathways of innovation to discover more about this elusive Arctic marine mammal.

0.9 Narwhal Science
*An international team of biologists and veterinary scientists have conducted experiments on captured narwhals in northern Baffin Island. Tests include basic biology and studies of tusk function. Whales are captured with a net and are held for a brief period before release. All studies are done in accordance with legal and ethical conventions established to protect animal safety and emotional status.
(photo: C. Wright)*

Though the narwhal is closely related to the beluga, we learn that the evolutionary background for the narwhal branches in varied and not always predictable paths. For example, we discover that whales share a common ancestor with the hippopotamus; we learn that the predecessors of modern whales are derived from artiodactyl origins—hooved animals like cows and deer. We are guided through studies concluding that toothed whales gave rise to toothed-plus-baleen whales (which are now extinct) and subsequently, living baleen whales.

How do we gather more information when there is such limited evolutionary background for the narwhal? A team of researchers has sequenced and assembled the genomes of the male and female narwhal. Often described as the blueprints and instruction manual, an organism's genome has the vital background information to provide scientists with a way to compare other genomes and discover similarities and differences that can help address evolution and the expression of various features. For example, four sensory genes associated with the tooth-producing area of the narwhal tusk were discovered, indicating sensory tissue and function. Investigators can then compare this gene expression with other tusked animals or with other whales as teams are now actively doing. Genetic similarities may provide a unique result that brings together animals with similar expression, the way biologic features like echolocation can expose the similarities between whales and bats.

An Arctic Nightingale

Part of the unfolding of the narwhal mystery is closely linked to its habitat in the world's icy and inaccessible High Arctic. Greeks of the fourth century BCE called the northernmost region of the known world "Ultima Thule," a place of frozen seas and terrifying storms hardly imaginable to Mediterranean peoples. How did they ever learn of such a place? Who brought back such information? How did early writers like the Roman naturalist Claudius Aelianus (170–235 CE) know to describe the unicorn tusk as a straight, spiraled form when it is unknown anywhere else in nature? By the middle ages narwhal tusks must have become available in the cabinets of royalty. Had they come from Saame or other Finno-Ugric peoples of the Arctic coast of Russia and Scandinavia, which is within the known range of narwhal distribution at least during cold climatic periods?

A more likely source of narwhal tusks, if not knowledge of the animal itself, would have been through Viking connections during the Scandinavian Iron Age and Viking times, between 500–900 CE. Narwhals are not yet known from European archaeological sites, probably because they lived well north of the Nordic coasts during the warm Viking and Medieval periods. Walrus ivory was well-known however, as documented in a report from the court of King Alfred the Great of Wessex, remarking on a walrus tusk presented by the Viking trader Ohthere around 890 CE. Elephant ivory, prized for Catholic Church relics, had become scarce in Europe after the Muslim expansion across North Africa and consequently became important to the Greenland Norse of the 11th to 15th centuries. But unlike walrus ivory, it was the form of the narwhal tusk—not its ivory—that gave value. Unlike elephant or walrus ivory, which is massive and dense, narwhal tusks are a rope-like construction of loosely-bonded strands, making them less suitable for large carvings or implements, although they were used by Greenland Inuit for hunting spears.

Greenland Norse harvested walrus with spears in the Nordsetr hunting grounds around Disko Bay during the open-water summer season. Disko was prime winter habitat for narwhals, but they abandoned it for the more icy waters of northern Baffin Bay during summer. And they had to be taken with harpoons, an Inuit technology not known to the Norse. For these reasons Norse may have obtained narwhal tusks second-hand from Dorset or Thule Inuit met during their annual hunting expeditions in the Disko region near Inuit homelands. The arrival of these tusks in Europe came with a mystique as elusive as the function of its famed tusk today. Their mysterious power lay in their origin from an imagined animal in an imagined place at the edge of the known world, a world well-populated in European myth by exotic creatures and beings. Not until Martin Frobisher's voyages of 1576–78 do we find the tusk attached to its proper Arctic owner. Frobisher is reputed to have presented a narwhal tusk to Queen Elizabeth, a principal supporter of his 16th-century North-west Passage expeditions.

Today this imaginary place is better known than the animal itself. Frobisher's desolate wastes are now traversed by military submarines, ore freighters, and sportsmen seeking the North Pole or circumnavigating Ellesmere and Svalbard in high-tech kayaks. Distant Early Warning radar bases have replaced Inuit skin tents. Cold War military installations opened up the North to biologists, oceanographers, anthropologists, and archaeologists who followed in the footsteps of pioneering navigators and explorers like Frobish-er, Hudson, Franklin, Parry, Rae, Peary, Rasmussen, and many others. The 20th-century arrival of planes, helicopters, snowmobiles, and motor boats,

replacing kayaks, dog teams, and foot travel, transformed physical access in the same way that satellite, GPS, and web technology revolutionized communication.

And yet, much about the narwhal habitat has not changed. The animals flourish in a circumpolar distribution coinciding with the southern fringe of the Arctic pack ice. These are regions where few, if any, peoples have ever lived. Even early Arctic explorers after the 1500s rarely encountered narwhals. Narwhals live where we

0.10 Narwhal Lance
This sea mammal hunting lance has a meteoric iron blade originating from the Cape York meteor fall in Northwest Greenland. Meteoric iron contains nickel, which resists rust, while the rivets must have come from smelted Norse or recent European iron. (photo: British Museum, Wikipedia Commons)

0.11 Narwhal Cup
Due to magical properties, drinking cups made from narwhal ivory were used by royalty to detoxify poison, a common cause of death for monarchs and tyrants alike. (Royal Danish Collections 5-320; photo: K. Weiss)

0.12 Drumming the Narwhal

This drawing by Dawn Katsak illustrates the reverence that Inuit have for an animal that figures prominently in their spiritual beliefs and subsistence activities. (photo: W. Richard)

cannot go: amidst the wind-blown, current-sensitive, shifting Arctic ice pack. Only for short periods in summer do they approach land or the shore-fast floe edge. No wonder they have continued to be so mysterious, even to naturalists. Inuit are more enlightened, but even their knowledge is based on a narrow slice of observation.

Some things we do know. Its food consists of Arctic cod, halibut, squid, and other species that range from the near surface to inky black waters thousands of feet deep. We are beginning to get inklings of its acoustic signaling, but how it communicates with its group and locates and eats it food, and whether the tusk plays a role in its diet, are all unknown. Most of this scientific work has to be done in summer, so its winter behavior is the least known of all.

Most of us imagine the narwhal habitat through the lens of a camera. We see the animals skimming the surface, breathing, and diving for food. Their skyhopping with heads and tusks in the air, sometimes with two animals rubbing their tusks in what appears like social grooming, suggest complex social behaviors. Recent recordings showing a range of narwhal sounds and investigation of their echolocation abilities begin to reveal the capabilities known for bowheads and other whales more accessible to scientists. Increasing reports of orca encounters and the responses of narwhals seeking safety in thick ice or shallow waters, reducing sound emissions, and other behavior adjustments, give us clues about narwhal survival strategies and intelligence. These scientific reports remind us how little we know and why it is important to preserve narwhal habitat and reduce pollution and other impacts resulting from Arctic warming and increasing commercial enterprise.

Despite their remote habitat and isolation, narwhals and humans share a history that began thousands of years ago. Until the invention of the toggling harpoon sometime around six to eight thousand years ago, whales and humans led largely separate existences. Small whales like pilot whales and beluga can be driven into shallow bays or rivers where they become stranded and can be killed. Petroglyphs depicting such hunts in Chinese rivers may be thousands of years old. But open-sea hunting of medium-size and larger whales relied on a complex technology including toggling harpoons and floats, techniques that were developed first by Asian North Pacific and Bering Sea peoples only after 500 CE. The prehistoric Palaeoeskimo peoples of Arctic Canada and Greenland hunted seals and by 2,000 years ago began hunting walrus with toggling harpoons. Narwhal tusk and bone implements are sometimes found in 3,500-year-old Greenland Saqqaq sites, in Labrador Dorset and Inuit sites, including Avayalik, Anniowaktook, and Adlavik, but there is little evidence of systematic harvesting of this animal until the 20th-century appearance of rifles (Chapter 8).

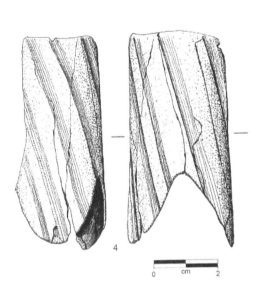

0.13 Narwhal Society
Narwhals travel in groups of related animals and their emergence above water often appears to reflect a curiosity about the world above water. (photo: G. Williams)

0.14 Saqqaq Container
One of the earliest finds made of narwhal tusk is a small tubular container excavated from a 3,500-year-old Saqqaq culture site in West Greenland. (B. Grønnow 1994: 232)

0.15 A Woman Who Became a Narwhal
This print illustrates the Inuit origin story of the narwhal by Canadian Inuit artist, Germaine Arnaktauyok of Yellowknife, and was loaned to the narwhal exhibition by Judith Varney Burch. (photo: S. Loring)

Until recently human activity in narwhal habitat has been limited or non-existent. Prehistoric human occupation of High Arctic Greenland and Canada has been sporadic since humans arrived 4,500 years ago. Pre-Dorset, Dorset, and Thule-culture occupations of these regions took place during warm climatic episodes when open-water polynias provided access to sea mammals, fish, and birds throughout the winter. Colder climates saw local extinction or southern retreat of these northerners to regions where game was more plentiful and open water was available in winter. None of the Canadian Thule and their Inuit descendants utilized narwhals to any great extent; but by the 19th-century, when Europeans first began document-ing traditional Inuit life, belugas and to a lesser extent, narwhals, were active-ly pursued. A similar pattern is seen in Greenland where Inuit communities, including Qannaq in the Thule District, and Uppernavik and Uummannaq on the mid-west coast, and Ittoqqortoormiit (Scoresbysund) and Tasilaq (Ammassalik) on the east coast, hunted narwhal consistently during the historical era. Introduction of the rifle and fast boats have contributed to the success of narwhal hunting, not only for food, but—as in Viking and medieval times—for income from sale of the tusk.

Narwhals and Inuit Today

In addition to studies directed specifically at the narwhal, our exhibition and book are concerned with their human neighbors, the Inuit. Early ethnographers like Otto Fabricius, Franz Boas, Kai Birket-Smith, and William Thalbitzer provide little information on the narwhal. They do however report a widespread myth that described the origin of the narwhal from a cruel mother who abused her blind child. Unknown to her, he magically regained his sight and while hunting with his mother asked her to tie the harpoon line around her waist while he searched for a small seal. But instead he harpooned a whale, which pulled her into the water where her hair became tangled with the harpoon line and she was transformed into a narwhal by Sedna, the goddess of the sea.

The association between Inuit and the narwhal became more pragmatic in 1953 when the Canadian government, wary of international claims on its northernmost Arctic Islands, recruited Inuit from food-stressed southern villages and placed them in new High Arctic villages like Resolute and Grise Fjord. Members of the existing Inuit community of Pond Inlet assisted the new arrivals, who struggled to survive during the first few years without

adequate housing and facilities. Protests from Inuit and others claiming that the government was using the Inuit as "human flagpoles" ultimately led to an official Canadian apology and reparations. One of the new resources these transplanted Inuit learned to hunt was the narwhal, which had long been a staple for the existing North Baffin Inuit communities of Clyde River and Pond Inlet. It is these villages, and those of northern Greenland, that have contributed most to the growing interest in, and knowledge about, the narwhal.

This book illustrates a profound change in the way information about the North is gathered and interpreted. Early explorers and later, anthropologists and ethnologists, documented what they learned from the Inuit about their lives, customs, stories, and technology. They collected artifacts and published ethnographies, and their collections and photographs were duly catalogued and stored in far-off archives and museums. By the 1980–90s these old ways of doing science became obsolete. Inuit had engaged in land claims leading to creation of a Home Rule government in Greenland (1979; extended in 2009) and the territorial government of Nunavut (1999). Inuit were receiving higher education; new transport systems facilitated the movement of people and goods; and satellite and mobile communications provided instantaneous contacts and emergency response to hunters and others in distress. Local people demanded

0.16 Pond Inlet Village
*One of the northernmost towns in the Canadian High Arctic, "Pond" (population: 1,617 in 2016) has a history stretching back to Dorset and Thule culture times. In the 1920s it was visited by Danish scholars during Knut Rasmussen's Fifth Thule Expedition, 1921–24. At that time a village in this location was called Mittimatalik, named after an Inuk who was buried here.
(photo: Getty 78711311)*

0.17 Qaanaaq Hunter
*In Qaanaaq, the Inughuit of Northwest Greenland have hunted narwhals since the arrival of the Thule Inuit culture in the 1300s. Today that hunt is conducted with a combination of traditional and modern vehicles.
(photo: B. Ovgaard)*

0.18 Arctic Bay Family
*During the narwhal
research projects friendships
blossomed in the several
communities visited in
Greenland and Baffin Island.
Here the Mucktar Akumalik
family gathered for a
memorable group shot.
(photo: J. Meehan)*

0.19 Entwined Narwhals
*These narwhals carved
from soapstone and ivory
by Kakee Peter (Kakee
Ningeeochiak) were loaned
to the Smithsonian's narwhal
exhibition by Drs. Michael
H. and Patricia Coopersmith.
(photo: J. Varney Burch)*

to play a part in the administration of their lands, the exploitation of their
mineral resources, and collaboration with authorities deciding on everything
from archaeological permits to hunting quotas. Changes in the conduct of
science came swiftly as well.

As reported in the pages that follow, a revolution has occurred in the way
cultural and biological research is being conducted. A good example of
the new approach is *The Meaning of Ice: People and Sea Ice in Three Arctic
Communities* (Gearheard et al. 2013). No longer are the Inuit seen as
"informants" or "by-standers" in the gathering and interpreting of data compiled by seasonal experts. Rather, everything from the formulation of the
research questions and project design to the field program and presentation
of results is being conducted in partnership with Inuit team members
who sometimes participate as co-authors in final publications. In researching narwhals outside investigators have learned that direct collaboration
unlocks centuries of Inuit knowledge (Inuit Qaujimajatuqangit) about
narwhal biology and behavior that scientists, with their limited exposure to
the animal, could never learn or access. With collaboration has come more
sensitivity to the local importance of the narwhal to Inuit subsistence,
gender roles, and community values.

*   *   *

During the past decade the narwhal has become one of the most
curious and iconic creatures on the planet. Known in disguise to
medieval Europeans and for thousands of years to High Arctic
Greenland and Canadian Inuit as a life-sustaining source of food
and raw materials, the narwhal today has become a messenger
from the Arctic about massive environmental changes taking place
in a little-known corner of the world. Even more than the polar
bear—its terrestrial partner of the icy cryosphere—the narwhal is
the sea-ice expert par excellence, hardly ever leaving the cover of
the Arctic ice pack. Its future and its very existence are linked to a
part of the world that, due to the surge in global warming, is

shrinking faster than any other ecozone on earth. Its habitat, the icy cover of the Arctic seas, is predicted to disappear in summer within the next few decades. What do we know about this majestic creature of the north? How can we learn more? How can we help ensure its future and the lives of the polar Inuit whose culture and sustenance, in part, depend on it?

This book, accompanying an exhibition produced by the Smithsonian Institution's National Museum of Natural History, reveals how little we know about an animal that has intrigued Arctic travelers since Viking times. Most of what was known from the middle ages was erroneous, like its ability to serve as an antidote for poisoned wine or to cure illness. A narwhal ivory cup made for King Frederick III of Denmark and Norway contains a miniature ship, also of narwhal ivory, that provided even more protection. Inuit used narwhal ivory for more prosaic purposes: harpoon foreshafts, sled runners, and small carvings. A small chunk of narwhal tusk in a 2,000-year old Dorset site near the northern tip of Labrador shows that early Inuit people near the southern geographic limit of narwhal distribution also knew this animal and must have told stories explaining its tusk during the long dark winter nights. Perhaps they, with their naturalist's age-old abilities of observation had come closer to solving the riddle of the tusk than five hundred years of intermittent glimpses by Western explorers and scientists.

Today narwhal science is advancing rapidly. New studies are benefitting from Inuit knowledge and participation in field projects; rapidly advancing technologists are allowing investigation of narwhal deep diving and foraging, echolocation and communication systems, dietary and physiology conditions. And yes, also the tusk! For the first time new questions are being asked, new methods applied, and Inuit are an integral part of these investigations.

Every week brings new findings. The mystery of the "the unicorn of the sea" is being replaced by solid facts. Our job now—as scientists, public, and Inuit—is to ensure new knowledge is put to best use to preserve and protect this marvelous creature that has inspired wonder, myth, financial gain, and curiosity for so many across the ages. At a time when our world is changing rapidly—especially in the Arctic—we need to see the narwhal through Inuit eyes, as a part of a shared world whose animals, peoples, and cultures need respect. Listening to Inuit and learning more about narwhals is a good way to advance that cause.

0.20 *Partnerships in Science*
Martin Nweeia and David Angnstsiak, among many other scientists and residents of Pond Inlet, have collaborated for more than a decade on narwhal science. The Smithsonian exhibition and this book, Narwhal: Revealing an Ancient Legend, *could not have been produced without deep and fruitful partnerships. (photo: J. Meehan)*

Part 1

The Narwhal World

"There are those that we call *Qirnajuktat*, blackish ones,

they are bull or male narwhal, stallions, and they are very big and are

much longer than normal and have long tusks...Every now and

then the female narwhal have tusks too, and their tusks are not as

wide as the male...and are more beautiful...that's what I know."

Cornelius Nutarak, Pond Inlet

What is a Whale?

Joy S. Reidenberg

What is a whale? It's easy to describe: it lives in water, lacks scales, has a spine that bends up and down, breathes air, gives birth to live young, nurses them with breasts, has flippers, is covered in a fat layer, and is warm-blooded. That definition is troublesome, though, because it also describes most marine mammals (seal, sea lion, walrus). How about if we add that they propel themselves with a horizontal tail and lack hind limbs? Equally troubling, because that also describes sea cows (manatee and dugong). Clearly, we're going to need even more definition here.

Let's start with the basics: whales live in the water. If you've figured out that a whale is not a fish, then you're way ahead of most people! Whales used to be considered fish merely because they lived entirely in water. Of course, there are a lot of other aquatic animals we call fish (e.g., catfish, dogfish, goldfish, swordfish, flatfish, starfish, jellyfish, cuttlefish, crayfish—you get the idea), but not all of them are fish either: starfish—more appropriately called sea stars—are actually echinoderms ("spiny" + "skin"), jellyfish are cnidarians (animals with "nettles"), cuttlefish are cephalopods ("head" + feet"), crayfish are arthropods ("jointed" + "foot"). Whales, however, are mammals, and thus possess key mammalian characteristics such as lungs, no scales, hair (sparse whiskers on the head), internal fertilization, placental pregnancy, live birth, breasts to nurse their young with milk, and the ability to maintain a warm core-body temperature. Some fish can do some of these things. For example, lungfish can breathe air, eels do not have true scales, and catfish have barbs that look like whiskers. Sharks, rays, and many freshwater aquarium fish are livebearers that have internal fertilization and give birth to live young, although they do not have a placenta. Some sharks and tuna can even raise their body temperature using heat generated by muscles. Whales, however, have all of these characteristics despite living in an aquatic environment. This makes them mammals and not fish.

Whales are not the only mammals living in the water. "Aquatic mammals" is a broad term that encompasses a range of mammals that spend a substantial amount of time in the water (e.g., beaver, river otter, muskrat, water shrew, platypus, moose, hippopotamus, sea cow). "Marine mammals" is a term used to describe those mammals that spend time in salt water: sea otter, polar bear, seal, sea lion, fur seal, walrus, and, of course, whales. While most aquatic mammals regularly haul out onto the land, only the whales and sea cows remain fully aquatic. To distinguish between them, one only needs to consider their diet: whales are carnivores, while sea cows are herbivores.

Previous spread:
1.0 Hunters at the Ice Lead
A group of Pond Inlet narwhal hunters gather at the ice lead, waiting to intercept the narwhal migration. (photo: J. Meehan)

1.1 Killer Whale Pod
Groups of killer whales, also known as orcas, arrive off Baffin Island in the summer. Traveling in pods, orcas are the major species that prey on narwhals besides polar bears and humans. (photo: G. Freund)

1.2 Major species of whales of the northern seas.

From top to bottom: blue whale, finback, right whale, minke whale, humpback, sperm whale, orca, beluga, narwhal (credit: M. Parrish, Smithsonian NMNH)

A predatory whale is not an intuitive concept when one considers that whales are evolutionarily related to herbivores, and their closest relative is the hippopotamus. All whales descended from a deer-like ancestor. Whales are part of a larger group, or Order, called Cetartiodactyla. The cetartiodactyls include both the cetaceans (whales, including dolphins and porpoises) and the artiodactyls (the even-toed ungulates). Artiodactyls are largely herbivorous mammals, and include ruminants (cud-chewers, e.g., cattle, sheep, deer, antelope, giraffe), but also include some species that do not have true hooves or are not true ruminants (e.g., camel, pig, hippopotamus). Whales, however, are predators that eat invertebrates, fish, or other marine mammals (see below).

Whales are Cetaceans

Cetacea derives from the Greek word "ketos" (large sea monster) and the Latin "cetus" (large sea creature), both words that include in their definition "whales." The infraorder Cetacea contains nearly 90 species. It is a very diverse group that includes the large whales as well as dolphins and porpoises. Although the lay public generally uses the word "whale" only when referring to the largest species, scientists include all of the smaller species (dolphins and porpoises) within Cetacea. Cetaceans are divided into two subgroups called odontocetes and mysticetes.

Odontocetes consist of a few larger species we typically call whales (e.g., sperm whale, beaked whale) as well as nearly all of the smaller species that include dolphins and porpoises. Many of these are species we often associate with the word "whale" (e.g., killer whale or orca, pilot whale, beluga whale). Even the narwhal is called a whale. Its name literally translates as "corpse whale," due to its unusual color pattern of white and brown patches that make it look like a drowned sailor. (I would have much preferred to call it the leopard whale because of its spots!) Odontocetes range in size from the great sperm whale (a large whale averaging 52 feet in length) to the tiny vaquita (a porpoise averaging 54 inches long). Many of the small whales are in fact very large dolphins (members of the family Delphinidae). Despite its large size, the orca is actually just a very large dolphin! Most odontocetes are marine (i.e., live in salt water), but there are a few dolphins and a porpoise that are estuarine or riverine (i.e., can live in brackish or freshwater) from the Amazon, Ganges, Indus, Irrawaddy, La Plata, and Yangtze rivers.

The parvorder name Odontoceti (literally "toothed" + "whales") refers to the presence of teeth. Most odontocetes have a single row of identically shaped teeth lining the upper and lower jaws on each side. The teeth have a cone shape in dolphins and sperm whales, a blunted spade shape in porpoises, and can take a variety of odd shapes in the beaked whales. Despite the "toothed whale" name, teeth are not always visible in odontocetes because teeth do not erupt through the gums of some whales. Sperm whales don't erupt the teeth of their upper jaw, and female beaked whales usually appear toothless because they don't erupt their single pair of rudimentary teeth.

The narwhal is unique in having only one erupted tooth. There are actually four teeth, but only one erupts in the male, usually on the left side. Rarely, a male specimen can be found with two erupted teeth, and females have been found occasionally with an erupted shorter tooth. The narwhal tooth, also called a tusk, is also unique in its shape: very elongated and spiraled. Amazingly, the legend of the unicorn's horn can be traced to the unusual shape of this tusk. They were once harvested as proof of unicorns, and sold for as much as ten times their weight in gold.

1.3 Dolphin Play
*Dolphins and porpoises
are highly social animals
that have a strong sense
of play, as every sailor who
has enjoyed their behavior
carousing in the bow-
wave or stern-wave of a
boat can attest.
(photo: W. Bradberry)*

The narwhal tusk is a fascinating mystery, as no one knows for sure what its purpose is (see Chapter 4). It has been proposed as a fish stunner (used by billfish to slap and guide prey fish into the mouth), sexual display (as it usually erupts only in males), and weapon (again, because it is much larger in older males). More recent research revealed pores in the tusk that appear to be sensitive to ion fluxes and/or tempera-ture. This indicates that the tusk might be used in navigation to detect fresh water or temperature differences. As narwhals often swim in narrow channels between ice floes, detecting where there is warmer melting ice versus an influx of colder salty water would be important for successfully navigating into and out of these channels. This theory presumes that the males of the pod are primarily responsible for determining the driving directions using their built-in "Global Positioning Tusk."

Dolphins and porpoises are both small odontocetes. The porpoise family includes only three genera, but the dolphin family encompasses 17 genera, including some with the word "whale" as part of their common name (excepting beaked whales and sperm whales). The smaller dolphins are very similar to porpoises in shape and size, but can be distinguished by a combi-nation of three main features: teeth, dorsal fin, and head shape. As men-tioned above, porpoises have spade-shaped teeth, a triangular dorsal fin (sometimes with serrations on the leading edge), and a blunted head shape. Dolphins have cone-shaped teeth, a swept-back sickle-shaped dorsal fin (with a smooth leading-edge), and usually a projecting beak (but there is great variation in the amount of beak exposed). The sperm whale family comprises two genera, including the great sperm whale and two smaller species (dwarf and pygmy). The beaked whale family includes six genera. There are four river dolphin families with one genus in each. The family Monodontidae has only two genera: the beluga whale (*Delphinapterus leucas*, literally "wing-less dolphin" + "white"), and the narwhal (*Monodon monoceros*, literally "one tooth" + "one horn").

Mysticetes consist of the larger species we often typically call whales, and are divided into four families: right whales (two genera including the bowhead), pygmy right whale (one genus), gray whale (one genus), and the rorqual whales (one genus of humpback whale, and one genus including minke, fin, sei, Bryde's, Omura's, and blue whales). The blue whale is the largest mammal to have ever lived and rivals the length of the largest dinosaurs (sauropods). The pygmy right whale is the smallest mysticete, averaging only 20 feet long (that's smaller than some dolphins).

Mysticetes are filter-feeding whales. Instead of teeth, they use baleen plates made of keratin (the same substance as your fingernails). The parvorder name Mysticeti (literally "mustached" + "whales") refers to the baleen appearing as a "mustache" across the mouth. Baleen consists of flat, triangular plates that are frayed along one long edge, sharp on the opposing long edge, and the shorter base of the triangle is embedded into the tissue of the roof of the mouth. They are stacked, flat surface against flat surface, in a long row. There is one row on each side of the upper jaw. The frayed edges resemble mustache whiskers or hairs and face the center of the mouth, while the sharp edges face outward. This arrangement creates a sieve. As Mysticetes feed, prey is separated from water by this sieve, with prey being caught on the baleen "hairs." Water leaves the mouth by passing between the plates, or it can be channeled along the plates to the back edge of the mouth's gape where is it released through a curved drainage channel.

1.4 Mysticete Baleen
Baleen whales, known as mysticetes, have fibrous plates of baleen hanging from the roofs of their mouths. Composed of hair-like strands made of keratin, they act as a strainer to trap prey engulfed in the mouth as the water is expelled. (photo: J. Tunney)

Whales are Carnivores

Whales have a multichambered stomach, similar to that of many herbivorous mammals, including the ruminant artiodactyls. Although the cetartiodactyl ancestor of whales may have been herbivorous, modern whales are not. They eat only meat. Odontocetes with many small teeth use them as a fish trap to grasp prey. The points of the teeth may be angled slightly backwards, making it difficult for prey to escape. Prey are generally immobilized by injuries from the whale's jaw compression, spit out, and reoriented so they can be swallowed head-first. This prevents the dorsal spines of the fish from catching on the lining of the throat. Odontocetes use a method of underwater prey transport called "suction feeding" to bring the reoriented fish into the mouth. The large hyoid bone in the neck is retracted, and this brings the attached floor of the mouth and tongue back-wards toward the chest. This movement is like a syringe or piston withdrawing, creating negative pressure in the mouth (oral cavity) that draws the fish in. Odontocetes without teeth (e.g., female narwhals) or limited tooth eruption (e.g., beaked whales, sperm whales) depend primarily on suction to bring prey into the mouth. Many of these whales eat soft-bodied prey such as squid, cuttlefish, octopus (cephalopods) in addition to, or instead of, fish. Some whales, such as orca, use their teeth to tear apart the flesh of larger prey (large fish or marine mammals), and then swallow the ripped pieces whole. The teeth are never used for grinding, shear-ing, or any other form of masticatory processing.

Mysticetes use baleen to trap prey (usually small fish, or small shrimp-like animals called crustaceans such as krill, amphipods, and copepods). The balaenid whales (bowhead, and three species of right whales) use a strategy called skim-feeding, in which they continuously strain the water as they swim forward. The lower lip is very tall, and creates a shield just outside the baleen that helps direct water flow toward the back of the mouth. The baleen plates are very long (some up to 14 feet in height), and provide a large surface area for filtering. The mouth is held open at a fixed gape while water

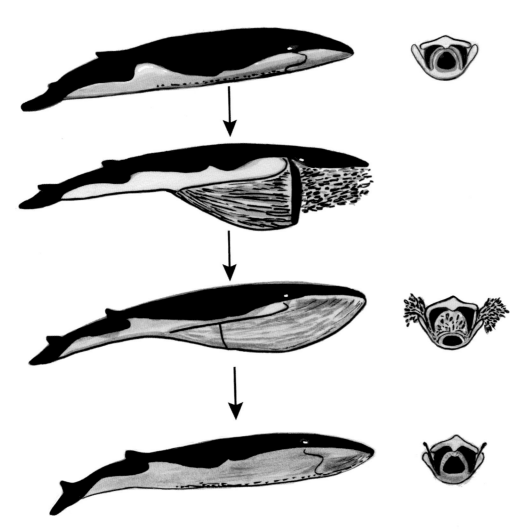

with prey flows in from the front, and water without prey streams out at the back of the gape. Prey is then trapped along the soft and delicate "hairs" of the baleen plates. Because the prey is very small, a smaller sieving mesh is needed. The angle of the baleen fringes directs everything toward the back of the mouth, channeling prey toward the gullet and diverting water laterally out of the mouth. It may not be necessary to wipe the baleen with the tongue in order to scrape the food off the "mustache."

The balaenopterid whales (also called rorqual whales) use a different strategy, called lunge-feeding. In this method, they seek (or actively corral) prey in a cluster, or bait ball. Then they swim directly at the cluster, open the mouth, and expand the throat to engulf both the prey and the surrounding water. The throat expands, with the water and prey, to a size that rivals the size of the whole whale. The throat can swell to accommodate a large volume, similar to the throat pouch of a pelican. The throat skin is comprised of folded pleats that can separate to expand, similarly to an accordion. The pleats extend from the lower jaw (mandibles) to the

1.7 Humpback Breaching
Humpbacks and a few other whales will often launch themselves almost completely out of the water in a behavior known as a breach. Whether for joy, display, or just to get a look around is unknown. The raised bumps are called tubercles; parasitic barnacles and symbiont crustaceans can be found attached to the skin around the tubercles. (photo: Wikipedia Commons)

mid-belly, ending just before the navel. As the whale swims forward, the throat distends with water similarly to a parachute filling with air. The mandibles disarticulate from the jaw joints of the skull (temporo-mandibular joints), are thrown forward, and rotate laterally. The mandibles also split apart at the front, stretching the tissue in the midline. This engulfs the largest possible volume in the mouth. The whale must then close the mouth to trap the prey inside.

If the whale is directed at the surface during its lunge, it may rise above the surface (a behavior called a breach), trapping the water with prey inside the walls of the mouth. It is easier to close the mouth in this position, as the mouth is in the air and thus will not encounter friction from movement through surrounding water. Also, the trapped water and prey are at the back of the oral cavity where the prey overlies the gullet and the water can stream out of the corner of the mouth, keeping most of the weight of the water off of the mandibles. When the mouth is closed, the mandibles make contact with the short baleen plates of the upper jaw. At this point, the trap is closed, and fish can no longer escape. Water is then forced out through the gaps between each baleen plate, but prey is retained within the oral cavity.

If the whale's mandibles lie in a horizontal position parallel to the water's surface after engulfing prey and the upper jaw is positioned vertically, it may be difficult to lift the mandibles up into the air to close them against the upper jaw. Instead, it is easier for the whale to literally swim its head over the mandibles. This is funny to behold, as the overflowing mandibles resemble a giant toilet bowl, with excess water spilling over the edge. The whale must then close the "toilet seat's lid" (upper jaw with baleen). The mandibles of

the "toilet bowl"–shaped mouth remain stationary, as they are too heavy
to move while containing so much water. However, the upper jaw is more
mobile, being held up in the air and away from the friction of the water.
It can more easily be lowered over the mandibles. As the "lid" almost closes
over the "bowl," it leaves a narrow gape covered by the baleen. The throat is
then contracted, and water is squeezed out through the narrow gape, separat-
ing water from prey. Whales that prey on fish have stiffer baleen plates
than those that feed on small crustaceans. The strong, wire-like fringes are
necessary to keep swimming fish from wiggling through the baleen to
freedom.

Whale Reproduction

The word "mammal" derives from the word "mammae," meaning breasts.
This is the most iconic of mammalian features. It's not so obvious that
whales have breasts, because they are not normally visible. Whales must
maintain a streamlined body shape so they can slip through the water at
great speed without the resistance of friction caused by protruding organs.
The teats of the breasts are therefore retracted inside the body and are
only extruded for nursing. For the same hydrodynamic reason a male whale
keeps the penis hidden inside until it is needed for reproduction. Interest-
ingly, there is no scrotum (skin over testicles), as the testes are permanently
internally positioned.

It's easy to understand now why ancient people thought whales were fish—
without breasts, penis, or scrotum, it could not be a mammal! If you want to
find out whether a whale is a male or a female, you will need to look at
the belly surface for the telltale pattern of the slit(s). One relatively short slit
in the midline surrounded by two very small slits indicates a female. The
midline slit is the common opening for the vagina (birth canal) and the
urethra (for urine excretion). Next to the very back portion of the slit (closest
to the beginning of the tail) is the opening for the anus (for stool excretion).
If the whale has one very long slit, then this is the opening for the penis
(for transporting sperm to the female), and at the back end of this slit is the
anal opening.

Whales have internal fertilization. Reproduction is a speedy affair, with
penetration measured in seconds (or fractions of a second in some porpoises!). The penis is coiled in a loop inside the body, resembling a spring. It
is kept in this coiled shape by a retractor muscle. When the male is ready to
mate, this muscle relaxes, and the penis springs out. Unlike most marine
mammals, the whale does not have a bone inside the penis (os penis) to keep
it rigid. This is a trait shared with humans and sea cows. However, unlike

humans, the whale penis does not need to fill with blood to be erect. It maintains its erect position with elastic tissue that helps it stay rigid, even in cold water. It appears to be able to bend in various directions, perhaps due to muscles at the base of the penis. This ability to bend helps direct the penis into the vagina—a trait that is helpful in water where they cannot use a pelvic thrust to assist with insertion. The controlling muscles, as well as the muscle that retracts the penis back to its spring-loaded position, are attached to the pelvic bones. It is interesting to note that although whales do not have hind limbs (see below), they do still have a pelvis. However, the pelvis is not weight-bearing or used for walking anymore. It is very reduced in size and no longer connects to the spine as it once did in fossil whale ancestors. Its main function now is to support the penis, stabilize the vagina and birth canal, and provide attachment of the abdominal wall muscles used to contract the belly (ventral) region during locomotion.

Dolphin and porpoise males often penetrate from underneath the female because gravity will assist in keeping her body positioned over the penis as she is pushed from below and lifted slightly above the water's surface. Larger whales sometimes mate in groups, with one male serving as the "couch" while another male penetrates. The male in the couch position stabilizes the female's position for insertion by keeping his body against her side or back. Another male on the other side can then penetrate the penis into her vagina. The males probably cooperate in this manner because each one will have a turn mating or being the couch. The real competition is among the sperm. Females may have some choice in the matter too. They may be able to protect the womb (uterus) from the sperm of unwanted males by covering the uterine cervix and diverting sperm into blind sacs along the vagina.

Pregnant whales carry a fetus for close to a year (15–18 months for some species such as orca). There is a placenta and umbilical cord with blood vessels that transfer nutrients and oxygen to the fetus and carry wastes away. Look at a whale carefully, and you will see a navel or belly button! This is a unique feature of placental mammals because the navel (umbilicus) is where the umbilical cord was connected to the belly of the fetus. When the fetus is ready to be born, it usually presents tail first. This would be the equivalent of a breech birth in a land mammal, and could be life threatening for both the mother and the baby if the fetus gets stuck in the birth canal. However, for a whale, this is the best way for the baby to emerge because the head is not exposed to water until the whole body is out of the birth canal. Therefore, the baby will not have the urge to breathe until it is capable of swimming to the surface where it can take its first breath. After the baby whale is delivered, the mother twists suddenly to sever the umbilical cord, freeing the baby to now swim unfettered to the surface.

A baby whale is called a calf, and the mother is called a cow. Just like their terrestrial cousins, a calf drinks milk from the cow's breasts (the equivalent of the udder of cattle). Also, similar to cattle, whale breasts are located near the genital opening. This is very different from sea cows that have chest breasts, similar to their closest relative the elephant. Other marine mammals, such as seals, sea lions, and walrus, nurse their young on the land. Whales and sea cows are the only marine mammals that nurse their calves underwater. However, unlike sea cows, whale calves do not have lips and cheeks to make a watertight seal around the teat. Therefore, a whale calf will roll its tongue into a tube that channels milk into the mouth. Fringes located along the edge of the tongue help zipper it closed and also grasp the teat, preventing any leakage of milk.

1.8 Maternal Instincts
Like other mammals, females give live birth, feed milk to their infant, and nurture them constantly until weaned and capable of living on their own. (photo: Camp Crazy Photography)

Whales Have Hair

Newborn whale calves are born with some sparse hairs resembling whiskers along the upper lip. In a few species, hairs are retained along the dorsum (top) of the head (e.g., humpback whales), or all over the head, including the face and underneath the chin (e.g., grey whales). Hair is another iconic mammalian trait, so its appearance on whales should not be a surprise. Hairs may assist in touch (tactile) information that may be useful when the calf is nuzzling the genital area of the mother to stimulate her to extrude the nipple. This might explain why hairs are found primarily along the newborn calf's lip.

The isolated hairs found on the head in some adult whales also appear to have a sensory purpose, much like whiskers on a cat. Bending hairs may inform the whale about water passing over the skin (and thus give information about swimming speed, or water currents when the whale is stationary),

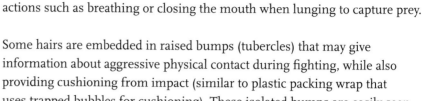

1.9 Tubercle Effect
Frank Fish, a whale biologist, discovered that the bumps and notches on the leading edges of humpback whale fins and tail create more stream-lined water flow over their surfaces, creating greater maneuverability in capturing prey. (Wikipedia Creative Commons)

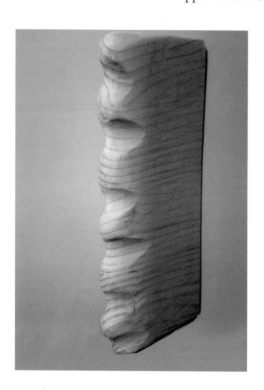

or whether it is about to touch another whale. Hairs on the top of the head may let it know it has reached the air at the water's surface, thus triggering actions such as breathing or closing the mouth when lunging to capture prey.

Some hairs are embedded in raised bumps (tubercles) that may give information about aggressive physical contact during fighting, while also providing cushioning from impact (similar to plastic packing wrap that uses trapped bubbles for cushioning). These isolated bumps are easily seen on the top of the head of a humpback whale. Other tubercles, without hairs, can be found on the leading edge of the humpback's flipper, possibly providing hydrodynamic efficiency. The same effect may occur along the irregular edge of the humpback's tail flukes. Other raised skin features, such as the head callosities of right whales, can provide camouflage by giving the appearance of a barnacle-encrusted rock. The irregular surface of the callosity provides a gripping site for many parasites, adding texture to the rock-like appearance. Many of the baleen whales (e.g., gray and humpback whales) also have real barnacles embedded in their skin, even without the presence of callosities. The barnacles provide a gripping surface for other invertebrates, including lice. Yes, even with the loss of fur, whales still have lice! However, whale lice aren't truly lice, but rather are crustacean amphipods of the genus *Cyamid*. They can be beneficial symbionts, as they help rid the whale of dead skin.

Hair is a mammalian trait, but in modern whales it is a vestige of their terrestrial mammalian ancestry. Whale ancestors likely used fur to trap air against the skin, where it could be warmed and used to insulate the body from the cold air. Wet hair is a poor insulator in the cold, and nature has developed many evolutionary solutions for marine mammals: sea otters frequently groom their dense fur with oil to repel water; polar bears have unwettable fur that feels like plastic threads and is spaced apart to allow water to drain off quickly before freezing; walruses have evolved hairless body skin; most marine mammals evolved a fatty layer around the trunk for insulation.

Wet fur also produces drag on the body, and so the fast-swimming seals and sea lions have shorter fur that lays flat to make a smooth surface. Whales have taken this evolution one step further: smooth, largely hairless skin devoid of sags and wrinkles. The skin is elastic and thus can allow regional deformation, from the local pressure of water flow, that helps streamline the body shape. They have also evolved a fusiform-shaped body (narrow front, smooth transi-

14

tion to a wider middle, and smooth transition back to a narrow tail) and fusiform-shaped projections (flippers, flukes, fin, tail keel) that are hydrodynamically efficient for slipping through water with minimal friction, or providing lift similarly to an airplane wing.

Whales are Warm Blooded

Fur-bearing marine mammals lose the air trapped within the fur when it is compressed during a dive. Nature's solution is the evolution of a non-compressible insulator. Fat is the ideal insulator for divers, as it does not compress. Whales traded fur for fat: they eliminated the drag-inducing and insulating properties of fur and evolved a fat layer that both reduced drag and provided better insulation. The layer of fat that insulates all whales (and most other marine mammals) is called blubber. It is thinnest in tropical freshwater dolphins and quite substantial in polar whales. Blubber acts as a thermos, blanketing the whale in a substance that keeps warmth in the core of the body.

While maintaining warmth is essential for whales that live in polar waters, such as narwhals, it is a liability in warmer equatorial waters. Whales that migrate between these regions must adjust their insulating properties so as not to overheat. Blubber thickness can only be reduced if it is used as an energy source. Whales do break down and use some of this fat to fuel their constant swimming. This is particularly true for female whales that have additional energy needs, such as maintaining a growing fetus during pregnancy (gestation), or nursing (lactating) a calf. This may explain why females are often larger than males in those species (mostly mysticetes) that regularly migrate between equatorial and polar regions. Some blubber is used to fuel the swim toward the pole. Feeding occurs at the poles, so the whales have an opportunity to replenish lost energy stores. The blubber layer must be built up quickly to keep the whale warm while in those frigid waters. A well-fed whale is better insulated, and also has the necessary energy stores to survive the long swim back to the equator. Once at the equator, the whale may be

1.10 *Sea Mammal Blubber*
In trading fur for fat, sea mammals have evolved an efficient method for retaining body heat, enabling those with thick blubber layers to inhabit cold-water seas.
(illustration: M. Bakry)

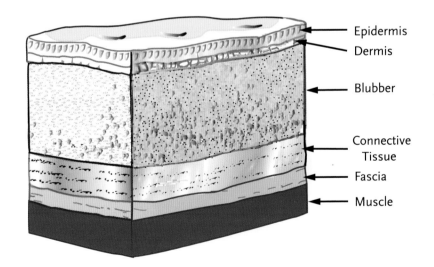

Epidermis
Dermis
Blubber
Connective Tissue
Fascia
Muscle

thinner again, but the need for insulation will decline. However, the whale will still keep a healthy layer of blubber around the body because heat is still lost (dissipated) to water, even when the water is warm. Tropical water is usually cooler than mammalian body-core temperature. It is rare for a whale to be in water that is at, or near, its body temperature (except tropical river dolphins, that therefore have a thinner blubber layer). The remaining blubber stores will also be needed in the tropics to fuel the remainder of a pregnancy or lactation once a calf is born, to fuel aggressive combats between males for mating rights, and to fuel the fleeing and pursuit of females in heat. Only those whales that can maintain good energy reserves after all of these activities will be strong enough to survive the next migration back to the poles to feed again.

The insulating properties of blubber can be detrimental to reproduction. Although mammals need to maintain a warm core-body temperature, this temperature can be too warm for proper development of sperm or a fetus. The blood vessels surrounding the reproductive organs are therefore directly connected to regions of the body where the blubber layer is very thin (dorsal fin, tail flukes). There are many of these vessels arranged in a parallel array similar to a steam radiator, and they do just that: radiate their excess heat across the skin's surface, thereby ridding the whale of excess heat. In addition, the hot arterial blood supplying the reproductive tract (particularly the testes and uterus) is cooled by venous blood flowing in the opposite direction from the periphery. As the hot blood in the arteries flows past the cold blood in the veins, heat is released to the veins. This heat loss lowers the temperature of the arterial blood, thus ensuring that cooled arterial blood is delivered to reproductive-tract organs. This vascular arrangement for thermoregulation is called counter-current exchange. Since whales keep their testes internal, they risk exposure to temperatures that would inactivate sperm. This body temperature probably does not inactivate sperm production, but it might inactivate sperm motility once the sperm is formed and stored. Therefore, it is particularly important for these cooling vessels to carry heat away from the tube that stores sperm (epididymis). Sea cows also share this trait of cooling the epididymis.

Whales can also adjust their body temperature by surrounding arteries with veins as they course to the perimeter of the body. As arterial blood flows toward the periphery, it brings heat from the core of the body. This hot blood begins to radiate heat to the surrounding veins. As the blood progresses to the periphery, it becomes cooler from losing that heat. By the time it reaches the skin, it should be close to the temperature of the surrounding water. Therefore, no heat exchange will occur along the skin. The returning cooled blood goes back in veins that are arranged around the artery. The cool blood in the veins picks up heat dissipated from the hot blood in the artery. Now, as those veins enter the core of the body, the blood is already warmed back up to body temperature. Thus, the core of the body stays warm, while the periphery

stays cool. This arrangement of blood vessels for heat conservation is called counter-current exchange. One can easily see why the early biologists, who were unaware of the counter-current exchange mechanism for heat conservation, thought whales were cold fish when they felt their cool-to-the-touch skin!

If a whale gets too warm, the thermoregulation process can reverse. The arteries can dilate and veins can constrict. This reduces the heat-transfer process by allowing less surface area between the vessels for the heat exchange, while allowing more heat dissipation at the periphery (particularly the flat surfaces of the flippers, flukes, and fin, where the vessels are closest to the skin). When a whale becomes stranded on the beach, out of water, it cannot dissipate heat efficiently, particularly when the air is hot. This is why people assisting a stranded whale may put ice packs on the dorsal fin and pectoral flippers.

1.11 Blowholes
Mysticetes (baleen whales) have two nostrils (blowholes), while odontocetes have one nostril. (photo: O. Perkins)

Whales Breathe Air

Breathing air is another trait that separates mammals from fish (except lungfish). All aquatic mammals must come to the surface to breathe air through their nostrils. Why, then, do whales look like they are spouting water when they breathe? The whale's spout is indeed made of air, however, there can be some water blown up into the air with each breath. This is because some water wells around the nasal opening(s) (blowhole), and gets pushed up with the exhalation. In addition, the air is rushing out of the blowhole(s) very quickly—almost like a sneeze! In order to evacuate all of that volume at once through the narrow passageways in the head, the air must be highly compressed. Then it greatly expands as it leaves the top of the head, where it is no longer constrained in a tube. This sudden expansion drops the pressure and this, in turn, causes water vapor to condense into small droplets. The appearance is similar to a fog—or the "smoke" of your breath on a cold day—and from a distance this water vapor looks like a spout of water (particularly visible on a cold day). The shape of the exhaled air (blow) is unique for each species of large whale, and that is how whalers, sailors, and today's whale watchers identify specific species from a distance. For example, the blow resembles a heart in humpback and grey whales, a V-shape in right and bowhead whales, a tall column in blue and fin whales, a short column in minke whales, and a left-sided forward-leaning column in sperm whales.

There are two blowhole openings in mysticetes, but only one in odontocetes. The blowhole is located on the highest point at the top (dorsum) of the head. In fossil ancestors of whales, the bony opening in the skull for the blowholes can be seen in various positions, migrating from the front of the snout in earlier forms to the dorsum of the head in later forms. The air passageway pipes traveling through the skull to the dorsal position resemble internal snorkels! A blowhole at the top of the head is in the best position for energy-efficient breathing while swimming. The whale does not have to lift its head out of the water. Instead, it can breathe (exhale and then inhale) while rolling forward in a natural swimming motion. The front edge of the blowhole region is guarded by a ridge of tissue that acts as a splashguard in mysticetes. The lateral edge of each blowhole can also be apposed against the medial edge to close the nostrils. In odontocetes, the leading edge of tissue is not usually raised up into a splashguard (probably because their heads are not flat on top, and so can shed water more readily). Rather, the tissue at the front of the blowhole is smoothly sealed against the tissue of the back of the blowhole to keep it closed when not breathing. This orientation is rotated 90 degrees in some whales (e.g., sperm whales) so that it appears as a slit running parallel to the long axis of the whale.

The connection between the windpipe (trachea), voice box (larynx), and nasal cavities is maintained by a soft palate that encircles the top of the larynx, creating a seal that separates the breathing and swallowing pathways. This is particularly important for preventing drowning, as the whale can be in any orientation during a swallow. It also separates and protects the two pathways, allowing open-mouthed prey-catching behaviors while using the respiratory tract for sound production.

Sound and Communication

Underwater sound production is generated by airflow. Mysticetes and odontocetes differ greatly in how they generate sounds. Mysticetes use the voice box to generate vibrations. This requires air to flow past the vocal "cords" (not "chords" as in musical notes) or vocal folds (this is the correct anatomical term, as the folds are not free cords of tissue but, rather, shelves of projecting tissue masses). As the air flows between the folds, it causes them to vibrate. This vibration in air is how we generate sound. Try making a sound and holding your finger to your "Adam's apple" (projection at the front of the neck). You'll feel some vibrations, but this is not the sound we hear. We hear only the sound emitted from the mouth or nose. The throat vibrations are lost, useless energy for us, because they are not transmitted very far. However, in Mysticetes whales, energy from throat vibrations through the skin is used to communicate. They close the mouth and nose, and don't let air escape from those openings during sound production. Air flows instead into a sac in front of the larynx. As the sac expands, it captures the air used to generate sound. Then the sac contracts and sends the air back to be reused. This recycling of air lets the whale make multiple vocalizations without having to return to the surface for more air.

Mysticetes generate low-frequency sounds. These low sounds have a longer wavelength and thus can travel very far. Think about what sounds you can hear when a car with the sound system on pulls up next to you at a traffic light. The treble melody attenuates too quickly, and all you hear is the bass beat because the low-frequency sounds have traveled farther. The larger the larynx, the lower the frequency and the louder the amplitude of the sounds that can be made. Blue whales, being the largest whales, make the lowest and loudest underwater sounds due to their huge larynx. Male mysticetes sing songs that are thought to be important for reproduction (although it is unclear if it is used for advertising for mate selection, male competition, defending a territory, or forming a male-male coalition). Humpback whales are particularly famous for their songs because of their complexity, as well as the social exchange of sharing sound units between groups as the song evolves into a new song every year. At any given time, all the humpbacks of a region will be singing the same song. It's as if they had been listening to the "top 40 greatest hits countdown," and knew which "hit" song to sing because it is the most popular one at the moment!

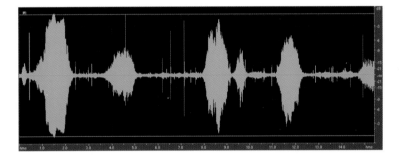

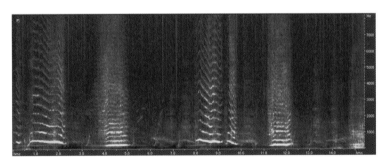

Whales are generally very social, so communication is important for bonding with other members of the pod. While whales make sounds for communication, only odontocetes appear to generate sound for prey tracking and navigation. The sounds are aimed at a target, and the returning echo relays information about the location, direction, speed, dimensions, texture, and density of a specific prey item. Sending and interpreting sound echoes is called echolocation (essentially radar, but used underwater). Echolocation can be used for navigation, as ships use sonar, to avoid swimming into obstacles. While echolocation as a navigational aid is probably not that valuable for open-water species, it is essential for whales that live close to shore or in a complexly shaped environment. Narwhals, in particular, need this to help them navigate between icebergs and within narrow water channels with sculpturally shaped walls.

1.12 Humpback Whale Spectrogram
As seen in this recording, a continuous tone is interrupted periodically by clicks (vertical bars). The bottom diagram reveals pulsing within the clicks. Humpback whales over vast regions sing variations of the same song, which evolves into a new song each successive year. (credit: O. Adam, CNRS, France)

Because narwhal males also have to manage navigating with a long tusk, echolocation becomes an essential part of their underwater "GPS." It could tell them how sharply an ice tunnel might be bending, thus helping them predict a travel route that would prevent the tusk from accidentally spearing into an ice wall. It may also help them find breathing holes in the ice, particularly at night when celestial cues of sunlight or moonlight are not available to shine down through the holes.

Odontocetes do not appear to use the larynx to generate these sounds, but instead, use a complex system of vibrating structures in the nasal region called phonic lips. The skin covering the phonic lips and surrounding nasal tissues is pigmented, even though it is internal and not visible outside the body. This pigment is an indication that these tissues were once external, and that they probably derive from an upper lip turned backwards against the openings of the nostrils. This created a valve to seal out water (nasal plug), but also provided a tissue that could vibrate as air is forced past it (phonic lips). It is similar to how we might make a rude flatulent-mimicking "Bronx cheer" or "raspberry" noise by passing air between loosely opposed lips. If you could make a similar noise by blowing air past your upper lip while it was curled up against your nostrils, you'd be making sounds the way a toothed whale does!

Surrounding these vibrating nasal tissues are multiple pairs of air sacs. These odontocetes' nasal sacs also recycle air, similarly to the laryngeal sac of mysticetes. This allows reuse for multiple vocalizations without losing air. In addition, the air sacs (of both mysticetes and odontocetes) keep the sound system from pressurizing. Try, for example, to make a sound while your mouth and nose are both held closed. The sound stops because the system pressurizes. With no place for the air to go, it stops flowing. No flow = no sound. Air sacs allow the air to keep flowing, and thus the sound to continue to be made, without releasing the air outside the whale.

The navigational sounds made by odontocetes are unique. They consist of high-frequency clicks that bounce off a target and are received by the whale. The clicks are generated by the vibrating tissue under the blowhole (phonic lips), and then filtered through a large fat body (e.g., the melon of dolphins and porpoises), or series of fat bodies (e.g., the spermaceti and junk organs of sperm whales) in the forehead. These fatty filters modify the sound (amplify or dampen, focus narrow or wide beam) and transfer the vibrations to water.

Whales do not have external ears (pinnae). In odontocetes, the returning echo is received by the fat in the lower jaw and surrounding throat region, and transferred to the ear. It is interesting that fat is used as a transducer for both outgoing and incoming sounds. The middle—and inner-ear regions are disconnected from the skull in odontocetes, and thus bony conduction would not be transmitted directly to the ear. Also, even if bony conduction were used, it would reach both left and right ears at the same time, thus making it difficult to localize the direction that the sound is coming from. This is probably why the middle and inner ears became detached from the surrounding bone. Those fine differences in high frequencies can tell the whale information about target size, distance, location, trajectory of movement, and even texture or density.

In mysticetes, the jaw fats may also receive sound, or it may be conducted through the bones of the skull and mandible to the ear region. The bony conduction appears necessary because the receiving instrument has to be very large to accommodate the very large wavelengths of the low-frequency sounds. These sounds are generally used for communication, but have been suggested to serve also as coarse sonar, much like a blind person tapping a cane and listening for the echo. Perhaps mysticetes can use pulses of low-frequency sound to navigate around large underwater obstacles, such as seamounts. Precise localization is probably unnecessary when the target is so large, and thus bony conduction reaching both ears at the same time would not be a detriment.

Whales are Divers

Blubber makes the whale float, but the density of the bones, muscles, and organs counter this and make the whale nearly neutrally buoyant. When the respiratory system fills with air, the whale is slightly buoyant. As the whale begins its dive, the air in the respiratory tract begins to compress with elevating ambient pressure. During the dive, the air volume in the respiratory spaces collapses, making the whale denser and therefore heavier. As the whale heads down for a dive, the air in the air sacs of the head naturally flows upward against gravity toward the chest and accumulates in the lungs. This makes the head heavier than the chest (particularly since it also contains a lot of bone from the skull), and thus the whale can maintain a head-down orientation. The whale follows its heavier head (that can be up to one-third of the body length in some species), as if attached to a sinking stone. After the first few swimming strokes, it should be able to cruise down without using much additional energy.

At depth, the whale may choose to vocalize. With collapsed air spaces, this would be difficult. However, the whale likely took extra air in the filled air sacs that was shunted to the lungs. This extra volume of air, now compressed and combined with what is left in the lungs, could be enough to shunt across the vocal folds or phonic lips to make sounds, as well as maintain an air space in the middle ear for the ear ossicles to vibrate and conduct sound to

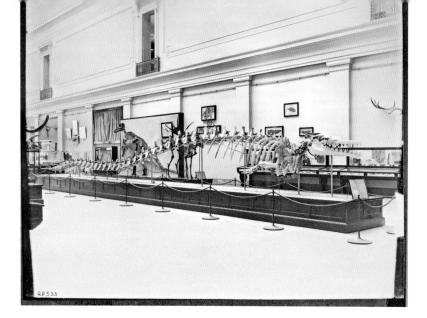

the inner ear. The chest-cavity volume will collapse to accommodate the collapse of the lungs due to air compression. This can be accomplished by both flattening of the ribcage and expansion of blood sinuses along the back of the lung (pleural) cavities. In odontocetes, jointed ribs allow the ribcage to fold under pressure. In mysticetes, the ribs may rotate caudally, creating the same flattening effect. The pleural cavity blood sinuses engorge to occupy space previously filled with inflated lungs. As these blood sinuses are fluid filled, they are relatively uncompressible compared with air.

As the whale begins its ascent, the process reverses. Residual air can be shunted from the lungs to the trachea, larynx, nasal cavity, and air sacs by contracting the chest musculature. This would make the head lighter than the rest of the body, and the whale would begin to follow the head up, as if following a rising balloon. After a few initial tail strokes to begin the upward ascent, the whale should rise effortlessly to the surface.

Whales can breath-hold for a long time while diving. Some large odontocetes are champion divers, with submergence times close to an hour for sperm whales, and over two hours for a Cuvier's beaked whale. Breath-holding implies less oxygenation to the tissues during a dive. Whales have adapted to this with three mechanisms. First, as mentioned above, they may use less muscle energy for swimming by regulating their buoyancy and gliding up

1.13 a,b,c
The Smithsonian Basilosaurus
These three images show the Smithsonian's fossil whale, Basilosaurus, from its early mount in the National Museum of Natural History's "Hall of Extinct Monsters" (1912, above), to the "Hall of the Ancient Seas" (1989), and the present "Sant Ocean Hall" (2010). Due to its initial composite assembly from incomplete individuals, later reconstructions have benefitted from new collections and more scientific study, including the addition of a hind limb proving its evolutionary land animal past. (photos: above, Smithsonian Archives; right and opposite, C. Clark)

and down. Second, they can slow their metabolism, including a slower heart rate. This means their bodies use less oxygen, so they can last longer before they "run out of air." Third, their muscles contain high levels of myoglobin. This substance helps retain extra oxygen where it is needed for muscle contractions, so they can handle the lack of circulating oxygenated blood during the dive. The level of myoglobin accounts for the various colors seen in some muscles. It's what distinguishes the white meat from the dark meat in chicken and the even-darker meat of beef. Myoglobin in whale muscle makes it very dark, almost black.

Walking and Galloping Whales

Modern whales do not have hind limbs, but they do have a pelvis. Some whale species also have a remnant thigh bone (femur) embedded in their flank, but it is not usually protruding as a limb. Rarely, a specimen will be found with protruding hind limbs, as was the case of a dolphin named Haruka discovered recently in Japan that had hind flippers. The reemergence of hind limbs proves that the genetic code for making hind extremities is present, but is usually suppressed in the DNA of modern whales. Although this genetic code usually lies dormant, a random mutation could reactivate it and cause the limbs to form again. The presence of this code gives credence to the idea that a whale ancestor once did have hind limbs. This  observation supports the evolution of limb reduction in modern whales from a terrestrial ancestor that was four-legged, weight-bearing, and walked on land.

A quick review of fossil whales shows the gradual reduction of hind limbs until none are visible and only a remnant pelvis remains. The bones of rudimentary hind limbs can be seen in some earlier whale ancestors such as *Basilosaurus*. These limbs are too small to bear weight and are not developed enough to perform locomotion. They remind me of a backward *Tyrannosaurus rex*! We may never know what these little legs were used for, but this intermediate form must have had some function. Nature doesn't make useless, vestigial structures. As structures morph from one shape to another, so do their functions. The similarity of these tiny hind limbs to the claspers of sharks and the mating spurs of snakes (also derived from reduced hind limbs) makes me think they could have been used for reproduction.

Another distinguishing feature of whales is their up-and-down (dorso-ventral) spinal movement, compared with the side-to-side spinal movement of fish. The side-to-side (lateral-to-lateral) movement is not unique to fish. We can also see it in non-hopping amphibians (e.g., salamanders) and non-shelled reptiles (e.g., lizards, crocodiles, snakes). Amphibians and reptiles are essentially swimming on land (and in the case of frogs, the tadpoles also move with fish-like swimming movements). Snakes even swim on land without the benefit of legs. Mammals, however, evolved longer extremities that didn't stick out laterally, but rather, were positioned underneath the torso. This brought the belly off the ground and placed the weight directly over the longer legs. The raised torso allowed carrying a pregnancy in an expanded belly, but also enabled longer strides, leaping, and galloping movements. The spine assisted in these actions, converting from a largely lateral-to-lateral movement to a largely dorso-ventral movement. This aided the leaping and galloping movements by extending the stride even further. Whales carry this vestige from their terrestrial mammalian ancestors: a dorso-ventrally bending spine. This movement is seen when whales swim. The up-and-down rolling movement looks like they are galloping through the water.

Some fast-swimming cetaceans (particularly small odontocetes) have spinal (vertebral) features that increase stabilization, compared to the more flexible coastal species. These include flattened vertebral bodies (round ones allow more range of movement), sharply angled neural spines and transverse processes (straighter ones allow more twisting), and prominent articular processes that nest on either side of the neural spine (reduced processes would allow lateral bending). In addition, the neck (cervical) vertebrae are often fused together into one unit. This unusual morphology does not break the rule for mammals—seven cervical vertebrae. If this fused unit is cut along the midline, the center reveals a stack of seven discrete vertebral bodies (even though they appear as one unit externally). The fused vertebrae are thought to give stability for head movements.

A swimming whale lives in a three-dimensional environment. Therefore, it needs to regulate movements in all three axes/planes. Circular movements around an axis are termed yaw (lateral deviation in the horizontal plane around an axis running dorso-ventrally in the vertical plane), pitch (dorso-ventral deviation around an axis running side-to-side in the horizontal plane. basically yaw, but rotated 90 degrees laterally), and roll (tipping over sideways along the long axis of the body running from front-to-back, in the transverse/transaxial plane). Linear movements along these three axes are called heave (up and down), sway (side to side), and surge (forward-backward).

The fused cervical vertebrae stabilize for yaw. They keep the skull aligned forward and allow only pitch movements that extend the dorso-ventral spinal undulations of swimming. Prevention of yaw minimizes the friction that would otherwise occur along the side of the face if the whale turned its head laterally to the left or right while it swam forward.

Additional projections from the whale's body increase stabilization of roll and pitch. The dorsal fin, located on the midline of the back, prevents tipping of the body in a roll. It resembles the keel of a sailboat, except that it is located on the back and not the belly. The vertical portion of the tail of an airplane, modeled on this same design, is an important feature that keeps airplanes from flipping over. Most fast-swimming cetaceans have a dorsal fin, but there are a few slower-swimming species that lack one (e.g., bowhead and right whales). The dorsal fin of porpoises is triangular and often has serrations on the leading edge. The dorsal fin of dolphins is swept-back into a hook or sickle shape (falcate), but there are some variations (e.g., the very tall fin of a male orca looks triangular, but the very top edge is curved backwards).

Two more stabilizers are found in the paired chest (pectoral) flippers, which project at approximately 33 degrees from the dorsal fin. This balances the keel function in one-third increments all around the perimeter of the trunk. In addition, the flippers can be angled to create lift (similar to the wings of an airplane), placed unevenly to bank turns, brought down and rotated forward to create friction for braking, or pulled into opposition or against the body in apposition to generate thrust (as a human swimmer might do with arm strokes). Flippers can have a large variety of shapes, including: falcate (found in most dolphins, porpoises, and rorqual mysticetes), paddle (orcas, belugas, narwhals, sperm whales, beaked whales), square (right and bow-head whales), triangular (some river dolphins), elongated (long-finned pilot whales), or very elongated with a bumpy leading edge (humpback whales).

The flippers can move in multiple planes because they are attached at a ball-and-socket joint where they meet the body. This joint is homologous to our shoulder joint (gleno-humeral joint) where our arm bone (humerus) meets our shoulder-blade bone (scapula). Whale flippers are supported by the same bones found in the flippers of other marine animals (e.g., seal, walrus, and sea lion flippers; manatee flipper/foreleg, turtle flipper, penguin flipper). The same bone pattern can also be found in the forelimbs of other four-limbed animals (e.g., hippopotamus foreleg, cattle foreleg, horse foreleg, dog foreleg, human arm, bird wing, bat wing, etc.). All of these species are tetrapods (descendants of a four-limbed ancestor). The whale flipper has the bones of the arm (humerus), forearm (radius and ulna), wrist (carpals), and usually five digits (phalanges of thumb and three or four fingers, with one of the fingers sometimes missing in some mysticetes species). Whales

1.14 Humpback Whale Tail-Prints

Humpback whales develop distinctive patterns caused by the black-and-white pigment patterns on the undersides of their tail flukes. Over time, due to natural growth patterns, scrapes or cuts, these patterns become virtual finger prints that can be used to identify individual whales and to track their migration movements and indirectly, their ages. (courtesy of Nathalie Ward, Stellwagen Bank National Marine Sanctuary, NOAA)

have hyperphalangy (extra elements for each digit) that extends flipper length while increasing flexibility (due to increased number of joints). This is particularly evident in the humpback whale, whose long flippers gave rise to its scientific name *Megaptera novaeangliae* (literally, "big-winged New Englander"). These elongated flippers help propel the whale, slap the water in a visual and acoustic display, caress another whale, or help herd fish ahead of the mouth.

Forward propulsion comes from the tail. The paired flat plates of the whale's tail are called flukes. Whale flukes are oriented flat in the horizontal plane (unlike fish tails that are oriented flat in the vertical plane). The flukes move dorso-ventrally during swimming (unlike fish tails that move lateral-to-lateral during swimming). The flukes press against the water and are slightly curved or held at an angle so that water is shed behind (caudally) relative to the fluke. This action is similar to the action of an angled fan blade, shedding air to create a breeze. As the water flows caudally, the whale is propelled forward (rostrally). The flukes are not supported by bones, but are comprised instead of dense connective tissue that has some flexibility (similar to rubber flippers). The tailstock (thick portion just before the flukes), however, is supported by tail bones (caudal vertebrae) of the end of the spine. The tailstock is flattened laterally so that its diameter is very narrow side to side, and is larger in diameter dorsally to ventrally. It is reminiscent of the shape of a broad sword, with the sharp dorsal and ventral edges cutting the

water with each up and down stroke. This allows the tailstock to move quickly through the water without encountering resistance from friction. The sharp blades of the tailstock can also act as a keel to stabilize the whale's position while gliding. Pigment patterns on a humpback whale's flukes allow these whales to be identified as specific individuals.

Whales are Smart

Whales are probably one of the most intelligent animals on the planet. It is very difficult to test intelligence in wild whales, particularly the very large mysticetes. Nevertheless, we can deduce intelligence from a combination of brain complexity and behaviors. Whale brains are among the largest of any animal, including humans (of course, one must adjust for the large size of the animals). Comparing a

human with a dolphin, for example, is reasonable as they are approximately the same size in body mass. The dolphin brain, while similarly sized, appears to be more convoluted. These convolutions provide more surface area for gray matter (the part that does processing), as opposed to white matter (the part that relays messages). Not all processing is thinking, though, depending upon your definition. Much of the gray matter of dolphins, for example, may be devoted to processing sound into a comprehensible "image" (or concept) of the topography of the environment or location of a target. Some is certainly devoted to communication, as all whales (not just dolphins) depend upon sound for social interactions. As mysticetes are extremely large, it is not clear whether the-brain-to body size ratio is a fair way to assess intelligence. The larger body requires very little additional brain tissue to coordinate muscle and organ activities, and the social interactions do not get more or less complex based on the length of the individuals of a given species. There are smart (perhaps we should we say complex?) large animals (e.g., elephants) and complex small one (e.g., crows), as well as simple large animals (e.g., whale shark) and simple small ones (e.g., worms). Some whales (e.g., humpbacks) have neurons that regulate emotions such as remorse. These have been found in a number of animals, but are most abundant in humans, great apes, and elephants. "Smart" is a difficult term, and can include learning, problem solving, creativity, tool use, play, language, emotion, social bonding, etc. Many of these concepts are extremely difficult to test.

1.15 Beluga Crooners
The complex—and sometimes comic—social behavior of many whales, like these belugas (perhaps expecting a meal in this case!) is an indication of high intelligence.
(photo: Navidim)

One aspect of intelligence, self-awareness, was tested experimentally in captive dolphins (as well as in captive elephants). In this experiment, the dolphins were first acquainted with mirrors. They did not ignore the reflection in the mirror and quickly appeared to surmise that the reflection was not from another animal. They did not attack the reflection or get scared by it. They played with it in a manner that indicated they were examining parts of their body they could not otherwise see (inside of the mouth, eyeball, back of the tail, etc.). Then, a mark was placed on several dolphins in a location on their back that could not be seen by them without the use of a mirror. Once they were marked, they swam directly to the mirrors and examined the part of the body that was marked. This is an advanced trait that even human toddlers have trouble with initially.

Another indicator of intelligence can be social complexity, although some may argue that insects have social complexity without high intelligence. In whales, evidence for social complexity abounds in all of their interactions, but some of the best examples probably relate to the cow-calf relationship. Cows and calves can be seen playing together. Cows will protect or "babysit" each other's calves. Odontocetes have been seen carrying a dead calf for days. The reason is unclear, but it has been suggested that they are emotionally bound to the calf, and are either mourning or hoping it will revive.

Social complexity is also apparent from the songs male humpback whales sing. Each group has a typical song, comprised of regular patterns of sound units. When a new whale moves into the territory of an existing group, it may not have the same song pattern. However, it can learn their song pattern and repeat it. Likewise, it may even help create a new song pattern by donating some sound units from the region it came from. All of the whales in a given area sing the same song, but every year, the song evolves into a new song that is learned by all of the whales. One might compare this to learning an evolving foreign language, or copying different accents. One can even make a case that whales have culture and share their culture with other whales in the group.

Sharing culture, or teaching the young, is also apparent in the following example from a group of hunting orcas. This group taught a calf how to hunt seals by repeatedly performing the same hunting maneuver. Each time, the adult orcas lined up in a row, and tried to usher the calf into position. Then they charged the ice floe with the seal, creating a bow wave from the water pressure in front of their bodies. The wave knocked the seal off the ice floe. They didn't kill the seal, but instead let it crawl back up on the ice floe so they could try generating the wave again and again—perhaps around 20 times before the seal was finally consumed.

Hunting in a pack is not unique to orcas, but cooperative interspecies hunting is very unusual. This occurs with dolphins that have trained local fishermen in South America to catch fish cooperatively. The dolphins herd the fish toward the fishermen, and then do a flip to signal that the fish are in position. The fishermen then throw their nets, haul the catch, and share it with the dolphins.

Using tools is another sign of intelligence. Dolphins have been seen using sponges covering the snout (rostrum) to protect it from scratches while probing into crevices between rocks or coral. They basically invented the glove! Dolphins have also been seen using a conch shell as a plow on the sea floor to rake out fish hiding in the sand. They have been documented slapping seaweed to herd fish into a bait ball. The have even corralled fish into a tight bait ball by swimming circles around the fish and kicking up mud to create a visual wall. Then, as the fish try to escape by jumping over the wall, the dolphins catch them in the air. Some dolphins use the beach as a tool, and drive the fish out of water onto the gentle slope. Then, they purposefully beach themselves (a foraging strategy called strand-feeding)

and pick up the fish flopping on the dry sand. They can also use the surface of the water as a barrier to trap fish. Humpback whales are famous for creating a bubble net to corral fish, trapping them between walls of bubbles on the side, the sea

1.16 Orca Pod
Orcas travel in family groups and have complex strategies for hunting their prey. (photo: G. Freund)

1.17 Killer Whale Crest Hat
The orca, or killer whale, is one of the crest images of the Tlingit people, a Northwest Coast tribe. The orca's habit of hunting in social groups and its curiosity about the world above water, which they observe by "skyhopping", has given rise to countless stories and mythological accounts. (Smithsonian NMNH E433020; photo: J. Di Loretto)

29

surface above, and the lunging whale swimming up from below to feed on them. While they cleverly use natural objects as tools (sponges, shells, seaweed), they are particularly creative in modifying natural features to create the geometry of a fish trap (e.g., bubble nets or mud corrals).

My favorite examples of intelligence involve play. Wild belugas trapped in a small breathing hole were caught on film as they spat water at a Russian reporter. This certainly wouldn't free them, or get them a fish reward, so the only reason for this behavior would be to get attention! Perhaps the most unusual example is of a dolphin and a humpback whale playing together. (This type of interaction has been seen in two locations in Hawaii: Kauai and Maui.) The whale allowed the dolphin to wiggle up onto its rostrum, and the humpback whale carried it around out of the water in this position. The humpback whale would then slowly lift its head, and let the dolphin slide down the slope. The dolphin immediately climbed back onto the rostrum to do it again! The slowness of the interaction, the repetitive nature of the play, and the cooperation between the two species indicates this was not aggressive behavior, but complex interspecies play. An unusual example of interspecies tolerance was documented when a dolphin with a crooked spine (presumably ostracized by its own pod) was seen swimming with a pod of sperm whales, as if the sperm whales had accepted the dolphin into their pod.

Whales are endlessly fascinating, and I hope this chapter has piqued your interest. The rest of this book is dedicated to learning more about one peculiar whale: the narwhal. There is very little scientific data on the elusive narwhals, in part because they live in an environment that is very unforgiving to most research operations. Much of what we know about them is through the generosity of the Inuit who have shared their knowledge of, and experiences with, narwhals. The narwhal is a very special whale indeed. In the following pages, you will see why.

1.18 Orca and Calf "Skyhopping"
The purpose of this behavior is unknown, but it occurs regularly among all orcas. This image shows a mother and calf of a "Type C" orca taken in the Ross Sea near Antarctica. Orcas that frequent Arctic regions do so only in summer and are not as comfortable in sea ice as their southern cousins. (Wikipedia Commons; photo: R. Pitman)

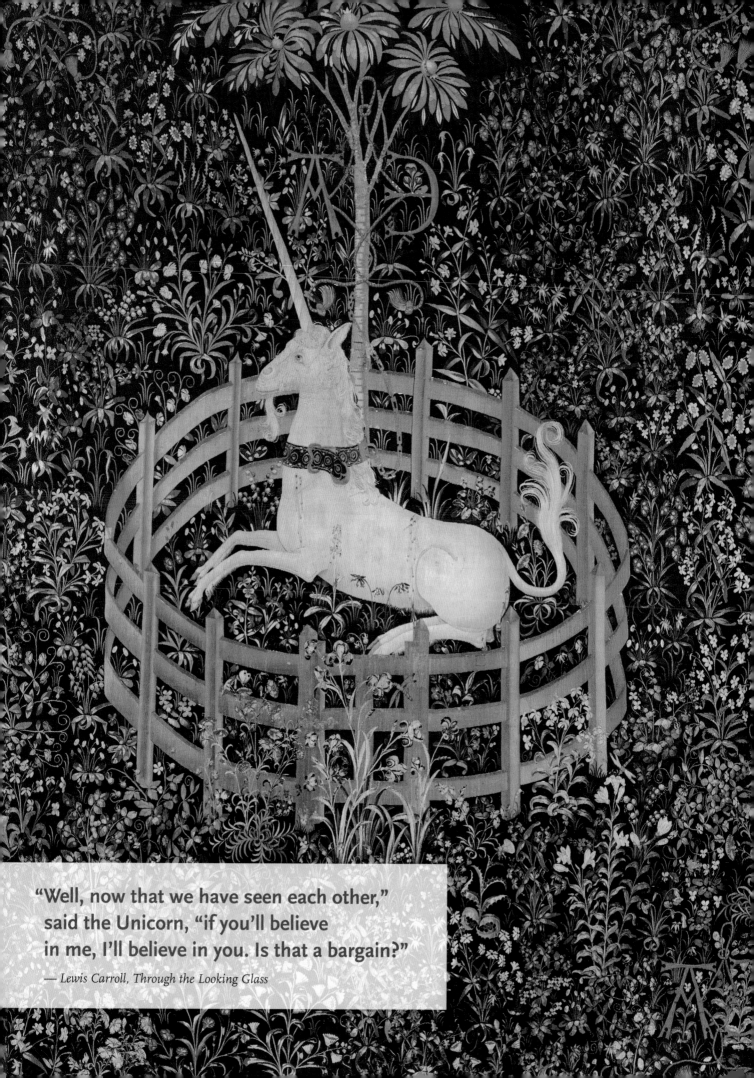

"Well, now that we have seen each other," said the Unicorn, "if you'll believe in me, I'll believe in you. Is that a bargain?"

— *Lewis Carroll, Through the Looking Glass*

The Universally Beloved Unicorn

Barbara Drake Boehm

For more than two millennia, men, women, and children have sustained an irrepressible belief in an elusive one-horned creature, possessed of magical powers (Shepard 1930; Gotfredsen 1999; Lavers 2009). The great, spiraling tusks of the narwhal, believed to be the horns of unicorns, were safeguarded in churches from London to Cracow. The royal abbey of Saint-Denis, outside Paris, possessed one legendarily given to Charlemagne in the ninth century by the Abbasid caliph Harun al-Rashid (Gaborit-Chopin 1991; Pomet 1694), while San Marco in Venice acquired one from Süleyman the Magnificent. Charles VI of France, the Duke of Berry, and the Duke of Burgundy all listed unicorn horns among their prized possessions. When Lorenzo de Medici died in 1492, the "unicorn horn" in his collection was valued at 6,000 florins (Lavers 2009: 94–99).

Stories embellished over the centuries and across the globe provided salient details about the nature of the unicorn, the health benefits associated with the creature, and its natural habitat; works of art echo these beliefs and bring the legendary creature to life.

Hebrew scripture repeatedly refers to a powerful, single-horned animal called the *re'em*, a symbol of strength and piety in Jewish artistic culture. In the biblical Book of Numbers, the strength of the unicorn is twice compared to God's own power (Wischnitzer 1951: 141–156). In the thirteenth-century *Meshal ha-Kadmoni (Fable of the Ancients)*, animals voice their opinions on various subjects. When the text was first printed and illustrated in Brescia, Italy in 1491, it was an image of a unicorn that appeared for the biblical *ofer*, deep in conversation with a ram, proclaiming the wickedness of hunters.

In classical literature, authors like Cstesias (a Greek physician and historian of the fourth century BCE), Aristotle, and Pliny all mention a one-horned beast, while the account of Julius Caesar's campaigns against the Gauls describes "an ox shaped like a stag, from the middle of whose forehead, between the ears, stands forth a single horn, taller and straighter than the horns we know" (Caesar 1952: 350–352). The *Physiologus* (meaning "the

2.1 Unicorn in Captivity
(MMA 37.80.6)

2.2 Unicorn and Ram Discuss the Wickedness of Hunters, *from 15th-century* Meshal ha-Kadmoni (Fable of the Ancients), *1491.* (credit: Jewish Theological Seminary)

**2.3 Woven Band Showing
Unicorns Purifying
Water at a Fountain.**
(MMA 22.106)

scientist"), a text penned in Greek but translated into Latin in the fifth
century, observes that the unicorn has the beard and cloven hooves of a goat
and could only be tamed by a maiden. This text echoed across the centuries,
from Europe to India.

Christian authors—from Basil, bishop of Caesarea in the fourth century,
to Timothy of Gaza in the sixth, to Isidore of Seville in the seventh—speak of
the unicorn. The Christian bestiary, a comprehensive encyclopedia of animals,
relied on the classical text of the *Physiologus* but drew on the observations
of churchmen like Isidore, concluding that the unicorn is a symbol of Christ.

As early as the 13th century the unicorn became an emblem of worldly love
and a common motif in works of art celebrating marriage. A plethora of
images, from portrait panels to tapestries, ceramics, and medals present the
unicorn as the lover drawn to a maiden, the only means of taming the beast.
Surely this is the theme of the *Unicorn in Captivity* tapestry, for no low fence
or slack leash could contain such an animal against its will.

Health Benefits of the Unicorn

Among the special powers repeatedly attributed to the unicorn is its ability
to purify water. Unicorns cleansing water poisoned by a snake so that other
animals might drink is found in some copies of the *Physiologus*. A similar
story appears in the Arabic-language bestiary written by Ibn Baktishu in the
ninth century. In that account, a two-horned beast, the *dabba*, miraculously
purifies the water on behalf of both carnivores and herbivores, and the water
remains clean for thirty days. This legend was embraced with enthusiasm
by European artists. On a delicately woven and colored band, the magical
beasts appear in pairs at either side of a fountain, gently dipping their horns
into the cascading water.

One of the hangings in The Met Cloisters' Unicorn Tapestries series shows the unicorn similarly posed.

There, an unlikely company of animals gathers, their open, red mouths suggesting their thirst. How surprising that these wild creatures should sit together peacefully and patiently, notwithstanding their natural antipathy to one another and the ominous presence of hunters. Such was the sway of the unicorn.

2.4 Unicorn at Fountion with Men and Animals.
(MMA 37.80.2)

35

The health benefits that unicorns offered humans were outlined by the twelfth-century nun and mystic Hildegard of Bingen, who proclaimed that unicorn liver mixed with egg yolk could be used to heal leprosy. Moreover, she asserted that shoes made of unicorn leather promoted healthy feet! (Lavers 2009: 101)

The thirteenth-century Persian physician Zakaria al-Qazwini believed the horn of the *karkadann*, a term sometimes used in Europe, to be effective in curing illnesses as serious as epilepsy and lameness, and as mundane as constipation. Al-Qazwini explains that, because *karkadann* horn was an effective antidote to poison, it was used to make knife handles. His thirteenth-century Arabic text was translated into both Persian and Turkish and was widely distributed (Stetkevych 2002: 121).

Three centuries later, Conrad Gesner, a medical doctor and professor of physics in his native Zurich, rigorously reviewed biblical, classical, and medieval tracts about the unicorn. He saw the long-tapered horns preserved in European collections as evidence of unicorns' existence (Bamforth 2010). Nonetheless, Gesner offers advice as to how to distinguish between authentic and false unicorn horns, and tells of a man cured after eating a poison cherry by drinking the marrow of a unicorn horn mixed with wine. Like al-Qazwini before him, Gesner believed that the horn could be used against epilepsy. In the 1554 edition of his book, Gesner joined the chorus of voices asserting the unicorn's ability to purify water with its horn.

2.5 "Iskandar Kills the Habash Monster," *by Abu'l Qasim Firdausi (935–1020). A folio from a* Shahnama (Book of Kings) *of Firdausi, Iran, ca. 1300, showing warriors in Mongol costumes slaying a unicorn-like creature.* (MMA 69.74.5)

2.6 Woodcut by Erhard Reuwich *illustrating animals, including unicorn, "seen" by German pilgrims around Mount Sinai, published in Bernhard von Breydenbach's* Sanctae peregrinationes (Holy Pilgrimages), *issued in Mainz in 1486.* (MMA 19.49.3)

The notion that unicorn horn was an antidote to poison was persistent. Pierre Pomet (1658–1699), pharmacist to the French king Louis XIV and purveyor of medicinal remedies from distant lands, made the same claim. Five engraved images herald the discussion of unicorns in his book on animals; several types are localized and described in the text. Citing the authority of Ambroise Paré, a French royal surgeon from the early sixteenth century, he asserts that the unicorn known as Camphur, which lives in the Arabian Desert, has a horn that can cure various maladies, especially poisoning. There are signs of change, however, for in his Chapter 33 Pomet discusses the narwhal, noting that what is known as "unicorn horn" is in fact narwhal tusk.

Habitat of the Unicorn

The natural habitat of the unicorn was a vexing question addressed in travel accounts and natural histories. In the Islamic world, Jibra'il ibn Bakhtishu, author of a ninth-century Arabic bestiary, noted that they are said to be common in Nubia and Abyssinia (Contadini 2003). The Persian *Shahnamah*, asserted that Alexander the Great hunted and killed the one-horned creature in Habash (Ethiopia).

Pilgrims accompanying Bishop Bernhard Breydenbach of Mainz to the Holy Land swore they had seen a herd of unicorns near Mount Sinai. The beast's image was illustrated by Erhard Reuwich, the artist who recorded their journey as one of the representative beasts of the region, along with camels and crocodiles. The caption accompanying the woodcut proclaims that they are all "truthfully drawn."

2.7 American unicorns as docile draught animals. (MMA 49.95.1524)

The sixteenth-century naturalist Conrad Gesner cited the authority of a traveler who saw two unicorns near Mecca. But the contemporary engravings of the Four Continents by Julius Goltzius after Maerten de Vos leaves no doubt: they are typically American!

Across the centuries, invariably, the unicorn has been perceived as just out of reach, inhabiting remote, unfamiliar territory. In that sense, medieval and Renaissance accounts are, of course, accurate. After all, the natural habitat of the narwhal could not be much more remote. The cold, scientific facts of their life in the Arctic seem quite incredible, far more difficult to imagine than a horse-like creature with a single great antler inhabiting the woods of Germany, the Holy Land, or even Ethiopia.

In the end, unicorns are emblematic of medieval notions of the magic inherent in the natural world, and while our understanding of the animal from which the beautiful spiral horn derives has changed, our sense of the magic of nature has not diminished.

"Upon another small island here was also found a great dead fish, which, as it would seem, had been embayed with ice, and was in proportion round like to a porpoise, being about twelve foot long, and in bigness answerable, having a horn of two yards long growing out of the snout or nostrils. This horn is wreathed and straight, like in fashion to a taper made of wax, and may truely be thought to be the sea Unicorn. This horn is to be seen and reserved as a jewel by the Queene Majesty's commandment in her wardrobe of robes."

(From the journals of Martin Frobisher expedition 1576–78, reported by George Best 1578)

Part 2

Tooth and Tail

Narwhal Biology: An Overview

Cortney A. Watt

Narwhals (*Monodon monoceros*) are medium-sized toothed whales. They are part of the family Monodontidae, which means one tooth, and their closest living relative is the beluga whale (*Delphinapterus leucas*). Narwhals are part of the annual subsistence hunt by Inuit in Canada and Greenland. Inuit communities eat the blubber and skin (referred to as *maqtaaq*) throughout the year. Typically in Canada and Greenland, Inuit hunt narwhals on their migration route along the ice edge, or in the summer when narwhals are in open water, from boats. Narwhals are also an important part of Inuit culture: The tusks are used for creating crafts and sculptures that are often sold in local craft stores.

The term *narwhal* is Norwegian and literally means "corpse whale," referring to the black-and-white mottled narwhal skin (Mansfield et al. 1975). Narwhal calves, when first born, are almost pink in coloration (personal observation), turning to a uniform grey color, and then eventually gaining the mottled skin coloration seen in adults (Hay 1984). As narwhals age, the mottling becomes whiter, which has led researchers to attempt to use coloration as one method for grouping narwhal into different age classes (Marcoux 2011). An average narwhal is 63 inches (160 cm) in length at birth. Adult females can achieve a length of 156–163 inches (401–414 cm) and a weight of 1,900 lbs. (862 kg), while adult males reach an average length of 180–185 inches (457–470 cm) and 3,625 lbs. (1644 kg) (Hay 1984, Garde et al. 2007). Although coloration has been used as one method for grouping narwhals into age classes, the most accurate age estimates use aspartic acid racemization of the narwhal eye lens and compare this to ages estimated by narwhal length (Garde et al. 2007). Aspartic acid racemization is a method for comparing the ratio of different forms of amino acids in the eye lens to determine age. As an animal ages one form is converted to another and thus, the ratio can be used as a marker for age (Masters et al. 1977). Using this method, researchers estimate that the oldest narwhal was a 115-year-old female from West Greenland.

Previous spread:
3.0 Narwhals in Ice Lead
(photo: G. Williams)

3.1 Brain and Heart Rate Monitoring
Martin Nweeia attaches monitoring equipment for narwhal physiology, assisted by Corey Mattews (left) and Fred Eichmiller. (photo: G. Freund)

3.2 Narwhal Skull and Tusk
Lateral cross-section view. (illustration: N. Rey)

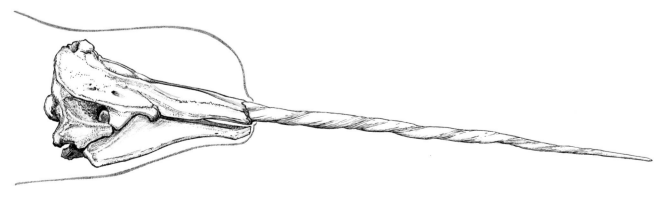

3.3 Narwhal Tusk Nerves
Collecting narwhal
blood and nerve tissue
from a tusk. (photo: J.
Meehan)

The Tusk

Narwhals are best known for their amazing spiral tusk. The tusk typically erupts from the left side of the upper jaw and is primarily seen in males, although approximately 15 percent of females have also been identified with tusks (Roberge and Dunn 1990). Tusks erupt when narwhals are young and can grow to be a maximum size of 8 ft. (2.44 m) (Tomilin 1967; Hay 1984). The right side of the upper jaw also contains a tooth, but this tooth typically remains embedded in the jaw and is not seen; it is referred to as the embedded tusk. A few narwhals have been seen with two tusks and are referred to as double-tuskers.

The function of the tusk is still hotly debated, but many researchers believe it is used for sexual selection, much like the antlers on a deer. Males display their tusk to females, and females will typically mate with males with larger tusks. Tusk length has also been correlated with testes size, indicating that it is a true display, letting females know who is the most fecund male (Kelley et al. 2015). Other research has indicated that the tusk has millions of tiny pores on it, and through these pores narwhals are able to sense their environment. Research by Nweeia et al. (2014) has found that narwhals respond through their tusk to different levels of water salinity, as measured through changes in their heart rate. Other hypotheses about why narwhals have these long erupted tusks and what they are used for include navigating in pack ice, for battle with other narwhals and predators, for hunting prey, for digging in the benthos and scaring prey off the bottom of the sea floor, and for use as a shovel for guiding benthic prey into their mouths (Dietz et al. 2007). Most of these hypotheses have little scientific backing, but it is also difficult to rule any one of them out. The tusk is one of the most unique characteristics of narwhals, and further research on why some whales grow two erupted tusks and why some females have the tusk is still needed.

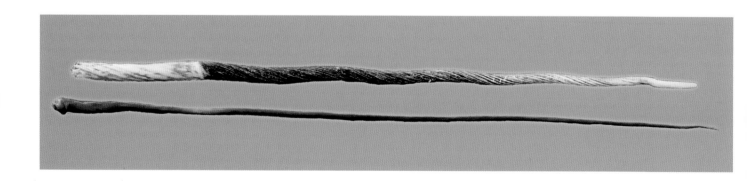

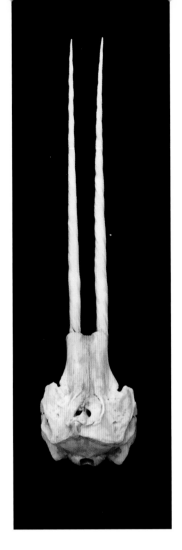

Narwhal Reproduction

No direct observations of narwhal mating have been made. However, the breeding season has been estimated to fall between February and June, based on the size of fetuses in harvested whales (Best and Fisher 1974; Heide-Jørgensen and Garde 2011). It is believed that narwhals have a polygynous mating system in which males mate with many females. Since tusk length is correlated with testes size, it is likely that males with large tusks are more successful at finding mates (Kelley et al. 2015). The narwhal's gestation period is estimated at approximately fourteen months (Best and Fisher 1974). Narwhal calves have been identified as early as late May during routine aerial surveys (Cosens and Dueck 1990) and into the month of August (Mathewson 2016). The rate of reproduction is generally unknown, but it is estimated that female narwhals calve every two to three years, with females becoming sexually mature between age six and seven and males around nine years of age (Garde et al. 2007). In general, what we know about narwhal reproduction is minimal and based on relatively few samples from the Baffin Bay population. Whether narwhals from other populations show different rates is unknown, and further research into reproduction is warranted.

3.4 Double-Tusker
In rare instances, narwhals may have two tusks, but when they do, they are hardly ever the same length, as seen in this narwhal taken on the north coast of Alaska, far from its normal range. (photo: C. Solhan)

3.5 Double Duty
Sandy Angnetsiak and Martin Nweeia package samples for preservation in cold locker. (photo: J. Meehan)

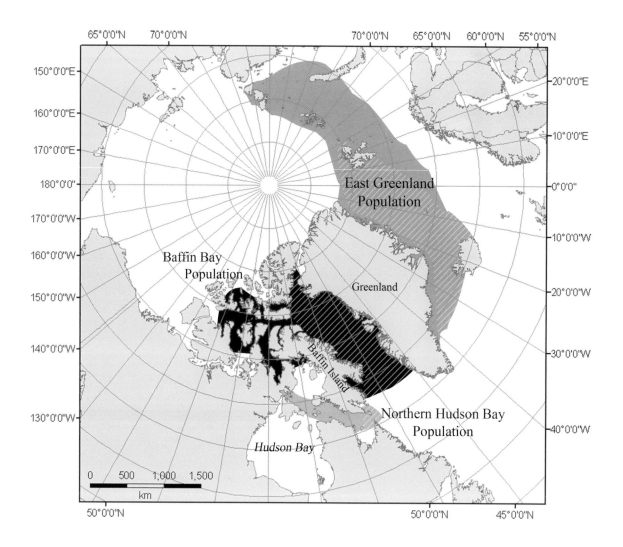

3.6 Narwhal Distribution Map

Summer (solid) and winter range (hashed) for narwhals from the world's three populations; Baffin Bay (black), East Greenland (dark grey), and Northern Hudson Bay (light grey) (Watt et al. 2013).

Where Do Narwhals Live?

There are three populations of narwhals in the world, all spatially and genetically distinct (Richard 1991; Petersen et al. 2011). It is believed there is no overlap in the geographic locales of these populations. The East Greenland population lives off the east coast of Greenland and has a large expansive range, estimated to encompass both Norwegian and Russian waters, but reports of these whales are rare and the range should only be considered a minimum estimate. Although relatively little is known about this population, it is estimated at approximately 6,000 individuals and is the smallest population of narwhals (Heide-Jørgensen et al. 2010). The second largest population in the world is in northern Hudson Bay, estimated at about 12,500 individuals (Asselin et al. 2012). Animals in this population spend the summer in northern Hudson Bay, Canada, and then migrate through the Hudson Strait and spend winter just outside the strait (Richard 1991). Finally, the largest population of narwhals in the world is referred to as the Baffin Bay population, which is estimated at 140,000 individuals

44

(Doniol-Valcroze et al. 2015). Whales in this population spend the winter in the Davis Strait, and summer in the fiords and inlets in northern Canada and western Greenland. Although this population is very large, whales form different summer aggregations, and it is believed the same whales return to the same summering region year after year (Heide-Jørgensen et al. 2003; Dietz et al. 2008; Watt et al. 2012). Narwhals typically remain in their summer region until approximately October, and then begin their migration to the wintering grounds in the Davis Strait (Watt et al. 2012).

Tracking Narwhals

We have a relatively good idea of where narwhals spend their time, as more than 100 narwhals have been tagged with satellite transmitters by researchers in Canada and Greenland since 1993 (Heide-Jørgensen et al. 2013a). Satellite tags are typically attached to narwhals' backs and provide information on their locations, dive behavior, and environmental conditions, such as water temperature and salinity levels (Laidre and Heide-Jørgensen 2007). A few whales have been tracked for over a year, but most tags quit transmitting before that time.

Instrumenting a narwhal with a satellite-linked tag takes a large group of people. Typically narwhals are caught by setting a net perpendicular to shore (Orr et al. 2001). When a whale is caught in the net, two boats (rubberized, low profile boats that allow you to get close to the whale with minimal risk of hurting them) with

3.9 Narwhal Migration
Narwhal group negotiating
an opening in the pack ice.
(photo: G. Williams)

three to four people in each, travel to the net, pull the whale to the surface, and bring the whale close to shore. There the whale is cut free from the net and is held using a rubberized tail rope attached to the tailstock. In addition, for females, a hoop net is placed over their head, and for males their tusk is held by a team member to stabilize the whale. Tags are attached to the dorsal ridge using two or three nylon pins. Anesthetic is not used for the tagging procedure, but a veterinarian monitors the tagging process and takes blood at the start of the capture and again just before the whale is released. Researchers can use this blood to measure stress hormones, such as cortisol, to determine how whales are responding to the tagging process, which usually takes less than thirty minutes. The tags provide valuable information for scientists, including about migration timing and corridors, which is communicated back to the communities that hunt narwhals.

Life in Ice

Narwhals are very well adapted to living in regions with ice cover. They lack a dorsal fin, which allows them to travel easier in ice. Whales have been seen in regions with over 95 percent ice cover (Laidre and Heide-Jørgensen 2011), suggesting that these animals are very good at navigating in the ice and finding areas with access to oxygen. However, sometimes entrapment events do occur. An entrapment is when a group of whales is stuck in the ice at isolated openings without access to open water. Ice-entrapment events are a concern for conservation of the species as a whole and sustainability

46

of specific narwhal stocks that are hunted as a food source by the Inuit. It is unknown how often these events occur as the narwhal's range is quite expansive and many events may not be found. However, a few entrapments have been reported.

In 2008 the largest entrapment in Canada occurred near the community of Pond Inlet, Nunavut. Over 1,000 narwhal were believed to be trapped in the ice after a period of cold weather caused the ice to freeze up very quickly overnight. Although narwhals are good at navigating in pack ice, they are not strong enough to break through ice, and therefore depend on leads and ice-cracks. When these leads and cracks are unavailable they may become entrapped. It was determined that narwhals at this particular entrapment were unlikely to be able to escape and a humane harvest of the whales was conducted based on consultations between the community members of Pond Inlet, the Nunavut Wildlife Management Board, and the Government of Canada. Six hundred and twenty-nine narwhal were harvested in temperatures of -40°C, with only a few hours of daylight. Scientists were able to sample 250 of the harvested whales, and genetically determined that more than 75 percent of these whales were females (Watt and Ferguson 2011). In 2015 another ice entrapment occurred near Pond Inlet, where at least 249 narwhal perished (Watt et al. 2016a). We do not know what causes entrapment events, but researchers linked the 2008 entrapment event to seismic testing that was ongoing off the coast of Baffin Island during the narwhals' typical migration period (Heide-Jørgensen et al. 2013b), and community members from Pond Inlet suggested the 2015 entrapment may have been correlated with increased shipping traffic in the area (Watt et al. 2016). Again, this entrapment event was composed of primarily females (more than 70 percent), suggesting females may be more vulnerable to these events; they could remain in the summer regions longer than males, or may be unable to dive as deep as their larger male counterparts. Alternatively, females with calves may be vulnerable as they are limited in their dive duration, due to the limitations of their accompanying calf. Entrapments are a natural cause of mortality for Arctic cetaceans; however, more research is needed to determine if the events are increasing in frequency or magnitude, or if they are correlated with anthropogenic activities.

What Do Narwhals Eat?

What an animal eats is one of the fundamental biological questions about a species. Monitoring foraging events is challenging for any marine mammal as they typically occur underwater where it is difficult to observe. Narwhals in particular spend part of the year in heavy pack ice and darkness; thus, no study has observed narwhal foraging directly. However, stomach

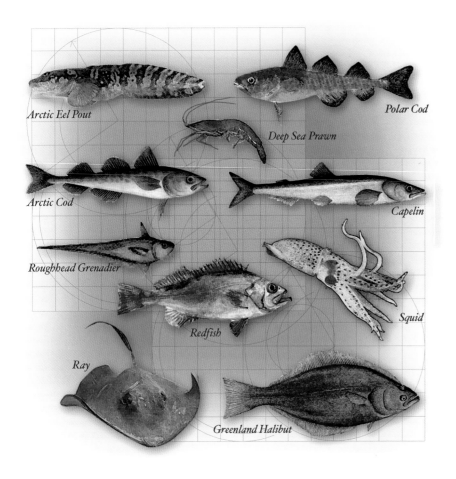

Arctic Eel Pout

Polar Cod

Deep Sea Prawn

Arctic Cod

Capelin

Roughhead Grenadier

Squid

Redfish

Ray

Greenland Halibut

3.10 Narwhal Diet
These are some of the
fish narwhals like to
see on their dinner menu.
(illustration: K. Hand)

contents have been analyzed from narwhals that are part of the subsistence hunt in Canada and Greenland. Stomach contents have suggested that narwhal consume primarily Arctic cod (*Boreogadus saida*), squid (*Gonatus* spp.), and Greenland halibut (*Reinhardtius hippoglossoides*) (Finley and Gibb 1982; Laidre and Heide-Jørgensen 2005b). Stomach contents provide an excellent snapshot of what an animal has recently ingested, but they cannot reveal anything about the long term diet of an animal or what prey is actually assimilated into their tissues, providing the needed source of energy. More recent studies have used chemical techniques that evaluate the tissues of a narwhal to evaluate diet and look at longer term trends in foraging behavior (Watt and Ferguson 2015). Fatty acids are transferred relatively unmodified from prey to predator tissues and can reveal what an animal has been foraging over the previous few weeks (Budge et al. 2006). Stable isotopes, on the other hand, are transferred with some enrichment from prey to predators and can reveal diet on much longer time scales, depending upon the tissue (Newsome et al. 2010).

Studies of narwhal skin have found that narwhals from the world's three populations forage differently (Watt et al. 2013). Whales from the East Greenland population forage more on pelagic (upper waters of the open sea) prey, such as capelin (*Mallotus villosus*), while whales from northern Hudson Bay forage more extensively in the benthic region, on prey such as halibut and shrimp (*Pandalus borealis*) (Watt et al. 2013). Whales from the Baffin Bay population forage approximately equally in both the pelagic and benthic regions. In addition, males from each population seem to have a slightly more benthic foraging signature. We suggest this may be a result of their larger body size that infers greater diving ability for accessing a greater proportion of benthic prey. Stable isotope analysis on different types of tissues can provide information on diet over various time frames (Budge et al. 2006). An analysis of both skin and muscle from narwhals from northern Hudson Bay and Baffin Bay showed that the whales foraged on different prey depending upon the season, and that these changes were more apparent in whales from the Baffin Bay population that migrate a greater distance (Watt and Ferguson 2015).

An evaluation of the long-term diet of narwhals from 1982 to 2011 using a combination of stable isotopes and fatty acids found there were annual changes in diet in both populations, and these changes were more apparent in the most southern population, the northern Hudson Bay narwhals (Watt and Ferguson 2015). This is likely a result of the greater reduction in summer sea ice that has occured in Hudson Bay compared to the High Arctic (Tivy et al. 2011). Changes in sea ice are shifting the food web in Hudson Bay (Gaston et al. 2012), and as a result, it seems narwhal have been adjusting their diet in this region to a greater extent than whales in the High Arctic. As sea ice in the Arctic continues to decline, it is likely narwhals from the Baffin Bay population will also have to further adjust their diet. Monitoring of the food web and narwhal diet will be important for determining how they will meet their energetic requirements and, if needed, for reducing the impact of competition with commercial fisheries in the region.

Diving

Satellite tags provide information on the migration and movements of narwhals. They also collect information on dive behavior. From these tags researchers have found that narwhals dive greater than 1400 m, and these deep dives occur frequently in the winter months (Laidre et al. 2003). Deep dives are energetically expensive, and it is assumed that they correlate with prey acquistion. In the winter, deep diving is likely related to the distribution of one of the narwhals' main prey sources, Greenland halibut (Laidre et al. 2003; Laidre and Heide-Jørgensen 2005b). There is variability in the dive behavior of individual narwhals, but at the population level there is also a significant difference in the way whales dive in the three populations (Watt et al. 2015a). By matching up dive behavior to ocean bottom bathymetry, researchers determined that narwhals from the East Greenland population foraged more in the pelagic zone, while those in Northern Hudson Bay and Baffin Bay foraged more in the deep water column (Watt et al. 2015b). Although it is difficult to prove that these dives are related to foraging, this was in line with diet estimates from stable isotopes for the three populations (Watt et al. 2013). New technologies in the form of stomach temperature pills that interact with satellite tags can tell us where

*3.11 **Flukes Up***
A male narwhal initiates a deep dive by lifting his tail out of the water, initiating downward thrust. (photo: D. White)

3.12 Summer Schooling
*Narwhals gather
in family groups known as
pods while on their
foraging migrations and
while hunting for safe
sanctuary locations during
the relatively ice-free
summer season.*
(photo: D. White)

foraging is occurring in the water column. Stomach temperatures drop
when prey is ingested and thus, a foraging event can be identified based on
temperature profiles. Currently only a few stomach temperature pills have
been deployed in narwhals (all from East Greenland) and most were rejected
within 48 hours; however, two pills provided information for more than a
week and suggested narwhals from this population were feeding in the
summer at depths from 13–850 m) (Heide-Jørgensen et al. 2014). Deploy-
ment of more stomach temperature pills in all narwhal populations throughout the seasons would assist with identifying where in the water column
foraging events are occurring, and could be paired with knowledge about the
relative availability of different prey in those regions.

Using deep diving as a proxy for foraging, areas important for foraging
have been identified for narwhals from northern Hudson Bay and Baffin Bay
(Watt et al. 2016b). Areas important for foraging were identified on the
summer, migratory, and wintering grounds for both populations. Many of
these areas correspond with regions used for shipping and oil and gas
exploration (Reeves et al. 2014). Consideration of how these anthropogenic
activities may impact narwhal foraging, and subsequently, the population
as a whole, will be important for narwhal conservation.

Narwhal Pods

Narwhals are social animals known to travel in large pods. Observations
of narwhals in Eclipse Sound, on northern Baffin Island, Nunavut, Canada
have indicated that within the larger herd animals are divided into many
smaller clusters. Each herd may have up to 600 clusters with anywhere from
one to 25 (Marcoux et al. 2009) or one to 50 (Cosens and Dueck 1991)
individuals in each cluster. Herds usually contain both males and females,
but clusters are almost always composed of a single sex (94 percent of the
time) or contain mature females with calves and immature males (Palsbøll
et al. 1997). Narwhals from Baffin Bay have not been amenable to photo-

identification techniques given their large population size, and the changing of their coloration with age. Nicks and notches on the dorsal ridge have been used for identifying narwhal successfully, but due to the large size of the population only two identified narwhals have ever been resighted (Auger-Méthé et al. 2010). As a result, little is known about the structure of narwhal clusters within larger herds.

A study comparing dietary signatures from fatty acid analysis with genetic relatedness among entrapped narwhals tested to see if there was a correlation between closely related individuals and foraging behaviour (Watt et al. 2015b). A correlation may suggest that animals that are closely related also forage together or share prey among the social group (Ford and Ellis 2006), which is common in animals that display a matrilineal social structure where closely related individuals remain in a social unit centered on the mother throughout their lives (Whitehead 1998; Ford and Ellis 2006). No evidence was found to support the notion that closely related narwhals have similar foraging signatures, which may suggest narwhals have more of a fission-fusion social structure in which animals change the size of their groups, or alter the size of subgroups depending on their activity and resource distribution and availability (Aureli et al. 2008; Watt et al. 2015a). This is common for animals that experience variable prey distribution and seasonally available food sources, and therefore may apply to narwhals that live in the variable Arctic environment; however, more information is needed to reveal their complex social interactions.

3.13 Echolocation
Narwhals use acoustic propagation to navigate and locate prey in the dark and in deep water and perhaps to locate open ice leads.
(illustration: K. Hand)

Communication and Echolocation

Vocalizations among narwhals are common and an integral part of their social behaviour. Narwhals make both pulsed calls and whistles (Marcoux et al. 2012a). Pulses function as both orientation and communication signals (Ford and Fisher 1978). Whistles and pulsed calls are more similar for whales within the same herd compared to whales in other herds, suggesting that narwhals produce unique group or individual calls (Marcoux et al. 2012a). A study of calls specific to two male narwhals found that the two males

3.14 Killer Whale Attack
*This rare photo shows a
killer whale (orca) lunging
at a narwhal in Admiralty
Inlet, Baffin Island.
(photo: G. Freund)*

produced significantly different whistles and pulsed calls. The authors
suggested that these individual specific calls may be used to reunite whales
with their group members (Shapiro 2006).

Narwhals have the most directional echolocation beam, used for foraging
and orientation, reported for any cetacean (Koblitz et al. 2016). Directionality
in the echolocation beam may provide an evolutionary advantage for reducing echoes off of sea ice, allowing the whales to scan a narrow area to locate
prey at far distances and thrive in the variable Arctic environment (Koblitz
et al. 2016). Vocalizations between mother and calf pairs are also likely very
important for the cognitive and social development of narwhals, but not
much is known about communication in narwhals in general. Much of what
scientists know about communication among other cetaceans comes from
studies of whales in captivity. However, there are no captive narwhals
anywhere in the world, and thus, field studies are the only method for
deciphering narwhal communication.

Predators

Other than humans, narwhals have two main predators in the Arctic: the
killer whale and the polar bear. Polar bears are known to forage primarily on
seals (Thiemann et al. 2008); however, beluga whales and narwhals are
also preyed upon (Smith and Sjare 1990). Polar bears take advantage when
whales become stranded in shallow
waters as a result of an outgoing tide.
They also hunt whales at the ice edge or
ice floes (Smith and Sjare 1990). Polar
bears also take advantage of entrapment
events in which whales are isolated at
small breathing holes. Narwhals that
have been tagged with satellite transmitters have displayed scars on the sides
of their body that indicate scratch marks
from polar bears. Although polar
bears are a predator of narwhals, the
bears do not seem to be exploiting
this potential prey to a significant extent
(Smith and Sjare 1990). Killer whales
are the other major predator of narwhals.
Killer whales are not adapted to living
and navigating in sea ice; however, they
tend to move north into Arctic waters in the summer. Summer sightings
of killer whales in the Hudson Bay region have increased exponentially and
the whales are now present every summer (Higdon and Ferguson 2009).

Narwhal behavior changes in the presence of killer whales; narwhals typically move slowly, in tight groups, in very shallow water close to shore in the presence of orcas (Laidre et al. 2006). During an attack, narwhals tend to spread out and travel far from the attack site. How important narwhal are to the killer whales' diet is still unknown, but the annual presence of orcas in the Arctic suggests they may be moving north to take advantage of this seasonal prey source. The Arctic covers a large expanse and it is likely that many interactions between narwhals and their predators go unseen.

3.15 Momentary Solace
A narwhal cruising in Admiralty Inlet on summer vacation. (photo: J. Meehan)

Looking Ahead

Narwhals live in some of the harshest conditions on the planet. They endure long, dark winters in heavily ice-covered waters and dive extremely deep to forage. They are well adapted to the Arctic environment, but how narwhals will fare in the face of changing climate and an overall reduction in sea ice is unknown. An increase in competitors from the south, and the increased presence of killer whales in the Arctic will pose challenges for narwhals. However, reduced sea ice may also mean increased productivity in the Arctic and an increase in potential prey species from the south.

While narwhal were considered specialized in terms of their foraging behavior (Laidre et al. 2008), new evidence suggests narwhal from different populations forage on different prey and therefore the whales may be more adaptable to a changing food web than originally believed. The increase in anthropogenic activities in the Arctic that is likely to accompany a longer open-water season and overall reduction in sea ice (Moore and Huntington 2008) may change narwhal migration behavior and alter the regions they use for foraging (Watt et al. 2016b), which could mean changes in narwhal distribution away from Arctic communities.

This, in turn, would have large impacts on the Inuit communities that rely on the annual harvest of narwhal for subsistence. The narwhal is an iconic Arctic species, and there are still many unanswered questions about their natural history. Further research is needed to uncover more about their elusive behavior, and as the Arctic opens up to more anthropogenic influences an understanding of narwhal biology will be essential for ensuring conservation of the species.

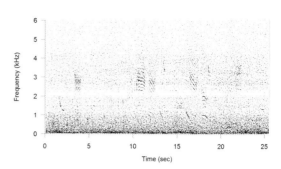

Listening to Narwhals

Marianne Marcoux

Passive acoustic monitoring (PAM) is a technique that uses hydrophones to make recordings to monitor the presence of marine life. We use PAM to monitor the presence of narwhals throughout the year at specific locations. The recording can also detect calls from other marine mammals as well as human-made sounds from boats, ships, and explosive seismic blasts used for oil and gas exploration.

We used PAM in Scott Inlet, Baffin Island, Nunavut, to monitor the presence of narwhals and other marine mammals over an eight-month period between October, 2012 and May, 2013. When marine mammals were detected on our recordings, we determined that sea-ice coverage strongly influenced the presence of marine mammals. Narwhals and bowhead whales were only present before sea ice fully covered the inlet in the fall. In contrast, mating calls of walruses and bearded seals were only heard during the full ice-covered period. Our study provides a baseline measure of the presence of marine mammals in Scott Inlet from fall to spring. We are planning to deploy hydrophones each year at the same location to see if the environmental changes that are occurring rapidly in the Arctic influence the patterns of marine-mammal presence in this location.

PAM is a promising method for research on narwhal ecology. Narwhals produce a distinctive "buzz" call. We hypothesize that this call helps them locate their prey just before they strike—a behavior known for other toothed whales. If our hypothesis is correct, the presence of buzz calls in our recordings could be used to identify key feeding locations. We are also hopeful that PAM can be used to count the number of narwhals present at specific locations.

3.16 Breaking news as we go to print: *Recently released video footage from a 2016 unmanned aerial vehicle (UAV) in Tremblay Sound, Nunavut, documented a previously unknown narwhal feeding behavior.*

The footage shows narwhals using the tip of their tusks to strike and stun fish before eating them. Narwhals then use their tusk to guide the fish into its mouth. Narwhals are very agile with their tusks, and their approach differs depending on whether they are targeting one or a school of fish. Tusk strikes ranged from small taps and circular motions to large strikes. Approximately 60 percent of approaches were successful. These findings overturn previously held ideas that narwhals mostly feed while diving and show that male narwhals feed during summer as well as winter. They also show the value of UAVs for studying narwhal behavior. (credit: Department of Fisheries and Oceans, Canada, Adam Ravetch and WWF, Canada.)

3.17 Narwhal spectrograph
Marine scientists record the sounds of marine mammals to identify different species, study their behavior, determine group sizes, and monitor their presence or absence. This spectrogram shows a series of intermittent narwhal calls recorded in Scott Inlet, Baffin Island. (credit: M. Marcoux)

3.18 Narwhal Fluke Cross-Section
*Profile of a narwhal fluke showing
streamlined fusiform design
with a rounded leading edge and
long tapering trailing edge.*
(credit: F. Fish)

The Physics of Flukes

Frank Fish

Flukes—the lateral extensions of the tail—are cetaceans' propulsive structures. Flexible collagen fibers give the flukes rigidity. Biomechanically, the flukes act like a pair of wings that generate lift. However, unlike the static wings of airplanes, the flukes move in a way to direct the lift force forward to generate thrust by pushing against the water—similar to the way a hand-held fan moves air. The thrust created by flapping tail flukes provides propulsion for swimming and resists the drag of the water. The amount of thrust is accomplished by controlling the angle of the flukes relative to the on-coming flow and by the speed and amplitude of the flukes' flapping or oscillatory movement. Thrust results both from the up-and-down oscillation (heave) and the angular change to the animal's direction of movement (pitch). In this way, the flukes act like a flapping bird wing.

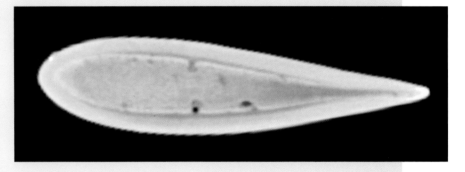

Another factor that influences hydrodynamic performance is shape. The shape of the fluke's cross-sectional profile and the planform outline determine the energy requirements for swimming. The cross-sectional design resembles streamlined, symmetrical airplane wings and hydrofoils. The streamlined fluke cross-section can be described as fusiform, having a rounded leading edge and a long, tapering trailing edge like an elongated teardrop. The maximum thickness of the section profile occurs at 25 to 40 percent of its chord length from the rounded leading edge. The chord length is the distance from the leading to trailing edges of the cross-section. The ratio of the chord length to maximum thickness for fluke profiles has values between 4.0 and 6.3. While this shape is optimal for generating lift, it is also the most efficient shape for reducing drag in the water. Well-performing flukes should possess a morphology that maximizes the ratio of lift to drag. The symmetrical design of the flukes indicates that thrust is generated on both up and down strokes, thus providing a balanced thrust throughout the entire stroke cycle.

55

Fluke planforms for whales and dolphins normally have a swept-back, wing-like design with tapering tips. A tapered wing with sweepback or a crescent design can achieve improved efficiency by reducing drag. A parameter known as the aspect ratio measures the effectiveness of hydrofoil design. Aspect ratio is the ratio of the square of the tip-to-tip span and the planform area of a wing or hydrofoil. Long thin flukes have a high aspect ratio; short broad flukes have a low aspect ratio. High aspect ratio flukes are able to produce high lift with low drag. Fast-swimming dolphins and whales possess relatively high aspect ratio flukes compared to slow-swimming animals. The combination of low sweepback with high aspect ratio flukes produces rapid, highly efficient, swimming.

The morphological design of the flukes is generally constant among most whales and dolphins. An acute departure from the typical fluke shape, however, is found in the narwhal (*Monodon monoceros*).

The flukes of mature male narwhals have a slightly concave leading edge without sweepback. On the other hand, immature male and female narwhals generally have flukes very similar in shape to that of the closely related beluga, which is sweptback like dolphins. In general, narwhals are regarded as very slow swimmers that seldom exceed speeds of 3.8 mph. Such low-speed swimming performance corresponds to the physiology of the propulsive muscles that run along the trunk of the body. These muscles are more similar to the muscles of endurance athletes rather than high-speed sprinters.

When the design of the flukes of male and females is examined, distinct differences are seen between the sexes with respect to cross-sectional profiles and planforms. The flukes of male narwhals have a higher ratio of chord length to maximum thickness compared to females. The average ratio for male narwhals ranges from 3.5 to 5.1, while female narwhals range from 2.3 to 4.8. Streamlined cross-sections have lower drags with higher ratios than fluke profiles with lower values. Conversely, as the ratio of chord length to maximum thickness decreases, as observed in female narwhals, lift is enhanced and stall is delayed. This hydrodynamic performance would be possible because the shape of the cross-section would allow the flow of water to move smoothly over the fluke surface. Similarly, displacement of the maximum thickness to a position further back on the fluke profile leads to delayed stall. Consequently, it would appear that the flukes of male narwhals have a hydrodynamic advantage in reducing drag; however, the cross-sectional design of the flukes of female narwhals would tend to increase lift and delay stall.

Female narwhals have a greater sweepback in fluke planform compared to males. Sweepback of a wing or hydrofoil can reduce the drag as the wing is canted at an angle to the flow by as much as 8.8 percent compared to a wing without sweepback. Sweptback wings produce maximum lift generation at high angles of attack. This would be advantageous, particularly at low swimming speeds when the angle to the flow is high. However, low sweep angles allow for high-efficiency, rapid swimming. Based on this information, it is deduced that female narwhals would have increased lift and thrust at low swimming speeds, whereas males would have high efficiency at high swimming speeds.

The difference in the three-dimensional design of the flukes may be reflected in the hydrodynamics and swimming performance between male and female narwhals. Narwhals are widely distributed in the ice packs found in the waters bordering Greenland and the Canadian High Arctic. There are no differences in swimming speeds between male and female narwhals during migrations. However, female narwhals make more dives to deeper depths when

foraging than males. Oxygen-consumption requirements related to deep dives necessitate increased swimming speed to get to a depth to forage with the available oxygen stored in the body. It is likely that at least during foraging dives, females could be swimming faster than males. The design of female flukes therefore may be associated with the need to swim to greater depths at fast speed. For males, the increased lift and concomitant increase in efficiency from the low sweepback fluke design may help compensate for the possible increased drag associated with possession of the elongate tusk. The lack of sweepback in the flukes of male narwhals may be an adaptation to counteract the added hydrodynamic resistance caused by the male narwhal's tusk, which logically should be a detriment to swimming performance. The physics of flukes helps us understand differences in narwhal behavior related to gender and foraging, just as experiments with tusk function have advanced our knowledge of this otherwise anomalous organ.

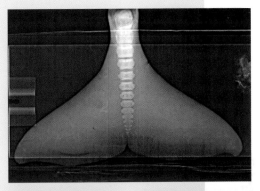

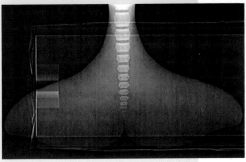

3.19 Fluke Design
Planform views show differences between the straight flukes of a female narwhal (top) and the convex curve of a male narwhal (bottom). These differences probably provide behavioral advantages that are not yet understood. (credit: F. Fish)

Narwhal Tooth Anatomy

The tooth organ system is a hydrodynamic sensor capable of detecting particle gradients, temperature, and pressure.

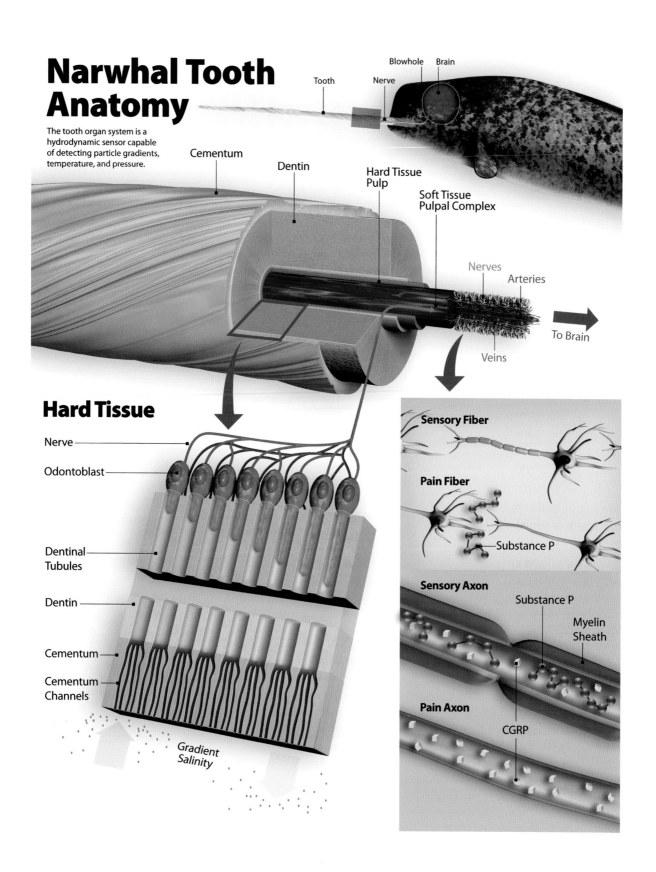

Tooth

Nerve

Blowhole

Brain

Cementum

Dentin

Hard Tissue Pulp

Soft Tissue Pulpal Complex

Nerves

Arteries

Veins

To Brain

Hard Tissue

Nerve

Odontoblast

Dentinal Tubules

Dentin

Cementum

Cementum Channels

Gradient Salinity

Sensory Fiber

Pain Fiber

Substance P

Sensory Axon

Substance P

Myelin Sheath

Pain Axon

CGRP

The Extraordinary Narwhal Tooth

Frederick C. Eichmiller and David H. Pashley

Few organ systems have evolved with more odd and unexplainable characteristics than the teeth in toothed whales. Some species, such as beluga (*Delphinapterus leucas*) and killer whales (*Orcinus orca*) have well-defined rows of teeth used in the typical manner for capturing and chewing prey, while other species have teeth that appear to take on completely different forms and functions, or lack any clearly defined purpose at all. Beaked whales, for instance, have only two teeth in the lower jaw that protrude upward and appear to have no real function. The strapped tooth whale (*Mesoplodon layardii*) also has only two long, curved lower teeth that can neither capture nor chew. Sperm whales (*Physeter macrocephalus*) have only lower teeth and no opposing upper teeth. Perhaps the most unique of all is the narwhal, with a single tooth that is nearly three meters long and is not even located within the animal's mouth. This and many other characteristics of the narwhal's tooth-tusk make it one of the most extrordinary examples of nature's mysterious oddities.

Certain features distinguish the narwhal tusk from all other teeth in both whales and land mammals. The first is the overall shape, with its straight, tapered form that is nearly three meters long in a mature male. This form would certainly provide hydrodynamic efficiency by cutting through the water with less resistance, but the length of the tusk would still make it very inconvenient while swimming. The most likely explanation proposed for the tusk's length is sexual expression. Males with the largest tusks are perhaps preferentially selected by females for procreation of the species, much like deer with the largest antlers. This would explain why tusks are found almost exclusively in males, but there are very few observations of mating behavior to confirm the theory of selective mate preference.

Another feature of the tusk is its helical or spiral twist. The spiral is always left handed, counterclockwise as viewed from the base to the tip. There are two dimensions to the spiral twist, a major spiral that forms the ridges that can be seen on the outer surface of the tusk, and a much smaller spiral that makes up the inner dentin that constitutes the bulk of the tusk's tissue. This minor helix can only be observed microscopically and is also left or counterclockwise. The current theory behind the spiral is that it controls growth along a straight axis down the length of the tusk. The twisting helix assures that as the tusk grows it does not bow or bend too far to one side because it is continually twisting around its central axis.

4.1 Narwhal Tooth Anatomy
Illustration of narwhal tooth sensory function. Dentinal tubules that detect changing environmental conditions connect to a tooth-pulp nerve that provides information to the brain. Lower right depicts sensory apparatus in narwhal nerve tissue. (illustration: K. Hand)

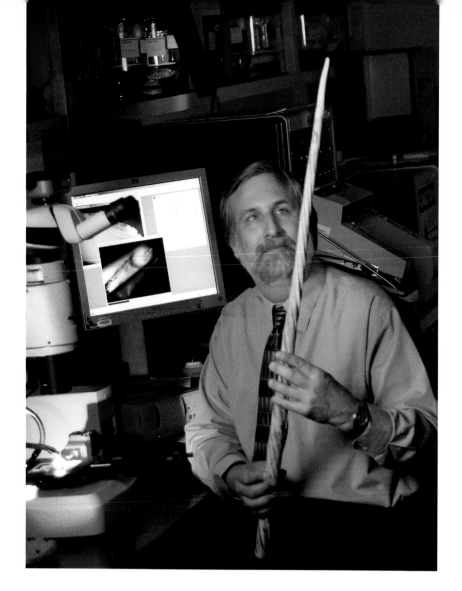

The narwhal tusk's location and direction is another unique example of nature's engineering. Most teeth originate inside the mouth and point either upward or downward with respect to the jaws, but the narwhal tusk erupts above the upper lip in a horizontal, forward direction. Except for narwhals there are no other known examples of teeth that erupt horizontally as part of their normal development. The narwhal tusk is found almost exclusively in males, and nearly all males have this distinguishing single tusk. Female narwhals have been observed with tusks, but they are generally shorter in length and are present in fewer than 15 percent of females. There are also rare examples of tusk expression, such as males with no tusk and the occasional expression of two tusks in both males and females. When a single tusk is present it always erupts from the left side of the upper jaw, the left maxilla, and angles slightly to the left. Actually, all narwhals have two tusks, but it is only the left one that normally develops into a tusk. The right side tusk is usually less than 30 cm in length and remains impacted within the upper jaw. Female narwhals usually have both short tusks impacted within the upper jaw.

Narwhals with two erupted tusks are asymmetric in that the left tusk is almost always longer than the right. Another example of asymmetry in the double-tusked narwhal is that both tusks have the same counterclockwise spiral twist or helix. With a single-tusked narwhal the left tusk is always much longer and larger than the right. Such asymmetry stands in contrast to most examples in nature, where organs or limbs on one side of the body are mirror images of those on the other side.

The narwhal tusk is an engineering marvel. This long slender tooth must survive in a hostile environment of ice and water where it is subjected to dangerous bending stresses and impacts with ice. Narwhal tusks have been used by native Inuit people as levers for lifting and prying sleds in journeys across the sea ice and are renowned for their strength and durability. An examination of the tusk morphology provides some answers on how this strength and toughness is achieved. The first feature is simply its shape. The straight, tapered shape reduces resistance to hydrodynamic stress as the animal swims through the water, thus reducing bending forces. A closer examination shows that the tusk is not solid but rather tube-shaped with a hollow center that caries blood vessels and nerves to nearly the entire length of the tusk. Its hollow form resists bending and minimizes weight—an important feature when considering the strength and energy required to maneuver, in the water, a three-meter-long appendage projecting from the upper jaw.

The tooth tissues that make up the bulk of the tusk are also uniquely suited to their purpose. In chewing teeth such as ours, the outer surface is coated with a very durable, mineral-rich material called enamel. Enamel is hard and wear-resistant, but also brittle and suscepti-ble to cracking. The enamel in chewing teeth is supported by an inner layer of tissue call-ed dentin. Dentin is a flexible and tough tissue that supports the overlying enamel and helps prevent cracking. If a narwhal tooth were formed in this same manner the bending of the long tusk would crack the outer enamel and fracture the tusk. To prevent this, the narwhal tusk is constructed in the

4.3 Strength and Flexibility
Frederick C. Eichmiller (left) and Martin Nweeia testing sections of narwhal tusk for physical charcteristics.
(photo: J. Meehan)

61

4.4 Tusk tubules
*Scanning electron micros-
copy of narwhal tusk
surface showing dentinal
tubule openings. Upper
image at 10,000 magnifi-
cation and lower at 2000 X.
(credit: A. Giuseppetti,
NIST)*

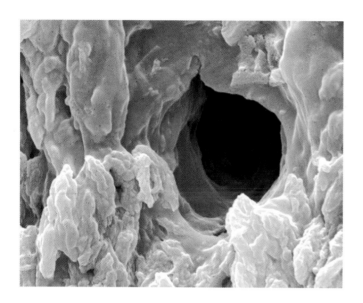

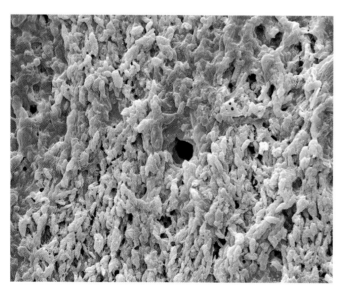

opposite manner, with the harder more mineral-rich tissue nearest the center and the toughest and most flexible tissue—cementum—on the outside. Cementum is found along the entire length of the tusk except for a few centimeters near the tip, where it is often worn away. Cementum consists of a high proportion of tough protein called collagen that can be thought of as a rubber-like coating to prevent cracks from forming on the tusk surface. Beneath the cementum the bulk of the tusk contains a mineral called apatite that can be thought of as nature's fiberglass. In the narwhal tusk, the dentin closer to the outside of the tusk is higher in collagen fibers and lower in apatite than the dentin nearer the center of the tusk. This provides a greater degree of flexibility and toughness to the outer tusk, allowing for greater resistance to bending without cracking or breaking. Overall, the narwhal tusk is a beautifully engineered system.

Maintaining the strength and durability of dentin requires a constant supply of body fluids and minerals. In chewing teeth like ours, these minerals and fluids are supplied by the pulpal blood vessels into the pulp chamber of the tooth and then through a network of small tunnels or tubules that extend through the dentin, ending when they reach the mineral-rich enamel coating. Nearly identical tubules are found in narwhal tusk, starting at the inner pulp chamber. These tubules extend through the entire thickness of the dentin and can be observed under a microscope to exit on the outer surface of the cementum. Since there is no outer layer of enamel these tubules traverse the entire thickness of the tusk from the inner pulp chamber to the tusk's outer surface. One important purpose of these tubules is to nourish the dentin and cementum tissues. This pulp and tubule system is present throughout the tusk and is critical to maintaining strength and integrity.

Sensation is an additional function of the pulp tissue and dentin tubules in teeth. Teeth are sensory organs in that they can sense such stimuli as tempera-ture, pressure, fluid movement, and changes in environmental chemistry. We rely upon this sensation to protect our teeth during normal chewing or when using teeth for other functions, for instance, as a tool to grip objects. Histori-cally, when dentists first began drilling into teeth with rotary drills to remove decay and make fillings, they were impressed that the enamel seemed to be

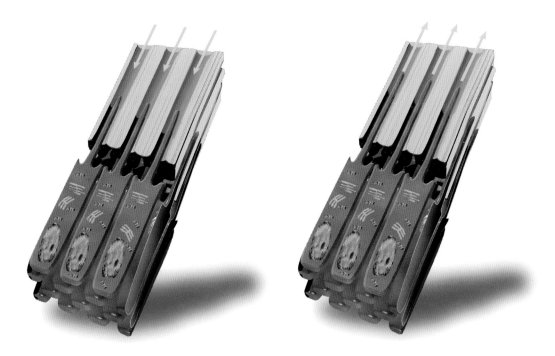

insensitive. However, as soon as the drill reached the dentin, sensitivity was extreme. So they asked their anatomy colleagues to perform histologic studies to investigate the junction between enamel and dentin, a boundary known as the dentinoenamel junction (DEJ). They expected to find pain nerves concentrated at the DEJ. Many careful studies were done, but no nerves were found at the DEJ interface where dentin was most sensitive. Instead, they found that most of the nerves in dentin were located in the pulp, 3 mm beyond the DEJ. How could the necks of teeth be so sensitive to the slightest touch of the dentist? Why did air blasts, directed toward exposed dentin, cause so much pain, while careful grinding of the same surfaces with water-cooled drills produced so little? Is there an obscure transducing mechanism that couples surface stimuli with deep subsurface nerve stimulation?

Dr. Martin Brännström and his colleagues in Sweden performed a series of experiments that demonstrated that dental pain results from minute fluid shifts in either direction within the dentinal tubules. It is this fluid movement that activates pain nerves in the pulp and links surface stimuli to subsurface nerve stimulation (Brännström 1986: Figure 2; Pashley 1986: Figures 3 and 4). A review of the mechanisms responsible for dentin sensitivity can provide insight into how narwhals might use their tusks for survival. For instance, when a male narwhal surfaces to breathe, his tusk extends into the air. If the air is windy, within seconds residual water on the tusk would evaporate, producing sensation, perhaps warning the narwhal of weather conditions. If there was no wind, raising his tusk would not cause water to evaporate from the tusk, and the lack of sensation could indicate calm weather. Sensory nerves within the tusk pulp contain fibers that detect

4.5 Tubule Dynamics
The graphic models show how sensory tubules react to changing environmental conditions by either stretching or compressing nerve plexsus, sending messages to the brain. (illustration: K. Hand)

4.6 Tusk Display
*Narwhals gathering
in an ice lead,
northeastern Baffin
Island, Nunavut.
(photo: G. Williams)*

both pain and sensation and connect through a nervous system network that communicates with the brain. Thus one possible function of the narwhal tusk, other than sexual expression, could be to monitor its environment.

Narwhals are mammals, and they breathe air. Although they can hold their breath much like seals and walruses, if they cannot find air holes in the overlying sea ice, they suffocate and drown from asphyxia. Sea water freezes at -2.7° C. When the fresh water in seawater freezes, the salinity of the residual seawater increases, making it hypertonic (having higher osmotic pressure) with respect to unfrozen seawater. Conversely, when ice melts, the released fresh water dilutes the salinity of seawater making it hypotonic (lower osmotic pressure). If a male narwhal is looking for an "air hole" in the ice in the dark, he may be able to sense hypotonic areas of seawater below the ice where air holes are more likely to exist. When this hypothesis was formulated, it was supposed that narwhal tusks might experience sensation. The sensory pathway begins with hypertonic ocean water permeating the full thickness of cementum through channels and a network of dentinal tubules extending from the cementum-dentin junction to the inner pulpal wall where tooth nerves reside. Changes in seawater salinity are thought to induce proportional changes in hydrodynamic fluid movement that, in turn, produce proportional changes in pulpal nerve activity. This activity is then transmitted via the maxillary division of the fifth cranial nerve to the brain.

To test that hypothesis, Martin Nweeia and colleagues participated in an Arctic expedition that included a veterinarian to temporarily capture male narwhals (Nweeia et al. 2014). A sealed tubular water jacket approximately 50 cm in length was placed around the base of the tusk. The animal's heart rate was monitored while water of either high salinity (41 PPT) or fresh water were injected into the tubular jacket. The order of injection was randomized, and experiments were repeated in six whales. The results showed that heart rates increased during periods when the tusk was exposed to the high salinity water and decreased when the tusk jackets were filled with the fresh water. These results demonstrated a physiologic response to tusks sensing an environmental stimulus related to changing salinity gradients. Other evidence included observation of sensory nerve fibers and neurotransmitter markers in pulp tissue, as well as the anatomical continuity of the nerve pathway from the tusk to the brain.

While sensory ability for teeth is not surprising or unusual, what is unique for the narwhal is the constant communication that occurs through the dentin tubules. In all other known biological systems this type of communi-

cation only occurs in circumstances where there is an unusual insult, such as loss of the protective enamel or unexpected exposure of the under-lying dentin. Sensation in these cases is protective in nature, warning the animal that something is awry with the tooth. For the narwhal the open communication via the dentin tubules is a natural and constant occurrence, suggesting the tusk serves more as an environmental monitor-ing-system than a warning system—another example of nature's amazing engineering.

4.7 In Vivo Monitoring
Field team with Fisheries and Oceans team in Admiralty Inlet, Baffin Island. (photo: G. Freund)

While much remains to be discovered about the narwhal and its tusk, this and other scientific evidence is beginning to reveal its mystery. Understanding this creature and its interactions with its environment requires both objective scientific measurements and the observations and knowledge contributed by Inuit who have been living with and observing narwhals for thousands of years. Their knowledge and collaboration with scientists from many disciplines will be needed to achieve a more comprehensive understanding of this extraordinary tooth.

4.8 Capture
Bringing a live narwhal
in for study in Tremblay
Sound, Pond Inlet.
(photo: I. Groc)

Whale in the Net!

Jack R. Orr and Sandra Black

How do you capture a narwhal and attach a transmitter to its back?

Begin by setting a net approximately 50 meters long and 10 meters deep, approximately 100 meters offshore. The netting is typically composed of a dark-colored nylon formed into a 16-inch mesh, which is almost invisible in the Arctic water. Nets are set with six to eight 12-inch inflatable buoys along their length, and one larger anchor buoy at the deep-water end. The deep-end anchor can be in 30 to 100 meters of water, and must weigh at least 150 kg; the net is also attached to an anchor and line on shore. Both attachment points are necessary to resist the strain of strong tidal currents, or the possibility of the net being dragged off by passing icebergs, ice floes, or struggling whales. Any ice in the area is carefully monitored, so that the net can be pulled before a four-story-high iceberg comes close enough to get tangled. The speed of the ice moving with the tide can result in a real race to save the net. At other times, when the ice is moving fast due to strong winds and current, it can get grounded close to camp, obstructing work for days.

Because whales or ice can be caught in the net at all hours of the day, it is absolutely essential for the team to get to the net as soon as possible. Even a few seconds delay could result in a net destroyed by ice or a whale drowning. With that in mind, all the field staff designated as primary aquatic responders can be called to action at any time of day.

When a whale is caught, one or more of the buoys are pulled underwater and the designated pair on watch springs into action, first by sounding a

portable marine signal horn and loud shouts of "Whale in the net!" to alert the entire team. Quick action is imperative to reach the entangled whale and pull it to the surface. In a frenzy of activity, everyone dons dry suits, and teams of three to four people run to the inflatable boats. One boat rushes to the spot where the net has been pulled down, cuts their motor and hauls the whale up; the second boat motors out to the buoy to cut the net away from the anchor. Once at the surface, the whale is safely restrained using a padded rope around the tail stalk and a rope on the tusk for males and tusked females, or a hoop net over the head for other females and juveniles. Other team members on shore are given an arm wave signal once the anchor rope is cut and, using the on-shore anchor rope, haul net, narwhal and boats to shallow water for study. Sites are carefully selected for a sand or gravel bottom and a slope that allows the captured

narwhal to float rather than touch the substrate, except at the tail end. This ensures safe handling. Once at shore a second tail rope may be attached to the tail stalk and team members gather alongside the whale to work quickly and gently to release it from the net. When the whale is freed, work must be completed within the narrow 20 to 35-minute window from initial capture to release. Careful restraint of the whale requires at least four people to attach the satellite transmitter to the whale's dorsal ridge area, which will provide location points and other data such as dive duration, depth, and temperature. One or two people are needed to collect notes, record measurements such as total length and fluke width, and pass instruments to the tagging team. Taking blood samples from the ventral

fluke vessels requires the expedition veterinarian and an experienced handler to restrain the tail and flukes. Data and samples may also be gathered to examine diet, genetics, and other subjects. Occasionally two, and rarely three, whales are caught together, which spreads the team more thinly. When all procedures have been completed, the project leader gives the signal for three or four people to gently walk the whale into deeper water and release it. There is a sense of profound accomplishment and privilege in working on such a fascinating animal, which the team shares in hugs and handshakes.

4.9 2010 Field Team
Narwhal research team joined by Inuit hunters. (photo: C. Wright)

67

4.10 Successful Catch
*Nweeia and Adrian Arnauyumayuq
with narwhal captured at Qaqqiat
Point, Admiralty Inlet, Arctic Bay.
(photo: C. Wright)*

Making Sense of the Tusk

Martin T. Nweeia

Stories within the field of science often start with a question. In this case, why does an elusive Arctic whale which consumes large fish as its primary diet have no teeth in its mouth? Why instead does one long tusk often form and the potential growth of twelve other teeth get switched off at birth? Why the spiral form of the tusk? Why straight? And ultimately, why this tusk at all?

Answering such questions requires a complicated series of scientific studies ranging across a variety of academic disciplines, including biology, zoology, physics, chemistry, histology, dental sciences, and others.

In this case, the research has to take place in one of the harshest environments on the planet. How does one find and catch a narwhal, and what experiments can be performed to help answer the questions? While science is predicated on forming a hypothesis—a proposed explanation based on evidence—what if there really isn't any evidence available or your gut feeling tells you that the standard hypothesis—in this case, males fighting with their tusks—may be wrong? That was exactly the case when we began to explore alternatives to the favored theory about the function of the narwhal tusk.

Research in the Arctic is difficult, unpredictable, and often frustrating. You can prepare for a year study and then never see a whale. Likewise, as happened in the summer of 2008, your field study can be suddenly shut down by severe

weather; just try to catch a narwhal in a 120-mile-an-hour Arctic hurricane! Jammed-up packed ice, appearing suddenly, can hamper or prevent field experiments during the normal August ice-free window when narwhals are usually seen in the inlets of Baffin Island where they are most often studied.

If the weather cooperates, what else can go wrong? Well, plenty of things, starting with catching a whale. Remember they are mammals, smart ones at that. We put out nets and then waited, monitoring them 24 hours a day in two-hour watches so we would know immediately if we made a catch. The nets needed to be a special color, depth, and length. Carefully-trained teams of twelve people were needed to coordinate the task of bringing in a 1,700-pound marine mammal to shore quickly, untangling it from a net, conducting tests, and eventually freeing it after 30 minutes of study. I guarantee

that such a project has plenty of surprises!

How does one design a live whale experiment in the Arctic? There you are, together with a narwhal in 36-degree water, so you'll need a dry suit to avoid hypothermia. The equipment must be powered by batteries that can withstand the cold. Even such a minor item as a suction cup, used to attach equipment to a whale's skin, needs to be selected and tested from more than 100 different types of rubber and silicone combinations and can determine the success of your work. Predictability of the experimental components takes years to perfect. Eventually, we built waterproof floating laboratories to house the equipment connected to a generator 100 meters away on shore to power electrocardiograms (to monitor heart rate), electroencephalograms (to monitor brain activity), and computers. The experiment had to be designed with a

stimulus, in this case alternating fresh and salt water, and a way to measure the animal's response recorded by a heart monitor.

Working conditions varied from crashing waves and bitter two a.m. cold, to warm sunlit afternoons with calm water. It is humbling working alongside a majestic, powerful animal that could easily overpower the restraining team. Narwhals are intelligent, graceful, and social. Our team included a veterinarian who monitored the captured narwhal and sensed if its family was waiting offshore for it to be freed, or if there were signs of fear and uneasiness that would be difficult for researchers like myself to notice. Of the twelve field expeditions we undertook to gather information, only two were fully successful, but they were well worth the effort.

From our research of anatomy and developmental biology, our team discovered that the

erupted tusk was likely a canine tooth; that it had unusual qualities of flexibility and strength; and that two other vestigial teeth embedded in the upper jaw were not functional and were on the evolutionary pathway to obsolescence. Our field experiments established that the extraordinary tusk of the narwhal is a sensory organ capable of monitoring its environment for particle gradients and potentially for temperature, pressure, and tactile sensation. Research continues; one question has been answered, but many more remain.

4.11 a,b Field Tests
With a narwhal captured and in stable condition, the team begins testing narwhal-tusk sensory function using a floating laboratory containing heart and brain monitors to detect physiological response to tusk sensation.
(photos: G. Freund)

Narwhal DNA

Winston P. Kuo, John Wilken, Alexander J. Trachtenberg,
Pedro A. F. Galante, Lucila Ohno-Machado, Baojun Beryl Gao and Jason G. Jin

Thanks to advances in the field of genetics, scientists are now able
to analyze and compare DNA and amino acid sequences to find hereditary
and evolutionary differences between organisms. These studies rely on
phylogenetics, a field dedicated to mapping the evolutionary histories and
relationships between extant and extinct organisms, to increase the
accuracy of phylogenetic trees. These relationships are visualized in phylogenetic trees that diagram scientists' hypotheses about the evolutionary
history of a lineage based on genotypic (genetic) and phenotypic (physical)
similarities. Molecular phylogenetics has also enabled scientists to address
questions surrounding the evolution history of whales through DNA; in
this chapter, we will discuss the separation of cetaceans from land mammals,
the division of the odontocetes and the mysticetes, and the difference
of the Monodontidae from the other odontocetes. We will present the basic
phylogeny of *Monodon monoceros*, the narwhal, compared to its marine
mammal relatives as determined by DNA analysis.

The taxonomic classification of the narwhal, *Monodon monoceros*, is:

Kingdom: Animalia
Phylum: Chordata
Clade: Synapsida
Class: Mammalia
Order: Cetartiodactyla
Infraorder: Cetacea
Parvorder: Odontoceti
Family: Monodontidae
Genus: *Monodon*
Species: *M. Monoceros*

This phylogenetic tree suggests that mammals shared a common ancestor
with reptiles but split into two separate lineages at some point in history.
Various dating techniques and molecular phylogenetics help scientists
estimate when splits like this occurred.

5.1 Molecular Phylogenetics
Model of DNA carrying the genetic code that programs life. Narwhal sensory gene vertical sequence and initial genetic results were published in the journal The Anatomical Record, *2014. (illustration: Kevin Hand)*

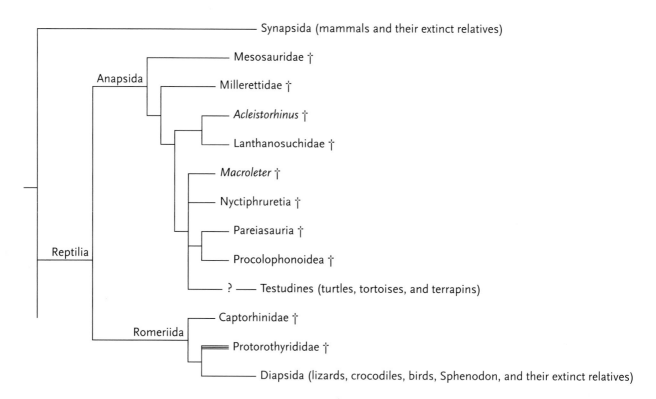

Synapsida (mammals and their extinct relatives)

Mesosauridae †

Millerettidae †

Acleistorhinus †

Lanthanosuchidae †

Macroleter †

Nyctiphruretia †

Pareiasauria †

Procolophonoidea †

? — Testudines (turtles, tortoises, and terrapins)

Captorhinidae †

Protorothyrididae †

Diapsida (lizards, crocodiles, birds, Sphenodon, and their extinct relatives)

Anapsida

Reptilia

Romeriida

5.2 Deep History
Phylogenetic tree showing the evolutionary history of the Amniotes. All but the Synapsida have gone extinct. (after Laurin and Gauthier 2012)

Important parts of the phylogenetic tree include the root, shown by the arrow, the branches, and the tips of the branches. The arrow indicates that the full phylogenetic tree extends further backward from the shown clade. The branches designate evolutionary differences between different clade members, and the tips represent the final descendant taxa for the clade. Note that these final descendants can be extant or extinct; only Synapsida, Testudines, and Diapsida have surviving members. Each of these extant groups has its own descending phylogenetic tree down to the species level, but we don't discuss them here. Our purpose is to present the phylogeny of the narwhal, *M. monoceros*, and its evolutionary relationships with other cetaceans.

The Narwhal's Hippo Sisters

The narwhal is an Odontocete, or toothed whale, that is best recognized by the modified canine "tusk" that protrudes from its upper lip. Narwhals are more closely related to other toothed whales than to the mysticetes, or baleen whales, though the groups do share some anatomical features and behaviors.

While the narwhal's physical traits are useful for taxonomic purposes, they are not perfect phylogenetic indicators. To determine where the narwhal falls in our molecular phylogenetic tree, we must first discuss the separation of cetaceans from other land mammals. As early as 1937, cetaceans were hypothesized to be a derivative of the order Artiodactyla (even-toed ungulates) because of similar fetal membrane structure and accessory uterine structures (Mossman 1937). Another study analyzed Artiodactyla mitochondrial

72

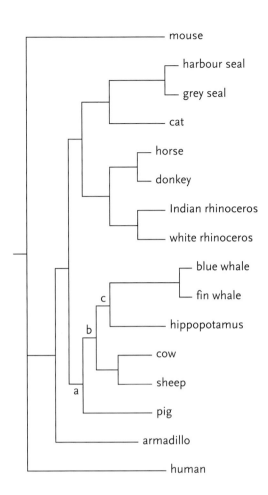

5.3 Ancestry Tree
Maximum-likelihood tree showing the position of the hippopotamus relative to that of a number of other mammalian species. (Strimmer and von Haeseler 1996)

5.4 Foot Structures
Physical comparison of the paraxonic foot of the A) human, B) hippopotamus and C) whale. Note that for A and C, the axis of symmetry runs bilaterally through the third and fourth digits. The paraxonic foot is an example of evolutionary similarity between contemporary mammals that live in very different environments. Paraxonia is a synapomorphy, or shared trait derived from a common ancestor, and is useful in phylogenetic analyses.

and nuclear sequence DNA and strongly supported a sister-group relationship between family Hippopotamidae and family Cetacea (Ursing and Arnason 1998). This phylogeny suggests that the hippopotamus shares more genetic similarities with cetaceans than with other even-toed ungulates like cows, sheep, and pigs.

Paleontological data revealed physical similarities between the Artiodactyla and the cetaceans as well, particularly through the paraxonic foot, in which the axis of the foot lies between the third and fourth digits (Gingerich et al. 2001). Though whales have single-digit flippers, the flippers' multiple metatarsal bones are arranged in the same paraxonic pattern, as shown below.

We currently believe that cetaceans have evolved from an even-toed ungulate ancestor during the Eocene era around 55 million years ago (Thewissen and Williams 2002). Thus, whales and the modern hippopotamus share a close common ancestor. This finding is surprising, considering the differences in behavior, physiology, diet, and habitat.

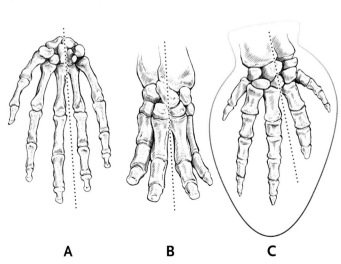

A   **B**   **C**

5.5 Evolution of Whales

Stepwise model of evolutionary separation of toothed and baleen whales. The 1–2a path represents the direct evolution of modern odontocetes, including narwhals, from an ancient toothed ancestor. The 1–2b–3 path represents the stepwise evolution of modern mysticetes from an intermediate "toothed mysticete" that has both baleen and tooth structures. This "toothed mysticete" evolved from an ancient toothed ancestor; whether this ancestor is the same as the modern odontocetes' ancestor has yet to be discovered.

Baleen vs. Teeth

Even among modern whales, there are disparities in body morphology great enough to warrant two parvorders, Odontoceti (toothed whales) and Mysticeti (baleen whales). When did this split happen? How? Molecular phylogenetic analysis proves to be a useful tool in answering these questions.

The fossil record suggests that mysticetes evolved from odontocetes, and that toothed mysticetes with pre-baleen structures existed in the Oligocene epoch (Deméré et al. 2008). That study shows toothed mysticetes dating to 34–24 million years ago and toothless mysticetes from the relatively recent past to 30 million years ago. These toothless mysticetes supposedly used baleen to feed. The study also compares the "nutrient foramina and associated sulci on the lateral portions of [the toothed mysticete] palate" to anatomically homologous structures that provide nutrients to baleen in extant mysticetes and proposes that toothed mysticetes had baleen structures. The study also provides molecular sequence data that indicates the presence of inactive, enamel-forming genes enamelin and ameloblastin in extant mysticetes. This would suggest a stepwise mode of evolution from toothed whales to toothed-plus-baleen whales, to extant baleen whales, as shown. This conclusion suggests that narwhals did not undergo stepwise evolution, but instead remained on a direct evolutionary path from ancestral toothed whales.

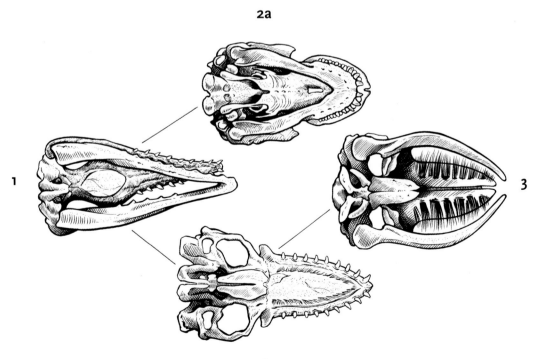

Narwhals and Belugas

A 1994 study attempts to resolve the phylogenetic relationships of the odontocetes and mysticetes, suggesting that from a common ancestor, the Odontocete lineage splits into three major subfamilies: Delphinoidea (narwhals, belugas, dolphins, and porpoises), Ziphiodea (beaked whales), and Physeteroidea (Sperm whales) (Milinkovitch et al. 1994). The study also stated that the position of the narwhal and beluga within Delphinoidea needs to be analyzed further due to morphological similarities and differences between their family members, but its support for Delphinoidea's separation from the other odontocetes with molecular evidence was nonetheless an important step in establishing the narwhal's phylogeny. The phylogenetic tree from this study is shown at right.

Since 1994, further studies have attempted to resolve the Delphinoidea trichotomy with molecular phylogenetics. A 2005 study on the phylogeny of freshwater river dolphins suggests that Delphinidae and Phocoenidae share a closer evolutionary history with each other than with the Monodontidae (Yan et al. 2005). However, more recent phylogenetic studies have questioned these observations.

5.6 Cetacean Evolution
Phylogenetic tree of Cetaceans based on genetic data. Pphoc to Lalbi represents Delphinoidea (dolphins, porpoises, narwhals and belugas); Igeof represents Platanistoidea (river dolphins); Bphys to Bmyst represents the mysticetes; Kbrev to Pcato represents Physeteroidea (sperm whales); and Meuro to Zcavi represents Ziphiodea (beaked whales). The three mammals—the cow, camel, and pecca—are related to the whales shown in the tree, but are less related to the whales than the whales are to each other. The cow/camel/pecca group can help root the phylogenetic tree and establish relative genetic distance between the individual whales, eventually forming the clades differentiated above.

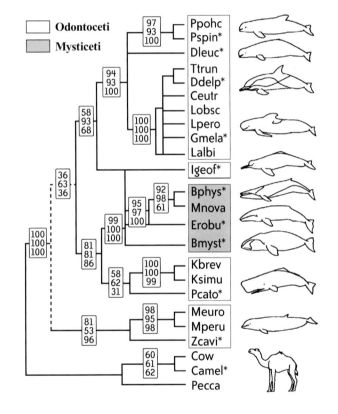

As of 2010, multiple studies on the molecular phylogeny of Delphinoidea support a closer relationship between porpoises, and narwhals, belugas with dolphins as a more distant "sister" group. A recent study analyzed DNA sequences from 110 protein-coding genes from 21 Cetartiodactyla species and found supporting evidence for a sister-group phylogenetic relationship between Phocoenidae and Monodontidae and Delphinidae (Zhou et al. 2011). Evidence from this study supported a sister-group relationship between

5.7 Narwhal and Beluga
Physical traits that differentiate a narwhal from a beluga include the narwhal's mottled coloring, protruding tusk, and larger size. The beluga's melon, or forehead, is far more pronounced than the narwhal's.
Both animals also lack dorsal fins.
(illustration: A. John Gregory)

Cetacea and Hippopotamidae, augmenting previous molecular and paleontological finding, thus supporting the formation of Cetartiodactyla. Another study analyzed non-coding DNA sequences for members of each family within Delphinoidea and also found a close Phocoenidae and Monodontidae grouping with Delphinidae (Chen et al. 2011).

A more recent study analyzed mitochondrial gene cytochrome b in cetaceans. Data supported placing superfamily Delphinoidea closer to superfamily Platanistoidea (river dolphins), more distant to super-family Ziphiodea (beaked whales), and furthest from superfamily Physet-eroidea (sperm whales) within parvorder Odontoceti (Urata 2014). The results from these studies suggest that within Delphinoidea, narwhals and belugas are most closely related to porpoises, and are progressively more distantly related to marine dolphins, river dolphins, beaked whales, sperm whales, and finally parvorder Mysticeti. However, molecular phylogenetics is an evolving field, and we should be prepared to examine new findings and observations supported by DNA analyses that may contradict what we currently understand about the narwhal's phylogeny.

Within the subclass Delphinoidea, the narwhal is most closely related to the beluga, the only other whale belonging to family Monodontidae. The narwhal and the beluga are anatomically similar; the most notable difference is the presence of the tusk in narwhals and the lack of such a tusk in belugas. Physical comparison of a narwhal and a beluga is shown above. Narwhals and belugas range from 12–20 feet in length, though narwhals are normally larger and heavier than their counterparts. Narwhals and belugas share the Arctic Ocean as their natural habitat. Narwhals also possess mottled grey-black dorsal skin that fades to greyish-white toward the under-belly. This color pattern serves as a counter-shading mechanism, helping the narwhal hide from predators, including polar bears and orcas. Belugas, on the other hand, are pure white and are easily identified.

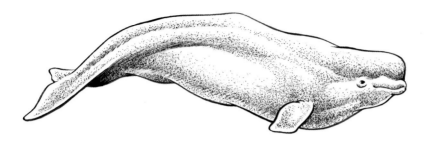

Narwhals and belugas also share large protracted forehead melons, spherical organs that help with communication and echolocation. While the narwhal's melon is mostly static, the beluga can change the shape of its melon at will and alter the frequency and direction of its echolocation beam. Furthermore, a characteristic that separates the Monodontidae from other Odontocetes is the lack of a dorsal fin; instead, narwhals and belugas share a "dorsal ridge," which is a low, rounded pronounced protrusion on animal's back. This ridge has the potential advantage of allowing the Monodontidae to swim directly underneath a frozen ocean surface, making it difficult for large-finned predators like orcas to pursue them without scraping against the ice.

As mentioned earlier, further DNA analysis is needed to fully demonstrate the phylogenetic separation of narwhals and belugas from their dolphin cousins, but we can return to the whales' dental morphology for a physical example of their genetic distance. While the beluga has eight erupted peg-shaped teeth on each side of its upper and lower jaws, the narwhal has no erupted teeth in its mouth. Rather, it has two pairs of maxillary teeth, from which one tooth normally protrudes through the left lip in a leftward-spiraling helix. Male narwhals nearly always possess one tusk, but only around 15 percent of females will grow one.

Although the narwhal and beluga belong to separate genera, there has been speculation around the idea of a potential hybrid between the two species. A 1993 study analyzed the skull of an Odontocete whale hypothesized to be a narwhal-beluga hybrid but was unable to provide proof of narwhal-beluga hybridization (Heide-Jørgensen and Reeves 1993).

To the best of our knowledge, this is the most current phylogeny of the narwhal, pieced together from various molecular phylogenetic analyses. The narwhal is most genetically similar to the beluga, the only other member of family Monodontidae. Within the superfamily Delphinoidea, the narwhal is more closely related to porpoises, and vice versa, compared to other marine dolphins. The narwhal holds a progressively more distant super-family relationship with the freshwater river dolphins, beaked whales, and sperm whales, comprising parvorder Odontoceti. The narwhal is even further genetically removed from parvorder Mysticeti, which is believed to have evolved from a toothed mysticete ancestor via stepwise evolution from toothed odontocetes.

Cetaceans share evolutionary history with land mammals as discussed above; however, three different mammalian phylogenies include species that, through convergent evolution, independently followed the path to aquatic life: Cetartiodactyla, Afrotheria, and Caniformia. These three orders have ancestors that split off into both land-dependent and aquatic-dependent species (Foote et al. 2015). The aquatic-dependent species such as narwhals, whales, dolphins, and porpoises; and land animals, such as, deer, warthogs, pigs, camels, and cows as well as the partially aquatic mammal hippopota-mus are all in the order Cetartiodactyla. The Cetartiodactyla superorder was created more recently because genetic studies have found that, what was thought to be two independent orders—Artiodactyla (even-toed ungulates), and Cetaceans—actually all evolved from a common land ancestor (Price et al. 2005). As a side note, the beaver, from the Rodentia order, also has aquatic abilities, unlike its exclusively land-based relatives—the rat, mouse, mole, and porcupine.

Through molecular studies, the order Proboscidea (elephants) and Hyracoidea (hyrax) have been found to be the closest living land animals to the order Sirenia (manatee and dugongs). Because of this, they are placed under the superorder Afrotheria, which also includes moles, shrews, and aardvarks. Most texts refer to the order Carnivora, but the third classifi-cation is the suborder Caniformia. This includes seals and walruses, which spend most of their life in the ocean, with the exclusively land animals such as the bear family, raccoons, skunks, dog/wolf family, and the partially aquatic otter.

Even though these three orders (super and sub) evolved independently of each other, they had adapted similar traits following convergent evolution. All forearms became flippers. The Cetacean order (whales, etc.) and Sirenia order (manatees, etc.) lost their hind legs, while the seals' hind legs became flippers, similar to the function of the Cetacean and Sirenia tails. The distinct orders containing the elephant, the warthog, the narwhal, and the walrus all developed an attribute that is unique their respective orders: the tusk. The tusk is a tooth that has grown to extend far outside the mouth.

The tooth of the narwhal, which has sensory ability (Nweeia et al. 2014), likely has multiple functions including the defensive function as that of the walrus, warthog, and elephant. The elephant tusks are incisors (Bracco 2013) while the tusks of narwhal (Nweeia et al. 2012), walrus (Winer et al. 2016), and members of the warthog/pig family (Locke 2008; Macdonald et al. 2016) are canine teeth.

As the genomes of new species are sequenced, it becomes possible to fill in the gaps in evolutionary history, adding greater certainty to our understanding of evolutionary relationships, especially those that are most distant in time, and giving us greater insight into the biology of extant species and genes and of their ancestors that are extinct today. Thus, with the completion of the narwhal-genome sequencing project, now well under way, we can anticipate a wealth of new information extending from and building on the pioneering work described in this chapter.

5.8 Curiosity: Narwhal and Human

The current program to sequence narwhal DNA, just getting underway, will likely reveal answers to many of the questions raised in this book. Who are their closest relatives and how long since they had a common ancestor? What kind of environments have they lived in? How will they fare if Arctic ice disappears? How did the tusk evolve, and why? These and many more questions may eventually be answered thanks to revolutionary developments in phylogenetics.
(photo: G. Williams)

Why Sequence Whole Genomes?

Daniel L. Distel

The work described in this chapter demonstrates the undeniable power of genetics and phylogenetics to sort out evolutionary relationships among species, as well as to uncover genetic changes that either explain, result from, or drive (it's often hard to tell which) the evolutionary differentiation of taxa. Amazingly, this work required knowledge of the sequence of just a handful of genes. So why sequence complete genomes?

In phylogenetic analyses, there are two recognized ways to increase the accuracy and certainty of inferred relationships. The first is to increase the number of characters (i.e., variable base pairs) analyzed, and the other is to increase the number of species examined. Both have the overall effect of helping to distinguish between relationships based on a preponderance of evidence and those that might be supported by a few anomalous results. Whales, like most mammals, have something on the order of 20,000 genes in their genomes. Therefore, sampling the complete genome provides increased statistical power to weed out sampling error (e.g. genes that may be evolving at anomalous rates or genes that have duplicated, sending one of the resulting copies on a new evolutionary trajectory). The analysis of whole genomes adds new dimensions not captured by the study of individual genes.

In addition to mutations in gene sequence, genome sequencing allows the study of genome content (i.e., presence or absence of genes in the genome), gene orientation (i.e., the direction in which the coding sequence of a given gene is read with respect to other genes in the genome), gene order (how the genes themselves are ordered along the linear length of the chromosomes), and the vast abundance of sequence that does not contain genes or encode proteins. These types of information add layers of nuance to interpretation of evolutionary processes and can help to sort out such subtle questions as the temporal order of evolutionary changes or whether groups of genes are evolving together under different constraints than others. Recognizing these types of subtleties not only helps to filter out evolutionary white noise that can hide true evolutionary relationships; it can also help reveal how genomic changes alter the biology of species. This analysis explains the differences that we observe among them and yields insight into the biochemical processes that underlie them.

For example, it's obvious how the absence of a gene could alter the biology of a species by eliminating the protein that the missing gene encodes. But changes in order and orientation can change the amount of proteins produced, and this can dramatically effect organismal biology as well. The majority of the mammalian genome, which contains no genes at all, contains regulatory elements and noncoding RNAs that turn genes on and off, and bits of ancient viruses and mobile elements that have entered the genome at some point in history through infection, leaving landmarks on the genomic terrain that can pinpoint the timing and direction of critical evolutionary events and processes.

As the genomes of new species are sequenced, it becomes possible to fill in the gaps in evolutionary history, adding greater certainty to our understanding of evolutionary

relationships, especially those that are most distant in time, and giving us greater insight into the biology of extant species and genes and understanding of their ancestors that are extinct today. Thus, with the completion of the narwhal genome sequencing project, now well under way, we can anticipate a wealth of new information extending and building on the pioneering work described in this chapter.

5.9 *Genetic Sample Preparation*
Dr. Martin Nweeia, working on an ice floe and assisted by Sandy Angnetsiak, prepares genetic samples to be preserved in liquid nitrogen within a dry shipper. (photo: J. Meehan)

The Narwhal Genome Initiative: A Progress Report

Martin T. Nweeia, Jeremy Johnson and Elinor Karlsson

Scientists from several institutions are working with the Principal Investigator of the Narwhal Genome Initiative Martin Nweeia, Harvard and Case Western Reserve Universities Schools of Dental Medicine, Smithsonian Institution and co-investigators Jeremy Johnson and Elinor Karlsson, The Broad Institute of MIT and Harvard; Winston Kuo, CloudHealth Genomics; Daniel Distel, Ocean Genome Legacy, Northeastern University; Sandra Black, University of Calgary and Calgary Zoo: Harris Lewin, College of Biologic Sciences and School of Veterinary Medicine, University of California at Davis; Lucila Oncho-Machado and Jihoon Kim, School of Medicine, University of California at San Diego; Jonathon Coddingon and Lee Weigt, Smithsonian Institution and Pedro Gallante, Centro de Oncologia Molecular Hospital Sírio-Libanês, Brazil and Dovetail Genomics to assemble and initiate biologic analysis of the genome sequence for both male and female narwhals. Institutional partners include the Broad Institute of MIT and Harvard, Harvard School of Dental Medicine, Laboratory for Innovative Translational Technologies, Harvard Medical School, the Science for Life Laboratory of Uppsala University, Sweden, the Global Genome Initiative, Smithsonian Institution's Ocean Genome Legacy, Northeastern University, University of California at Davis, Stanford University, and Centro de Oncologia Molecular - Hospital Sírio-Libanês in Brazil. The project utilizes equipment developed by Illumina and cutting-edge software developed at the Broad Institute. Technology has advanced at a rapid pace since the first human genome was sequenced in 2003 by the Broad Institute, where the Human Genome Project took more than ten years, involved hundreds of researchers at twenty different institutes worldwide, at a cost of almost $3 billion. By contrast, the narwhal genome sequence was recently completed in a few months, involved fewer than a dozen researchers, and cost $10,000. The larger expense ($30,000) was for collecting and transporting narwhal tissue from the Arctic by Martin Nweeia (Harvard, Smithsonian, and Case Western Reserve), Sandie Black (Calgary Zoo), Winston Kuo (Harvard-MIT), and John Wilken (University of California at Santa Barbara).

From this genomic assembly our scientific team has already identified four genes for tusk sensory function that are expressed in living narwhal. Investigators are currently examining genes DLX2, Fam134B, NGFR and TFAP2A,

*Four genes of the male narwhal identified with tooth sensory function
and found in significant amounts in and around the tooth pulp tissue.
(illustration: K. Hand)*

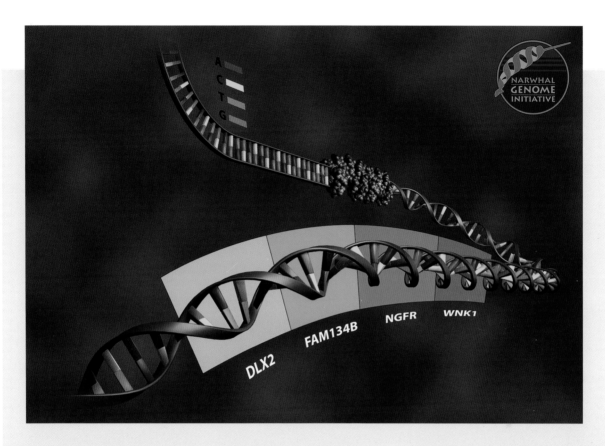

for unique characteristics tied to sensory ability of the male tusk (Nweeia et. al. 2014)

By locating the genes specific for tooth development, researchers are asking why six pair of developing teeth in the narwhal embryo are genetically silenced (turned off) at birth; why one tusk, typically in males, grows to such extraordinary length and forms such an unusual left-handed spiral; why the expression of teeth on both sides of the male narwhal are so different in size; why the teeth of males and females are so different;

and looking at the evolution of toothed whales, how and why did such an unusual example of whale teeth evolve?

Questions of narwhal phylogeny —the evolutionary development and diversification of the species —will be addressed in future studies to better understand how such an extraordinary expression of teeth formed. Genomic studies will also give insights into the expression of this unusual odontocete (toothed whale) when compared to other odontocetes and the evolutionary branching from

mysticetes (baleen whales). Insights into the narwhal's relationship to other tusked animals such as walrus, elephant, and warthog will also be investigated, providing insight into the various expressions of tusks, more specifically of the narwhal. Thus, studying the genome of the narwhal and comparing it to other related animals and their described genomes provides another pathway to better understand the expression of a unique tooth organ system, its evolutionary origins, and its functional significance.

Deep Time: the Narwhal and Beluga Fossil Record

Ryan Paterson, Natalia Rybczynski, David J. Bohaska, and Vladimir V. Pitulko

Finds of narwhal fossils are exceedingly rare and those that have been discovered are geologically recent. The oldest member of the family is late Miocene (12 million years old); the genera and species of the modern narwhal and beluga date to the late Pleistocene (Ice Age), 43,000 years and less. DNA studies show the narwhal—*Monodon monoceras*—diverged from its closest living relative, the beluga—*Delphinapterus leucas* (white whale)—just over six million years ago (McGowen et al. 2009). Together they are the only two living species in the family Monodontidae.

Ice Age Narwhal Fossils

The largest group of early narwhal fossils is known from a single death event in High Arctic Russia. In the mid-1970s, the Russian paleo-geographer V. M. Makeyev found fossil remains of narwhals on Severnaya Zemlya Island (known in English as October Revolution Island) in the archipelago north of the Taimyr Peninsula. A age of 43,000 (+/-1,000) years ago was obtained on a narwhal tusk unearthed from an exposure that included seven nearly complete narwhal skeletons, along with separate tusks and bones of few others. The fossils were found 45 meters above modern sea level along the bank of the Ozernaya River on the western coast of Severnaya Zemlya (Bolshiyanov and Makeyev 1995). In the same area Makeyev observed bones of whales, bearded seal, ringed seal, and walrus. All of these finds probably

resulted from natural entrapment when sea water remained open near the river mouth due to the discharge of warm fresh water in summer. Under such conditions sea mammals feeding in the open water can be trapped and will drown if the sea ice freezes rapidly and the animals are unable to find new breathing holes.

Pleistocene (Ice Age) fossils of narwhals and belugas all seem to be of the modern species and have been found within modern or near-modern ranges. Owen (1846) mentions narwhal tusk fragments from Great Britain, Germany, and Siberia, and illustrates one from England. More common, but still exceedingly rare are skulls and partial skeletons of beluga. In North America some have been found in deposits of the Champlain Sea, which formed between 12,500 and 9,500 years ago when the last continental glacier retreated and the Atlantic Ocean flooded into the depression. Its sediments contain the remains of various other Arctic-dwelling creatures including walruses, bearded seals, ringed seals, and bowhead whales, along with belugas and narwhals (Harington 1977). Champlain Sea remnants include Lake Champlain, which was a southern spur of the sea. Considering that belugas still occur in the St. Lawrence River up to Quebec City, many of the Canadian specimens are within the modern range. One beluga skeleton found in Vermont in 1849 was named "Charlotte" after the town where it was found (Thompson 1853). Today "Charlotte" is the official state fossil of Vermont and is on display at the University of Vermont Museum in Burlington.

Like the narwhal, the beluga inhabits cold Arctic waters, and so it has long been thought that the common ancestor of belugas and narwhals was similarly adapted to a cold Arctic climate. Yet, remains of their fossil relatives show that early Monodontids would have splashed about in balmier waters, off the coasts of the United States, Mexico, and even near the western coastline of central South America. The known fossil record of these extinct Monodontid species extends from 7.2 until 2.9 million years ago. During this interval, the Earth was warmer than today and polar forests reached the Arctic Ocean. Other than the Pleistocene records of modern species, only two early belugas have been formally named and described.

The beluga *Bohaskaia*, named in 2012, is a tuskless fossil monodontid that inhabited the subtropical waters of Virginia and North Carolina during the Early Pliocene (3.8–2.9 million years ago) (Vélez-Juarbe and Pyenson 2012). *Bohaskaia monodontoides* was described from a skull from the Pliocene Yorktown Formation exposed in a pit in Hampton Roads, Virginia. Another skull fragment was reported from the same formation at the Lee Creek Mine in Aurora, North Carolina (Kazár and Bohaska 2008; Whitmore and Kaltenbach 2008). Additional beluga specimens come from Lee Creek Mine, and since they are the same age, some are likely *Bohaskaia*. The size range of flipper elements suggests the possibility of two species. Some of the larger humeri are in the narwhal size range.

Fossils of *Denbola*, another fossil monodontid from the Upper Miocene (7.2–5.3 million years ago) have similarly popped up far from the Arctic, along the northwest coast of Mexico. *Denbola brachycephala* is based on a ca. ten million-year-old skull of upper Miocene age from Isla Cedros, Baja California, Mexico (Barnes 1984). A briefly mentioned but undescribed new species related to *Denbola* has been informally reported from the Upper Miocene of San Diego, California dating five to six million years ago (Barnes and Demere 1991).

Perhaps the only whales more peculiar than the modern narwhal are the ancient relatives, *Odobenocetops peruvianus* and *Odobenocetops leptodon* (de Muizon 1993; de Muizon et al. 1999). Although classified in their own family, the family is generally thought most closely related to the narwhal and beluga. These five-million year old fossil oddities, found in Peru and Northern Chile, were the first known whales to experiment with prominent tusks. Whereas the modern narwhal's single canine (usually the left) points ostentatiously forward, both species of *Odobenocetops* sport a pair of downwards-facing tusks, prompting the moniker 'the walrus-whale.' However, unlike the walrus, the tusks are asymmetrical with the right canine being disproportionately longer. Like the walrus today, *Odobenocetops* appears to have been a suction feeder, using its grossly enlarged upper canines to dig up or pry apart molluscs. Despite its walrus-like appearance, multiple skull traits, particularly in the eye socket and temporal region, suggest a link between *Odobenocetops* with narwhals and belugas, though recent research on freshly unearthed fossils from Chile have prompted some researchers to question this relationship.

6.3 Odobenocetops
This creature, whose name means "walrus-faced Cetacean," was about two meters in length and lived in the Early Pliocene about five million years ago. Like the narwhal the function of its meter-long tusk, which in this case extended to the rear, is unexplained. Unlike the beluga and narwhal, Odobenocetops *lived in temperate and tropical seas. (illustration: Mary Parrish)*

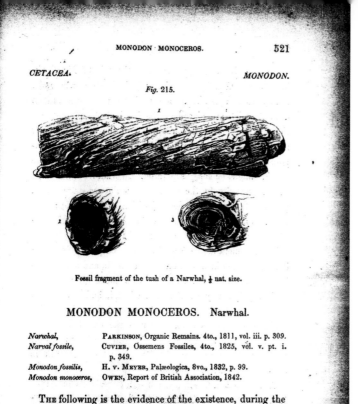

Fig. 215.

Fossil fragment of the tush of a Narwhal, ⅓ nat. size.

MONODON MONOCEROS. Narwhal.

Narwhal,	PARKINSON, Organic Remains. 4to., 1811, vol. iii. p. 309.
Narval fossile,	CUVIER, Ossemens Fossiles, 4to., 1825, vol. v. pt. i. p. 349.
Monodon fossilis,	H. v. MEYER, Palæologica, 8vo., 1832, p. 99.
Monodon monoceros,	OWEN, Report of British Association, 1842.

THE following is the evidence of the existence, during the deposition of our tertiary strata, of the very remarkable species of Cetaceous animal, whose spiral tusk so long perplexed the older naturalists, and still figures in heraldry as the horn of the fabulous Unicorn.

Mr. Parkinson, in the work above cited, states that two fossil fragments of the long-projecting and spirally-twisted tooth of the Narwhal were formerly in the museum of Sir Ashton Lever; and he adds, "One of these I now possess, and strongly suspect it to have been found on the Essex coast."

6.4 Narwhals in Britain
Richard Owen was the first to illustrate a narwhal fossil in his 1846 A History of British Fossil Mammals, and Birds. *He noted that "two fossil fragments of the long-projecting and spirally-twisted tooth of the Narwhal were formerly in the museum of Sir Ashton Lever," adding "one of these I now possess, and strongly suspect it to have been found on the Essex coast."*

In conclusion, the fossil record of monodontids shows two things: They have a relatively late origin, and were more widely distributed in the past. Whether they were warm- or cold-adapted, they were in warmer waters than they are today. Do they have a relict distribution or did they take advantage of a new opportunity?

Warm vs. Cold

The distribution of monodontids suggests the last common ancestor of belugas and narwhals may have been adapted to life in warmer waters and calls into question whether or not some of the supposed Arctic adaptations shared by narwhals and belugas actually arose due to selective pressures in an Arctic environment. Conspicuously, both narwhals and belugas lack a dorsal fin upon their back, a feature otherwise common among cetaceans. Reduction of the dorsal fin is believed to either lessen the difficulty of maneuvering under the sea ice or to aid in heat retention. However, if the dorsal fin arose from a warm-water dwelling ancestor, this trait may actually represent a "preadaptation"—a feature evolved in one environmental context that is retained in a new environment because it fortuitously also provides a selective advantage in that new environment. An example of preadaptation may be the case of the modern camel, whose giant ancestors have been uncovered in the High Arctic of Canada. With fossil evidence in hand, researchers have suggested that the modern camel, an icon of the sweltering desert as well as 'Arctic' Inner Asia, may have inherited its hump from an ancestor adapted to living in the High Arctic, at a time when the Arctic was covered by a boreal-type forest (Rybczynski et al. 2013). In this context the hump may have originally served as fat storage to survive dark, frigid winters, and so would have been a preadaptation in the modern desert-dwelling descendant.

Unfortunately, the fossil record of monodontids is sparse, and most specimens are incomplete, making it difficult to reconstruct the evolutionary history of this group, particularly as it relates to the Arctic. As the Arctic and other landscapes continues to be surveyed for fossil remains, and as paleontologists remain eternally vigilant for odd specimens in museum collections, more fossil relatives and ancestors of narwhals will likely be found, helping us to understand how the narwhal became one of the most fantastical of all living creatures.

Narwhals and Climate

R. Ewan Fordyce

The narwhal lineage is an ancient one that has endured the great climate fluctuations of the ice ages during the last 2.5 million years. Narwhals live only in cold Arctic and Subarctic waters, closely associated with ice. Most narwhal populations are in the North Atlantic. The species migrates seasonally, feeding on cold-water fish and squid. Migrating narwhals generally return to the same location each season. Thus, narwhal biology is strongly linked to Arctic climate.

Narwhals occasionally range south beyond their usual limits, into waters around Britain and northern Europe. It is thought that narwhal ranges were affected during the historic "little ice age," a time of cooler climate from about 1300 to the 1800s. This "little ice age" included several marked short cold snaps. Narwhals experienced these climate fluctuations, but the exact affect on the species is uncertain.

The "little ice age" is one of several climate fluctuations that narwhals encountered since the last major ice age. The time since the last ice age, which is known as the Holocene interval, spans the last 11,700 years. Human populations expanded widely during the Holocene, and Arctic cultures were established. Ancient remains of narwhals have been reported from Holocene marine sediments around the North Atlantic, suggesting that the species had a distribution like today's.

If we look back beyond the last large ice age, we discover a history of major warming and cooling with a global impact. Those changes form climate cycles on time-long scales. For example, the last 800,000 years had eight climate cycles roughly 100,000 years long. Glacial advances, cooling, and lowered sea level alternated with glacial retreats, warming, and rising sea level. In cool intervals, glaciers spread across the northern continents, and ice expanded southward in the Atlantic. The cool-warm climate cycles extend back some 2.5 million years. Collectively, these cycles represent the Pleistocene time interval. There are a few narwhal fossils from Pleistocene sediments, but not enough to show a detailed history for the species. However, studies of molecular signals from living narwhals and the closely related beluga reveal narwhal history on a longer time scale.

Molecular signals from living animals—like whales and dolphins—provide "genetic fingerprints" to show which species are related closely. The molecular signals can also be used to predict when any two living species had a common ancestor. Such methods suggest that narwhals and belugas had a common ancestor about 6.3 million years ago, long before the Pleistocene ice ages. This means that the narwhal lineage is at least 6 million years old, and that it originated before the onset of major cooling cycles.

Global warming will reduce the area of the ice that is linked so closely to narwhal habitat. Narwhal ranges will probably contract to the north as ice cover reduces. How much ice is needed to maintain narwhal habitat? Narwhals clearly survived the conditions of the last interglacial, 125,000 years ago—a time of minimal ice, warmth, and high sea levels—and should survive them again. But, conditions of the last interglacial were not complicated by humans.

Part 3

Narwhal and Inuit

"The Inuit inhabit the whole Arctic coast of America and many
islands of the Arctic Archipelago. Their habitat extends on
the Atlantic side from East Greenland to southern Labrador, and
thence westward to Bering Strait. A few colonies are even located
on the Asiatic shore of Bering Strait. Their culture throughout
this vast area is remarkably uniform."

(Franz Boas, "The Folk-lore of the Eskimo" Journal of American Folk-Lore, 17(64), 1904)

Qaujimajatuqangit:
Inuit Knowledge and Modern Life

Henry P. Huntington and Kristin H. Westdal

To a visitor, the view from Pond Inlet in northeastern Baffin Island is beautiful, if austere. The community sits on a hillside sloping down to the waters of Eclipse Sound. In July melting sea ice fills much of the sound, trapping an iceberg here and there, an expanse of slippery surfaces and dangerous holes. Bylot Island's sharp mountains and rugged glaciers rise from the far side of the sound. "Remote," "trackless," and "wilderness" may come to mind. In winter, when the sea ice is solid, the sun has set for months (from late October to early February), and cold winds carry a blur of snow over the land, a visitor may also think of "harsh" and even "hostile."

For the Inuit who live here, none of these words would seem apt. The land is indeed beautiful, and it is well known. Every feature has a name, often a descriptive one that will help in finding one's way. Inuksuit—cairns and human-like figures of stacked stones—can be seen on hilltops, a reminder that people have long called this home. The sea provides food in the form of narwhal, seal, and fish, and winter sea ice is a pathway for travel. In the days when people lived in smaller camps and settlements across the landscape, winter was a time to visit, to socialize, a time for telling stories and playing games.

This stark contrast in perspectives illustrates the distance we must traverse to share Inuit ways of knowing and living with those who have lived very different experiences. This chapter's authors started on the visitors' side but we have, nonetheless, learned enough about the people through friendships and collegial relationships, and shared enough experiences on the Arctic land and sea and in Arctic communities, to develop knowledge to better understand this part of the peopled world.

One starting point is an appreciation for the deep knowledge and wisdom gained by Inuit, transmitted through the generations, and continually increased and adapted through experience. In Nunavut, this knowledge is

Previous spread:
7.0 Narwhal Hunt in Qaanaaq
Greenland Inuit hunters in the Thule District of Northwest Greenland hunt narwhal in kayaks with harpoons. After a successful strike the animal is dispatched with a rifle shot. Use of a harpoon ensures retrieval if the animal sinks. (photo H. Saxgren)

7.1 Pond Inlet
Known by the 19th-century Inuit as Mittimatalik, Pond Inlet derives much of its "country food" from narwhals, walrus, seals, and halibut. Mineral deposits have recently figured prominently in its economy. (photo: Getty Images)

7.2 Inuksuit
An ancient South Baffin Island Inuit construction is said to "stand in place of a human." (photo: N. Hallendy)

7.3 Walrus Hunt
Although times and technology have changed, traditional methods like harpooning remain the only way to manage a sustainable sea mammal harvest. If an animal is shot and sinks before it has been harpooned, the modern technology is not efficient but wasteful.
(photo: G. Williams)

called Inuit Qaujimajatuqangiiqt, "that which has long been known by Inuit." Without this knowledge Inuit could never have survived in this region. With this knowledge they developed a remarkable material, social, and spiritual culture far from the tropical origins of humanity. Their knowledge has stood the test of time, as Inuk after Inuk has staked his or her life on the ability to find food, travel safely, make tools and clothing, and cooperate in small groups.

Today, Inuit Qaujimajatuqangit is no less relevant for being safe and productive on the land, the ice, and the water. Modes of travel have changed, from dog team to snowmobile, from kayak to motorboat. Synthetic clothing has replaced much that was made from skins and furs. Radios and phones allow instant communication. But the animals remain the same, the sea ice still has its perils, and the differences between success, failure, and disaster remain small.

There is more to living on the land than survival. Inuit recognize their role in caring for the land and the animals, the system of which they are part. Respect for animals is paramount for hunters, to make sure the animals will continue to give themselves to those who need them. Even if television shows and the National Hockey League provide the same distractions in Pond Inlet as they do in the south, thriving in Pond Inlet depends on heeding the hard-won lessons of one's ancestors.

Inuit Qaujimajatuqangit in Action

Many facets of Inuit Qaujimajatuqangit seem straightforward to visitors. Animals are understood in terms of their food, their habitat, their migrations, and behavior. Sea-ice terms reflect such conspicuous features as the jumbled pressure ridges created by colliding ice floes, or cracks that can widen and trap a traveler on the far side. Clouds and wind help in predicting weather. Much has been documented in the past few decades about the details of such knowledge in many communities across the North. Indeed, early explorers often relied on Inuit and other indigenous peoples to keep them safe and fed and to show them the way to their "discoveries." What Roald Amundsen learned from Inuit during his transit of the Northwest Passage was instrumental in his later success in being the first to reach the South Pole.

The observations on which Inuit Qaujimajatuqangit is built can also be easy to understand and yet awe-inspiring. Navigation in poor visibility can be difficult and mistakes can have dire consequences. When crossing largely featureless ground near one community, hunters in a whiteout are advised to dig through the snow to see which way the blades of grass are pointing on the ground. If they have been paying attention to wind direction during freeze-up and the first snowfall, as they should have done, they can then use the grass to orient themselves. Crucially, however, one hole is not enough to stake one's life on. Travelers should dig four holes to make sure the grass is all pointing in the same direction, a much more likely indicator of the overall wind direction, rather than a chance of local topography or swirling wind.

Inuit also see deep connections in their ecosystem, which may not be so apparent to visitors. In western Alaska, during a study about traditional knowledge of beluga whales, a group of Elders was discussing whales but then moved into a conversation about beavers. Noting the puzzled look on the researcher's face, one of the Elders asked if the researcher understood why beavers were important. The researcher admitted he was confused. The Elder explained that beaver populations in the area were increasing, leading to more dammed streams. These streams were the spawning habitat for many of the fishes that the belugas eat in the nearby bay. Hence, beavers were affecting belugas. The connection seems obvious once explained, but few scientists study both the marine and the terrestrial realms together and rarely have the depth of time in one place to recognize such patterns of influence as that connecting beaver dams and beluga prey (Huntington 2011).

In a traditional knowledge study of killer whales in Pond Inlet, eastern Nunavut, another perhaps more obvious example emerges. Numerous elders spoke of marine mammals such as seals and narwhal being easy to hunt at certain times during the open-water season when the animals would bunch up close to shore. These times would occur when killer whales were in the region (Westdal et

7.4 Winter Travel
Traditional Inuit knowledge and clothing crucial to survival for millennia is still important for safe travel and subsistence activities despite the introduction of modern technologies like satellite phones and snow machines. (photo: G. Williams)

7.5 Summer Camp
*Today, as in ancient
times, summer camp is
a time when families
came together at good
hunting and fishing
locations. Plentiful food,
calm weather, and long
sunlit days encouraged
the sharing of information.
In this undated photo,
a polar bear kill provides
an opportunity for
youths to learn from an
experienced hunter.
(photographer unknown)*

al. 2013). Though not seen often by the hunters, and certainly before killer whales would be spotted, the behavior of other marine life would indicate to the experienced eye that they were there.

Inuit understanding reveals a worldview that can be very different from what visitors are used to. On St. Lawrence Island in the northern Bering Sea, Yupik whalers recognize a behavior of bowhead whales that they call *angyi*. A whale will swim alongside the whalers' boat, on the side away from the harpooner, and roll partway on its side to take a good look at the crew one by one. If it is satisfied, the whale may then offer itself to the whalers by surfacing where the harpooner can strike it. The word *angyi* shares a root with the word for "gift," and is also the root of the word *angyaq*, the walrus-skin boat the whalers use. This behavior, and the cognitive ability it requires, is not part of scientific understanding of bowhead whales. Yet the St. Lawrence Island whalers continue to hunt the whales successfully, so dismissing their observations and understanding seems unwise (Noongwook et al. 2007).

In the Eastern Canadian Arctic, we find another example of a local relationship and understanding of wildlife that may be quite different from a visitor's understanding. Killer whales, which have a long but still-evolving

history in the north, are respected and considered very wise. Numerous participants in a traditional knowledge study across Nunavut noted being advised by elders never to harass, hurt, or shoot killer whales as they and their pod will remember and seek vengeance. Individuals who knew of people who had shot at killer whales would steer clear of boating on days when killer whales were thought to be in the area, even years after.

Inuit Qaujimajatuqangit is at heart a collaborative undertaking, in which individuals share experiences and insights so all can learn, all can be safe and successful when out on the land and sea. The transmission of knowledge from elder to youth is important in a community that retains many traditional practices like Pond Inlet on northern Baffin Island. This sharing is arguably more important now than historically, with a much larger population, time obligations, and so many distractions and activities available to youth. Programming with elders exists in the community, but camping in individual family units and in

larger groups in more permanent hunting camps are common in the
summer. This is where much intergenerational learning takes place.
"A family that hunts together stays together" is a favorite saying. The largest
camp, at the north end of a large inlet, Saviit, will often have five to ten
families camped at any given time during the open-water season. Activities
such as tool repair and preparation, hunting out on the water, meat preparations, fishing, and fish preparations such as gutting and smoking, occur
simultaneously with all age groups involved, observing or partaking in some
way. It's easy to see how this transmission might occur when, for example,
mothers work with babies looking on inquisitively from their safe place
in the *amauti* (traditional Inuit parka) on their mother's back.

In addition to learning from one another and from experience, Inuit are
typically eager to add new information from any good source. Once when a
bowhead whale was being cut up on the ice, an elder described to a young
researcher the details of the remnant pelvic bones of the whale. He talked of
the differences between males and females, and what these differences
meant in terms of reproductive physiology and behavior. The young researcher was amazed at the depth of understanding beyond the relevance for
any practical purposes in butchering or use of the whale. Then he asked the
elder how he had learned so much about this small feature. The elder smiled
and said, "The biologists told me," adding that since then, he had paid
attention at each whale he helped with. The elder considered this interesting
information part of his own understanding of bowhead whales and was
proud to know it: that mattered far more than any concern about what might
be "traditional."

7.6 Amauti
*The mother's parka with
a huge hood, known
as amauti, doubles as a
baby-carrier, allowing
Inuit women to go about
their chores while keeping
their child warm. Bottles
are convenient add-ons.
Alice Erkloo and her
daughter Rebecca Erkloo.
(photo: J. Meehan)*

Life in the North

For many Inuit, life on the land is fundamentally different from life in the community. In the community, there are the pressing quotidian concerns of going to work, paying the bills, doing the chores, and so on. On the land, there is a sense of freedom, following the rhythms of the surrounding world, doing things that have been done since time immemorial. Physically, life on the land may involve much more work. Mentally, it may require close attention and care. But emotionally, life on the land confers a sense of wholeness, with everything as it should be, in one's relationship to the land, sea, and animals, and one's sense of purpose. Even visitors fortunate enough to travel with Inuit can experience a taste of this feeling, living in the present and very much attached to place.

The split between life in the community and life on the land creates many challenges for Inuit today. This can be seen across age ranges. One can see the struggle in high school-aged youth in Pond Inlet for example, who want to get an education, know the value in it for their future, but are drawn to snowmobiles, boating, and hunting much more than the class-room. It can also be seen in experienced hunters who provide for their families and the community, yet have full-time jobs and schedules that don't correspond with the timing of migrating wildlife. Finding a balance between the two is not easy.

Food is, for Inuit as for many cultures, an essential part of continuity and a way of connecting a community. For many visitors, cold is the key characteristic of the Arctic. For Arctic peoples, however, food is central. Hudson Stuck, archdeacon of the Yukon in the early 1900s, traveled throughout northern Alaska by dog team (Stuck 1917). He noted that the village site of Point Hope was exposed to high winds, snowdrifts, and other meteorological discomforts. The one saving grace, however, was that no matter the wind direction the ice on at least some part of the local coastline would pull away, leaving open water for hunting seals. In other words, putting up with bad weather was a small price to pay for reliable food. Later on the same trip, he preached in Barrow (now Utqiagvik) about tropical locales where food fell from trees. An old woman made clear to him that she was ready to move there immediately, not for the sunshine and warm breezes, but for the food that could be obtained without effort. To that end, if one wants to find biologically productive places and important wildlife habitat in the north, it should come as no surprise that regions surrounding community locations are a reliable place to start research.

Similarly, Inuit from Utqiagvik, Clyde River (known today as Kangiqtugaapik on Baffin Island, southeast from Pond Inlet), and Qaanaaq in northern Greenland were involved in a sea ice project that included members of each community visiting the other locales to see things firsthand (Gearheard et al. 2013). Participants would travel out onto the sea ice, where the local residents would point out important features or indicators of danger or opportunity. Then all would discuss the day's events back on land. The academic researchers would typically start a conversation by talking about some aspect of sea ice. When the Inuit took the lead in the conversation, however, the discussion immediately turned to food. "How do you catch seals?" "What kind of fish do you have?" It became clear that sea ice, no matter how interesting and no matter how well-known in detail and nuance, was simply the means to an end, the end being food.

The procurement of food, harvesting the same animals in the same places as one's forebears have done through time, is central to continuity. But this is just one part of the story. Sharing food is vital to a healthy society, and so, it is essential to show respect for animals by treating them properly after they are caught. Here, too, is a difference in outlook between Inuit and visitors. In many societies, especially mainstream North American culture, wealth and prosperity are derived from procuring and accumulating abundance. For Inuit, status and well-being are typically measured by how much one can share. A young hunter gives his or her first seal or caribou away,

7.7 Food Sharing
Throughout the North the sharing of a hunter's catch among members of a community is widely practiced even when most of one's food comes from the store. This Arctic Bay family is preparing narwhal maqtaaq. *(photo: J. Meehan)*

usually to an elder. A mature hunter is recognized both for skill and for generosity. One who hoards food or anything else may be regarded as unwell. Incorporating old and new, today it's not uncommon to see hunters sharing their catch on social media and calling for those wanting meat to stop by their home and pick some up.

Sharing is a reciprocal act, calling for something in return. That return, however, does not cancel a debt, but increases the strength of the sharing bond between individuals. These bonds create lasting partnerships of mutual benefit. In modern terms, this phenomenon might be called a form of resilience, providing some protection from, say, a change in health. To Inuit, connections among people are simply a matter of being fully human, of living one's potential as part of a community rather than as an isolated individual. This philosophy is at odds with the materialistic culture portrayed on television and in movies, pervasive now throughout the North as it is in the rest of the world. Such mixed messages contribute to the sense of dislocation felt by many Inuit as they straddle traditional and modern worlds and values.

A similar clash can be seen between the Inuit values of humility and respect, on the one hand, and, on the other, glorification, boasting, and celebratory triumph. A successful hunter does not speak of his or her skill, but of the animal that shares itself. An individual may feel proud of contributing to the well-being of the community, but will not expect extravagant praise. Indeed, teasing is more likely, both for the prospect of enjoying a good laugh and to help reinforce the notion of humility as a boon to social harmony. This is not to say that skilled hunters are not recognized or respected, simply that they are unlikely to be the ones to label themselves as such.

Continuity and Change in Today's Arctic

It is easy to point to the many things that separate life today in Pond Inlet and other Arctic communities from what Inuit experienced in past generations, even within living memory. Permanent communities in Nunavut are relatively new, historically speaking, and there are many elders who were born on the land and remember what it was like prior to "town life." The things that connect Inuit past and present may not be quite so obvious, but they are just as real and often stronger.

To be Inuk today is to have experience of two vastly different ways of looking at the world. Yet the difference need not demand a choice. Instead, Inuit have the opportunity to draw on both worlds to create a new way of living. Most obviously, Inuit use modern technology—the internal combustion engine, electronics such as GPS, rifles—to continue traditional harvests of

7.8 Recovering Voices
Here Martin Nweeia interviews Pond Inlet elder, Elisapee Ootoova, one of five Canadian women to receive the Governor General's Award and author of the Inuktitut Dictionary, Tununiq Dialect. The translator is Tracy Kyak-Savard. (photo: J. Meehan)

7.9 The Nunavut Crest
The official crest of Nunavut shows a globe framed by a caribou and narwhal, surmounted by a crowned igloo. Land and sea are represented on its base, while the globe carries an inuksuk, a seal, the pole star, and five positions of the midnight sun. (courtesy of Nunavut Assembly Clerk)

seals, narwhal, and other animals. Less obviously, Inuit also combine borrowed practices with traditional ones to provide leadership and governance in communities, to steward their land and the sea. Scientific methods and Inuit Qaujimajatuqangit are used together to manage wildlife, a process undertaken by organizations composed of Inuit and non-Inuit. In some places, this approach is known as co-management, reflecting the joint enterprise and collaboration required. In Nunavut, the organizations are called institutions of public governance, reflecting the degree of Inuit self-rule in the territory.

A glass-covered case in the lobby outside Nunavut's Legislative Assembly chambers in the territorial capital of Iqaluit holds a jeweled narwhal tusk encrusted with seal carvings and carried by soapstone carvings of parka-clad Inuit. This symbol of authority, based on the sceptre held by the Queen of England, is an apt joining of Inuit and Canadian culture. The form of the sceptre clearly connects the governing power of Nunavut to that of Canada's head of state and leader of the Commonwealth. The substance of the sceptre is wholly from Nunavut, held aloft by Inuit figures carved in Inuit style from Nunavut stone. It is fitting that the narwhal should hold such a place, since most of the world's narwhals are found here, and narwhal continue to mean so much to the people of Nunavut.

Nunavut Government Symbols

Nunavut Legislative Assemby

The narwhal figures prominently in the political and social
life of Nunavut and is present
in its official emblems: the
Nunavut Coat of Arms and the
Mace of the Legislative
Assembly. The following text has
been adapted from the official
description of these government
symbols. (Permission to use
these emblems in this publication has been given by the
Clerk of the Nunavut Legislative
Assembly, John Quirke.)

The Mace of Nunavut

The Mace of the Legislative
Assembly of Nunavut was first
unveiled to the public on
March 30, 1999 at the first
sitting of the Legislative Assembly of Nunavut on April 1, 1999.
At the beginning of each day's
sitting of the Legislative Assembly, the Sergeant-at-Arms carries
the Mace over his or her right
shoulder, leading a procession
of Pages, Clerks, and the
Speaker into the Chamber. In
the Chamber of the Legislative
Assembly, the Mace rests in
the hands of a man and
woman carved in granite and
labradorite representing the
equal respect for both genders
of the population.

Following British Parliamentary
traditions, there are upper and
lower positions for the Mace.
The upper is used when the
Speaker of the House is presid-
ing and the lower is used when
the House takes a recess during
the sitting day or convenes as
the Committee of the Whole. In

the 12th century, the
mace was a weapon to
protect English and
French kings. Now, the
mace symbolizes the
authority of the Legisla-
tive Assembly. The mace
is made of narwhal
tusk. The animals on the
mace represent the
connection between land,
sea and a food source.
The common loons
carved from Nanisivik
silver form a crown with a
cross on top. The cross
symbolizes the respect for
the British monarch. The
carved people carrying
the mace represent a
family working together.
The elder helps lead the
way to the future. The
man and the woman
represent gender equality.
The big ball is blue lapis
lazuli, from Kimmirut,
which is one of the only
three deposits of lapis
lazuli in the world. The
gemstones around the
crown were hand-cut by

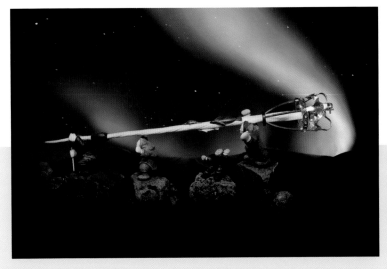

artists. The clear stones are quartz, the purple stone is amethyst, the red is garnet, the black quartz, the green citrine, the blue lapis, and the white marble. At the tip of the mace is a 2¼-carat diamond from the Jericho diamond deposit in Western Nunavut.

All the materials on the mace come from Nunavut, as do the artists: Inuk Charlie of Cambridge Bay, Paul Malliki of Repulse Bay, Simata Pitsiulak of Kimmirut, Mathew Nuqingaq of Iqaluit, Mariano Aupilardjuk of Rankin Inlet, and Joseph Suqslaq of Gjoa Haven.

The Nunavut Coat of Arms

On the Nunavut Coat of Arms the dominant colors—blue and gold—symbolize the riches of the land, sea, and sky. Within the gold part of the shield the *inuksuk* symbolizes the stone monuments that guide the people on the land and mark sacred and other special places.

The *qulliq*, an Inuit stone lamp, represents light and the warmth of family and the community. In the blue portion, the concave arc of five gold circles refers to the life-giving properties of the sun arching above and below the horizon, the unique part of the Nunavut year. The star is Niqirtsuituq, the North Star and the traditional guide for navigation, which more broadly stands for the unchanging leadership of the elders in the community.

In the crest, the *iglu* (igloo) represents the traditional life of the people and their means of survival. It also symbolizes the assembled members of the Legislature meeting together for the good of Nunavut, with the Royal Crown symbolizing public government for all the people of Nunavut and the equivalent status of Nunavut with other territories and provinces in Canadian Confederation. The *tuktu* (caribou) and *qilalugaq tugaalik* (narwhal) refer to land and sea animals that are

part of the rich natural heritage of Nunavut and provide sustenance for people.

The compartment at the base is composed of land and sea and features three important species of Arctic wild flowers. The motto, in Inuktitut, NUNAVUT SANGINIVUT means "Nunavut, our strength."

The Coat of Arms was designed by Andrew Karpik from Pangnirtung.

7.10 a-d The Nunavut Mace
These images illustrate the complex design, materials, and iconography of the Nunavut Mace, built on a narwhal tusk staff. When the Legislative Assembly is in session the mace rests on the shoulders of an Inuit man and woman, made of granite and soapstone, representing the burden of office. Details of the symbolism and the artists' names are found in the accompanying text. (text and photos courtesy of the Assembly Clerk, John Quirke)

Inuit and Narwhals

David S. Lee and George W. Wenzel

The narwhal is an iconic animal of the Canadian Arctic, perhaps only second to the polar bear. The Norse and other early European voyagers associated the spiraled tusk of the narwhal (in Inuktitut, *tuugaalik*, from the root word for tusk, *tuugaak*) with the spiraling horn of the mythical unicorn. Despite the "unicorn" mythology, no people have as intimate a relationship with narwhals as the Inuit. Today narwhals are a more important resource for the Nunavut Inuit and Inughuit of northern Greenland than at any time in the past, due to changes in technology and subsistence patterns.

This chapter focuses on Canada and explores the many ecological, economic, political, and, most importantly, cultural dimensions of the relationship between Inuit and this unique marine animal. We will examine this relationship by inspecting the archaeological record, scientific evidence, and the voluminous ecological knowledge the Inuit have accumulated about this animal. Important issues include management, Inuit hunting methods, the whale's role within the traditional economy, and finally, how changes in the Arctic ecosystem may affect this relationship.

Overlapping Geographies of Narwhal and Inuit

Narwhal range around the entirety of the Arctic and are a true ice-associated species, meaning that they do not migrate out of Arctic waters with the arrival of winter sea ice (Dietz et al. 2001). Although narwhal are distributed worldwide, no populations are of more importance to any indigenous culture than the two populations that have their winter homes in polynyas—persistent winter open-water zones surrounded by pack ice—between Baffin Island and Greenland and in northern Hudson Bay where they are able to feed on deep-water stocks of Greenland halibut (Heide-Jorgensen et al. 2002). Together, these two groups of whales are estimated to number 142,000 animals (DFO 2015). Because the wintering areas are ice surrounded and far from Inuit communities, neither commercial shipping nor subsistence hunting disturb them.

When narwhals leave their winter homes and disperse throughout the waters of West Greenland, Canadian High Arctic, and northern Hudson Bay, the opportunities for people to interact with the whales becomes apparent. The movement of whales from their winter refugia to their various summering areas can, depending on summer ice conditions, place animals

8.1 Inughuit Retrieving a Narwhal in Thule District, Northwest Greenland.
(photo: H. Saxgren)

105

in proximity to nearly all the communities in Nunavut as well as the settlements along the West Greenland coast from Disko Bay north to the Qaanaaq district. At each place there are Inuit hunters eager to add narwhal to the community menu after a winter diet mainly of ringed seal.

Narwhal and Inuit Historically

It is likely that Inuit-like peoples have been aware of narwhals since humans, generally referred to by archaeologists as Paleoeskimos, first began occupation of North America's Arctic coasts about 4,500 years ago. Because narwhal are very much a part of the seasonal diet of contemporary Inuit and because Inuit possess voluminous IQ (*Inuit Qaujimajatuqangit* [Inuit Knowledge]—see Chapter 7) about the species, it is surprising that there is almost no physical evidence of Inuit use of narwhal in the prehistoric record (Savelle 1994). Even more perplexing is that the Thule Culture people, who migrated from Alaska across the Canadian North and into Greenland between 900 and 1200 CE and are known to have been both well-adapted large whale hunters and the direct biological ancestors of today's Inuit, also left almost no archaeological evidence of narwhals.

This lack of evidence is worthy of speculation. In terms of the scant archaeological record, Savelle offers a number of possible explanations. The first is that recognizable bone remains, even in the Arctic, may not have been preserved over the millennia. Second, it is possible that early Palaeoeskimo hunters may not have had the technologies—large harpoons, floats (*avataq*) or watercraft, like the kayak—needed to efficiently hunt and recover the swift-swimming narwhal.

These may explain the lack of evidence for Palaeoeskimo narwhal use, but they do not explain why Thule Culture (1300–1600), known to possess the tools and organization (such as the large multimanned open skin boats known as an *umiakand*, as well as specialized harpoons and floats), to hunt the bowhead whale which can weigh in excess of 40 tons. Savelle suggests that because the seasonal presence of narwhal is simultaneous with bowheads, Thule hunters may have made the economic decision to invest their effort in hunting the bowhead, because the successful capture of even a small bowhead could feed a village of one hundred people through the succeeding winter.

The reasons for the apparent absence of narwhal hunting by Palaeoeskimo and Thule peoples remain speculative. What is clear is that as the Little Ice Age (1300–1870) helped precipitate an end to Thule bowhead whaling, the descendants of that culture adapted in several ways. One was by living in smaller extended-family groups. Another was broadening the post-Thule food system (McGhee 1972) into the one European explorers met and that today we call the Inuit subsistence system, an adaptation made possible by combining specialized clothing and harpoon technology with advances in kayak design. When narwhals became part of this transition remains uncertain, but we know from the detailed observations by Parry (1821) and others that both narwhal and beluga (*Delphinapterus leucas*), were important summer sources of food, blubber, and other materials for Inuit by at least the early 19th century.

8.2 Narwhal Migrations
Map of North Baffin and Bylot Islands showing Pond Inlet, other locations, and movement of narwhals along the floe edge.
(illustration: D. Lee 2004)

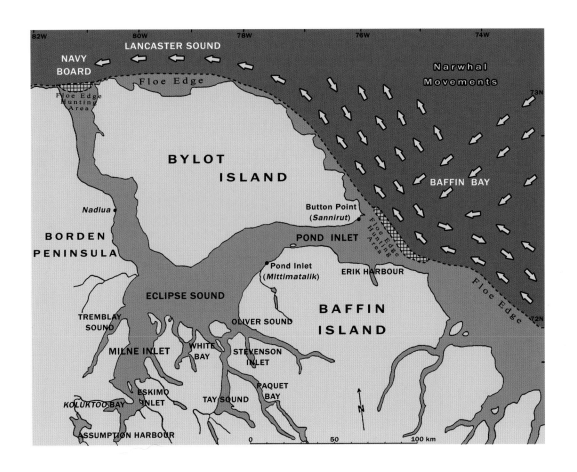

8.3, 8.4, 8.5, 8.6
Greenland Kayak and Hunting Gear

Due to geographic isolation, traditional Inuit life and culture persisted in East Greenland longer than in most other areas of the North American Arctic. This model kayak illustrates the refined technology and style employed by the East Greenland Tunumiit for hunting seals, narwhals, and walrus. The hunting parka, throwing board, harpoon head and line were collected in the 1880s in West Greenland. Similar but stylistically different kayaks, clothing, and technology were used in the Canadian Arctic. (Kayak: USNM E432494, photo: S. Loring; parka E74126, photo: J. Di Loreto; NHB2017-00203; throwing board and line, E74126-5, E37547, photos: S. Loring).

8.7 Toggle Harpoon and Lance

The harpoon used by Greenland Inuit today has a 4,000-year ancestry in the Eastern Arctic. Once the animal is struck, the head toggles sideways beneath the skin and blubber. A leather line held by the hunter prevents the struck animal from escaping or sinking. The animal was then dispatched by a lance like the one at upper right with a wood and narwhal-tusk foreshaft. (photos: J. Mehan and J. Di Loreto, lance)

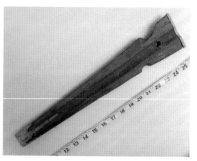

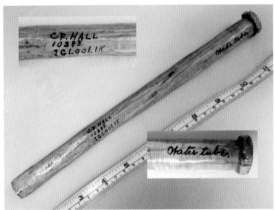

Governance of Modern Narwhal Hunting

Inuit narwhal hunting is co-managed by a regime that involves a variety of governmental agencies and Inuit organizations. This arrangement, referred to in official Canadian government documents as a "fishery," in recognition of the constitutional right of Indigenous cultures to hunt, fish and trap, gives Inuit a voice in the management system that affect the use of wildlife within the Nunavut Territory (Armitage 2005). Co-management is a governance approach meant to invite public participation and promote the confidence of Inuit in the management system.

Governance of narwhal hunting, therefore, brings together bodies that range from the federal government, Wildlife Management Boards, to indigenous organizations. The Nunavut Wildlife Management Board (NWMB) was created through the Nunavut Agreement, a constitutionally protected document. The NWMB is an institution of public government comprised of Inuit and government representation. It acts as the primary instrument of wildlife management in Nunavut where both science and IQ are sought in the decision-making process. The management process is substantially different in Greenland where access is governed by licensing and technological restrictions.

This arrangement is meant to procure the best scientific and cultural information about narwhal into the decision-making process. Parties may engage in management plans that identify putative narwhal stocks and form the basis for establishing total allowable harvest levels (TAHs) and non-quota limitations (NQLs) that are limits on subsistence hunting based on principles of conservation and estimation of sustainable harvest levels.

8.8 Hunting Visor
*Visors were worn to shield the hunter's eyes from glare off the water and ice. East Greenland visors used by the 19th-century Tununmiit were decorated with ivory inlays and beaded straps.
(photo: R. Ohern, USNM E168939)*

8.9 Drinking Tube
*Hollowed-out narwhal tusk sections were used to suck fresh water from shallow pools on the sea ice. This piece was collected from the Igloolik Inuit in the 1860s by the American explorer, Charles Francis Hall.
(USNM E10383; photo: S. Loring).*

Many Nunavut communities, through the local Hunter and Trappers Organization (HTO), also have customary IQ rules about narwhal hunting. One example is that animals should be harpooned prior to a ballistic penetration in order to minimize the possibility of loss in deep waters. Another is that the hunter that harpoons an animal, even if it has first been shot by another hunter in a different boat, has the right to make decisions about the distribution of the meat, *maqtaaq*, and tusk.

For management purposes, the Northern Hudson Bay and Baffin Bay narwhal populations are divided into six narwhal "stocks or management units" that cover virtually the entirety of Nunavut. In fact, a number of communities located in southern Hudson Bay, the westernmost part of Nunavut and southeast Baffin Island may have several years when no narwhals are sighted. Consequently, there is a wide range in individual community quotas (Furgal and Laing 2012), from 236 animals for the community of Arctic Bay to 20 for the community of Grise Fiord. The Total Allowable Landed Catch for four of the summering stocks of the Baffin Bay narwhal population is 1,123 whales (DFO 2012).

The narwhal harvest is also managed by a tag system: each community receives the number of tags equivalent to the total allowable harvest. Further, depending upon the community, the HTO may receive either summer, migratory, or all-season narwhal tags. Because narwhals are available to some communities as they migrate, the migratory tags accommodate this circumstance. For example, Pond Inlet and Arctic Bay have access to the Somerset Island narwhal stock during the spring migration. Once the tags of a season are used or the season ends, hunting is terminated, even if unused tags remain. In addition, all tusks must have a Marine Mammal Tag attached; otherwise possession, whether by an Inuk or a non-Inuit person, is illegal (Morgan 2013).

Inuit Hunting Strategies, Technology, and Methods

Inuit begin to pursue narwhals as soon as they appear and continue for the entire time animals are present. However, while Inuit can expect to interact with narwhals during the time the animals leave their winter home areas, how frequently (if at all) depends on a variety of environmental factors. These include the timing of break-up and freeze-up of the sea ice, whether broken ice impedes boat use, the position and stability of the ice's floe edge (an interface between the open water and landfast sea ice or *sini*), and weather. Fog can hinder locating whales and high winds can disrupt accurate shooting and safe retrieval of kills.

Although narwhal are considered a "summer" resource, it is more accurate to think of them as an open-water one. In fact, in the early part of their post-winter dispersal, they can be encountered when ice, either as a land-fast shelf bordered by open sea or one with leads and cracks and holes, dominates the hunting situation. In the first case, narwhal may move along this border and in the second they may swim under the ice to surface and breath in the openings. True open-water conditions may occur as late as July and there have been occasions along the East Baffin Island coast when there was no break-up and narwhal hunting was not feasible.

The range of environmental conditions under which Inuit engage narwhal—floe edge, open sea, ice leads—mean that different approaches are required for successful narwhal hunting. Four major situations in which Inuit pursue narwhal are: the early season floe edge; in open water; at *sapput* (holes surrounded by ice that are large enough for narwhal to surface to breathe); and ice leads. Needless to say, these scenarios are highly general and in reality Inuit employ a number of tactics that are specific to a particular situation.

Inuit employ a multitude of strategies when pursuing narwhal. One foraging strategy is to "sit and wait" or ambush the narwhal. Because narwhal are known to be acutely sensitive to any noise disturbance, this strategy is most often used during the early part of the hunting season (April to June, depending on the area and ice conditions) along the ice edge. It can also be used later in the season when narwhal may venture into embayments. The other strategy Inuit employ is to search actively for narwhal. This strategy is sometimes used at the floe edge, but only when the sit-and-wait ambushing has been unproductive or remaining time becomes low. Active searching is part of narwhal hunting later in the season when it is ice free and whale activity becomes less predictable.

Hunting at the floe edge is carried out as long as the *sini* is stable, although there is always a risk that a shift in wind direction, a sudden wave, or undercut ice behind the floe edge can cast hunters adrift on floating ice pans or, worse, into the water. Hence, hunting at the floe edge requires a high level of vigilance. Because of the potential risk, and because retrieving and

8.10 Hunters at the Floe Edge
Hunters from Pond Inlet may have to wait for days at the spring ice edge for narwhals. Some years the animals never appear or ice conditions prevent hunting.
(photo: J. Meehan)

8.11 Processing Narwhals at the Floe Edge
Preliminary work at the capture site involves gutting, and severing the head, flukes, and fins. (photo: E. Loring)

butchering a narwhal is a considerable task, hunters rarely travel alone. co-author George Wenzel observed a Clyde River floe edge hunt that included 11 men, six snowmobiles, and four boats.

Accessing the spring floe edge requires an array of equipment including a snowmobile, a boat for retrieving a kill, *qamutiik* (a large sledge), plus high caliber rifles, one or more harpoons, a tent, stove, sleeping bag, flensing knives, extra clothing and provisions as a hunt can last several days. Today, almost every hunter travels with a VHF radio that allows them to communicate with hunters or the village up to 20 miles away. The VHF allows information of whale sightings and ice conditions to be exchanged. It also enables men to call for assistance should an emergency arise. Some hunters also carry GPS locators, although travel routes and the topography of the *sini* are generally well known.

When the narwhal are away from the ice edge, it is often necessary to rely on rifles. In such situations, hunters use another technique. They know that after the animal surfaces to breathe, its lungs are full, making it buoyant. When narwhals sharply arch their backs as they prepare to dive, they are preparing to make a deep dive and expose the area behind the blowhole. Hunters aim for this exposed area, knowing that a strike while the whale's lungs are full will prevent it from immediately sinking.

Once a whale has been secured by harpoon, it is brought to the floe edge and pulled up on the ice, sometimes using a block and tackle or more often today by pulling with several snowmobiles. Once the animal is on the ice, the *maqtaaq* is removed in slabs that can weigh 20–25 pounds, after which the meat is removed. While they are processing the animal, which can take up to two hours, the men examine the whale for evidence of previous wounding, noting its age and sex, body condition, and disease. If it is a male, they remove the tusk and sometimes, if present, the second, unerupted tooth. The main tusk may go to the oldest hunter or by agreement to the one who harpooned the animal. Regardless of who receives the tusk, all of the hunters initially share in the *maqtaaq* and meat.

Open-water narwhal hunting begins as soon as the sea ice opens and is sufficiently dispersed, usually by mid-July around northern Baffin Island, when boats are able to navigate the open water. Because there is little ice, narwhal can potentially be found anywhere. The most common summer hunt strategy is active searching, especially for hunters who have wage positions in their community and, with limited time available to hunt, may spend five or six hours after work or an entire weekend searching for whales in nearby fiords and bays. Most narwhal hunting trips at this season include two to four or five men—normally a father, sons, his brothers, and cousins—who come together as a crew.

Open water hunting requires only the use of a boat with an outboard engine, plus harpoons, rifles, extra fuel, and a radio for emergencies and to rally other boats, as successful narwhal hunting by a lone boat in the open sea is problematic. Active searching is a strategy that creates noise from the outboard engine that invariably alerts narwhal. Boat crews are constantly scanning for any signs of whales. Under ideal conditions, such as calm waters and absence of fog, Inuit are able to detect narwhal several miles from the boat. When a pod is spotted, the boat engine is immediately shut off and the boat is allowed to drift; movement in the boat stops to minimize further noise. If people are working together, a radio message is sent to other boats about the location of the whales and to alert any that are nearby to cut their motors.

When a whale is either killed or wounded seriously enough that it can only weakly dive, the boats rush to harpoon the animal with a float, as whales often sink rapidly and hunters may have barely a minute before the dead whale is lost. When the whale is secured, one or two boats tow it to shore or an ice pan where the carcass undergoes the same cooperative process described for floe edge hunting. Again, the boat that lands the first harpoon, regardless of which shot the whale, takes charge of the animal and, if a male, the tusk; with the butchering complete, any boat crew that stayed to assist in the processing usually receives a share of the *maqtaaq*, although the harpooning crew retains such preferred parts as the tusk, flukes, and fins.

Hunting narwhal in summer in deep open water can be challenging as whales often escape or on occasion sink before they can be harpooned. However, hunting narwhal in summer can be very successful if conducted

ON "SAVSSATS": A CROWDING OF ARCTIC ANIMALS AT HOLES IN THE SEA ICE

By MORTEN P. PORSILD

Director, Danish Arctic Station, Disko, Greenland

FIG. 1—Over 200 narwhals' tusks planted in the snow at Godhavn. They were obtained from the two savssats in the winter of 1914-15.

On the west coast of Greenland, at the 69th parallel, is situated Disko Bay, to the north of which lies the large island of Disko. Aligned across the mouth of the bay are several groups of islands, formerly called Whale Islands, in the modern Danish charts named Hunde Öer (the southern

8.12 Savssat Bounty

This image from the front page of an article by Danish Greenland scholar, Morten Porsild in The Geographical Review *(1918: 215) shows a harvest of tusks taken from narwhals caught in a* savssat, *or breathing hole, that occurred in Disko Bay in 1914–1915.*

under different circumstances. This involves a sit-and-wait strategy that can only be employed when a crew or family have more than a couple of days to establish a camp. In these cases a camp is established at the mouth of a small bay or adjacent to a river estuary where whales are known to pass by with regularity. If a pod enters the bay, the hunters launch their boat and by driving back and forth across the bay entrance use the sound of the motor to drive the whales closer to shore. Hunters can also repeatedly aim their rifle fire so as to drive the animals toward shallow water. As the narwhal are driven into the more restrictive area, the boat (or boats) begin to move close enough to either fire or harpoon the whales. This method often results in the take of two or three animals and loss through sinking is rare; even when an animal sinks, the shallow water often allows hunters to use grapnels to recover the animal or, if out of reach, the carcass usually rises in a day or two due to bloating. While the meat from "risers" is unusable, the *maqtaaq* and tusk are salvaged.

A third hunting situation arises when narwhal, following cracks and leads in the ice that are wide enough for them to surface to breathe, swim beneath the ice between *sapput,* which are essentially breathing holes. Whales may also become trapped in a *sapput.* These situations usually occur in the early part of the season and allow narwhal to divert from cruising along the floe edge. A *sapput* can also occur in the late autumn as a result of a sudden freezing and may cause narwhal pods, and even hundreds of narwhal, to be entrapped in a hole too far from other holes or the pack ice—a condition known as *sikujjausimajat*, which happened in 2008 when nearly 1,000 whales became trapped.

Late winter-spring lead and *sapput* (*savssat* in article illustrated in 8.12 is the Greenlandic equivalent of Canadian Inuit *sapput*) hunting differ little from that done at the floe edge. If a breathing hole is located, hunters adopt a sit-and-wait strategy. Sometimes, when there is a series of closely spaced holes, a number of hunters may spread out to cover several of them. In a lead situation, Inuit may choose to combine the two strategies, searching by snowmobile until whales are sighted and then either waiting in place if the animals are approaching or taking a wide detour to set an ambush ahead of narwhal that are moving away from the hunter. Unless a lead or hole is very wide, no boat is needed to accomplish retrieval; instead a harpoon or grapnel with a line attached is used to pull the carcass to the ice edge.

Sometimes *sikujjausimajat* are found when the *sapput* is clearly icing over, leaving little or no prospect that any animals will survive. After approval by the NWMB and DFO, hunters, and even families, will harvest and process as many of the whales as they can secure. Samples are also taken for scientific purposes. Unfortunately, this is a situation in which mortally wounded animals may dive and be lost before a harpoon and line can be attached.

8.14 Maqtaaq Sharing in Qaanaaq, Greenland
Sharing a bit of the harvest at the kill site is a widespread tradition among Inuit. Here the hunting team eats maqtaaq *after the animal's capture at the ice edge. (photo: H. Saxgren)*

Sharing and Use

In describing narwhal hunting we noted that sharing begins at the kill site, but is very limited compared with the widespread distribution that takes place when hunters return to their community. On the ice, the only sharing is with non-kinspersons who may have participated in the hunt or helped with the hauling out or butchering. Along with eating *maqtaaq* during the processing, non-kin generally receive a slab or two of the *maqtaaq* as well as meat. In parts of Greenland (Robbe 1994: 278) distribution of narwhal appears to be more formal, with up to four men who assist in the hunting and butchering receiving meat and *maqtaaq* from either the hip or shoulder area of the narwhal. The desirability of narwhal meat differs among different Inuit groups; Inuit from northern Baffin Island do not place a great premium on the *maqtaaq*; in the fall some meat on an abandoned carcass may be left for polar bear and Arctic fox.

8.15 a, b Community
Sharing
Once landed, narwhals are
processed for sharing
throughout the community
following traditional
butchering plans shown
in this illustration by
Ilannguaq Qaerngaaq.
(credit: (a) E. Loring,
(b) S. Gearheard et al. 2013,
Meaning of Ice, IPI Press)

Inuit sharing, termed *ningiqtuq*, is a complex system that can be likened to an onion. It is a "layered" system in which the passing of food begins with a hunter's close relatives and potentially extends across the entire community. In fact, it is rarely the hunter who makes the decision of what, how much and with whom food will be shared. This responsibility belongs to a hunter's grandfather, father, or other older kinsperson who is *isumataq*, a term that can be loosely translated as thoughtful. In fact, much Inuit food sharing is not by "hand to hand" transfers, but is done through an *isumataq* hosting meals in which kin and non-relatives partake.

Narwhal can appear to be something of an exception to the more controlled process that is directed by *isumataq*. A boat that has successfully hunted a whale is met upon its arrival home, regardless of whether it is day or night, by a crowd of men, women, and children, alerted by the hunters' radio report, waiting with plastic bags. The scene is celebratory and seemingly chaotic as the large slabs of *maqtaaq* are unloaded from the boat onto plastic sheets or the snow and immediately divided into smaller parcels of a few pounds, stuffed into bags and taken home; some is also always delivered to elders unable to come to the beach. By the time the last person leaves, as much as half the *maqtaaq*, perhaps 100 or more pounds (an adult narwhal may provide up to 200 pounds of *maqtaaq*), arrives in homes across the community.

Such scenes are, however, only part of the sharing story. The enthusiasm of those participating underscores the commonly held idea that *maqtaaq* is a "delicacy." The fact is that narwhal are a seasonal and very unpredictable resource. (The unpredictability of narwhal hunting is illustrated by the

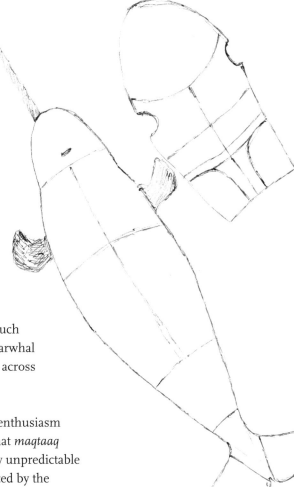

average annual harvest at Clyde River between 1971 and 1990. While the annual quota for the community is 50 narwhal, the yearly average over this time was 24 animals; in three summers, sea ice prevented any use of boats.) Unpredictability, and the fact that narwhal tastes distinctly different from most other foods certainly does make it desirable. So the activity at the beach by no means ends the distribution. The younger people who met the boat divide their parcels and pass a few pounds to their various kin. Elders host meals for family and neighbors called *nirriyaktuqtuq*. Within a few hours, most people have had at least a taste of fresh narwhal.

Maqtaaq preparation is typical of Inuit cuisine. When fresh, *maqtaaq* has a slightly nutty taste, so eating it un-cooked is favored; as the skin is a rich source of Vitamin C, this has health benefit, but as vitamin C is soluble, it is lost depending on how *maqtaaq* is prepared. When *maqtaaq* is cooked, boiling is the preferred traditional method and the broth can be drunk. Today, whether eaten raw, fresh, or boiled, many Inuit dip pieces in soy sauce or sprinkle it with salt.

8.16 Maqtaaq *Feast*
The inner skin and outer blubber of cetaceans like bowhead, beluga, and narwhal—called maqtaaq *and known for its nut-like flavor—is considered a delicacy by the Inuit and contains nutritious vitamins and nutrients. Among those sharing* maqtaaq *here several years ago are (l to r): Jeeteeta Merkosak, the late Martha Merkosak, Dina Koonoo-Arreak (child), the late Martha Koonoo, and Simon Merkosak.*
(photo: J. Meehan)

Narwhal meat undergoes different processing. Because it is oily, it is less often consumed fresh. Instead, it is traditionally prepared in one of two ways: either air-dried into *nikkuk* or packed with seal oil as *misigaak*. *Misigaak* can be stored for a considerable time and is generally eaten as is, while *nikkuk* typically is taken with seal oil as a dip or boiled.

The other important by-product is the ivory tusk of the male narwhal. While early Inuit found various uses for the tusks (such as tent poles or carved to create amulets), because the narwhal's tusk is a tooth and hollow for much of its length, they are fragile, and it is not uncommon to find the male whale's tusk chipped at its tip or broken along its length. Still, narwhal tusks have been exchanged with non-Inuit since at least the 19th century, when British and American whalers appeared in the Eastern Arctic.

8.17 Cash Income
*Narwhal products, seen
in this shop in the village
of Arctic Bay, provide
important cash income,
both as whole tusks and as
small articles like jewelry
and animal carvings.
(photo: J. Meehan)*

Regardless of a tusk's condition, there is a market among tourists and
collectors of Inuit art for narwhal ivory, either as whole tusks or carved to
create sculptures, rings, and other ornaments (or even cribbage boards).
A general rule of thumb is that each foot of a tusk is valued at $150 CAD, and
a complete, undamaged tusk, depending on its length, can fetch as much as
$2,500 CAD; a double tusk skull has sold for $10,000 CAD. Narwhal ivory
is also an important medium for Inuit sculptures, but, because of the twisted
tusk, it is especially preferred for jewelry, like rings and bracelets. Thus,
even damaged and incomplete tusks are utilized. In no small sense, therefore, as a by-product of food production, the tusk, whole or partial, is an
important source of income that offsets the high monetary costs of hunting.

Climate Change

There is considerable discussion today about the possible impacts on narwhal as the Arctic continues to warm. At present, the precise impacts remain uncertain. However, narwhal have been subject to climatic shifts as brief as a few decades. Using historical meteorological and narwhal tusk trade records for Greenland extending back more than 150 years, Christian Vibe (1967) identified how warming episodes precipitated a movement of narwhal northward away from Inuit communities along island's southwest coast. This shift in range correlates with northward shifts in the species' primary foods—Greenland halibut and Arctic cod. Understanding how climate change may affect narwhal will likely require understanding complex changes taking place with other species and especially prey (see Chapter 10 for details).

However, some of the changes on the surface of the Arctic Ocean that impact narwhal are obvious. As the Arctic waters become free of ice for longer periods, industrial activities planned or already underway will test how compatible large-scale ship transport through narrow marine passages and offshore seismic exploration are with narwhal. Several ships carrying iron ore for Baffinland Iron Mines Incorporated already traverse Eclipse Sound and Pond Inlet each day during the open-water season; a proposal by a Norwegian consortium to carry out oil-related seismic studies using high-decibel air guns is presently on hold, awaiting the outcome of a case before the Supreme Court of Canada brought by several Baffin Island communities, Inuit rights organizations, and Greenpeace Canada (see Chapter 11).

Inuit knowledge (Remnant and Thomas 1992; Stewart et al. 1995) and scientific reports (LGL and Greeneridge 1986; Cosens and Dueck 1986; Finley et al. 1990) suggest that narwhals are sensitive to acoustic disturbance and can display changes in migratory behavior as a result. It remains uncertain how vulnerable narwhals are to the increasing level of acoustical sisturbance as more and more ships pass through areas used by migrating whales. However, there is some evidence that narwhal make the most directional biosonar signals reported to date (Koblitz et al. 2016). The directional beam may be advantageous for detecting prey items at long distances and for reducing clutter from the periphery. The recent decision to allow the passage of ore ships through Eclipse Sound and surrounding areas, both being summer narwhal and narwhal-hunting areas, may soon test the reaction of the animals, and Inuit hunters. Thomas et al. (2016) report that narwhal did react to the presence of shipping activity. Results from both the extensive and photographic surveys indicate that narwhal numbers are reduced during periods with large vessel activity. Thus, an increase of ship activity will likely have a large influence on narwhal behavior and ultimately, narwhal distribution.

120

Inuit Contributions to Narwhal Knowledge

Martin T. Nweeia, David Angnatsiak, Pavia Nielsen, and Cornelius Nutarak

Nweeia Journal, June 3, 2002:

I was on the ice floe edge outside Pond Inlet, Baffin Island, in May of 2002, waiting with my guide and hunter, David Angnatsiak, for the spring migration of narwhal. Our campsite was on the edge of the shore-fast ice between Pond Inlet and Bylot Island at the northeastern end of Baffin Island. After camping here for nearly two weeks, with no sightings of narwhal and with other hunting teams regularly passing by exploring for areas where narwhals would first appear, I asked David, "Do these other groups know something that we don't?" I asked because I know there are two film teams hoping to record the migration, and they are armed with technology like hydrophones to monitor the sounds of narwhal arriving. David looks at me for a long time, pensively, and then responds, "The other teams can look all they want for narwhal; the narwhal will be coming here, to this spot." Within days, hundreds of narwhal came exactly to our spot on the ice."

Later when we got back to Pond Inlet, I discovered that none of those other teams that had ventured out for weeks had sighted narwhals.

Nweeia Journal, August 5, 2005:

During an expedition to Kaqqiat Point in Admiralty Inlet off Arctic Bay, I listened to Issaic Shooyook, an elder who was telling me about narwhal tusks being used to dislodge the runners of a sledge frozen to the ice because they had so much strength and flexibility. He explained that when swimming, the narwhal's tusk is readily bendable. I doubted his story, since I had examined many tusks and could not imagine such flexibility.

Results from studies three years later concluded that Issaic was indeed correct about the tusk's flexibility and strength. When tusks were analyzed by Dr. Frederick Eichmiller, then Director of the Paffenbarger Research Center at the National Institutes of Standards and Technology, he determined that a 2.5-meter tusk could flex two degrees in every direction. What a surprise!

These are just a few of the hundreds of observations and results of Inuit knowledge in a study the author has compiled from sixty-three hunters and elders. They include field observations passed down among the Inuit for hundreds if not thousands of years. So insightful, accurate, and descriptive are these observations that much of our recent science on the function of the narwhal tusk has been guided by Inuit oral knowledge. In 2010, with support from the National Science Foundation, we set out to collect oral knowledge

9.1 Cornelius Nutarak (1924–2017)
One of the most respected elders of Pond Inlet, Nutarak was an experienced hunter who observed narwhal behavior for many years. He assisted several groups of scientists in their studies of narwhal ecology and biology. (photo: J. Meehan)

9.2 Narwhal Migration Changes

Jens Jeremiassen and his daughter Hunde Ejland describes changes in sea-ice distribution and narwhal-migration routes observed during the current period of climate change. (photo: J. Meehan)

from ten communities in the High Arctic—five from northeastern Nunavut and five from northwestern Greenland. Sound and film recordings were collected that added significant information to knowledge of the narwhal. Such results highlight the value of traditional knowledge in scientific studies.

Publications on Inuit knowledge (e.g., Wenzel 1991; Berkes 1995; Broadbent 1996; Krupnik and Jolly 2002; Krupnik 2009) are insightful and help all fields of science in the Arctic. Inuit knowledge has advanced understanding of environmental change (Nadasdy 1999; Ford and Martinez 2000), Arctic wildlife management (Huntington 1992, 1998, 2005; Berkes 1999; Dowlsey and Wenzel 2008; Moore and Huntington 2008; Huntington et al. 2011) and Arctic marine mammals (Bogoslavskaya 2003; Noongwook et al. 2007; Clark et al. 2008). In these cases the combination of traditional science with Inuit knowledge has provided a more complete picture of the Arctic environment. Inuit knowledge has also contributed to a better understanding of the narwhal (Finley et al. 1979; Silverman 1979; Remnant and Thomas 1992; Stewart et al. 1995; Gonzalez 2001; Stewart 2001; Lee 2004; Lee and Wenzel 2004; Westdal 2008), adding observations of seasonal aggregation, migration routes, populations, and anatomic variations (Rosing 1999; Nweeia et al. 2009).

The Inuit and their ancestors have been associated with the narwhal ever since they arrived in the North American Arctic. Their observations have accrued over thousands of years, passed down from one hunter to another. This knowledge was essential in understanding narwhal behavior and their environment and helped guarantee human survival in a dangerous, unpredictable region. Inuit see their world from experience and do not separate or isolate environmental variables such as weather, ice patterns, or animal behavior. Rather, their knowledge is contextual; everything is related, linked, and understood as one story.

In this regard, the Inuit view stands in stark contrast with western science, which is reductionist and attempts to understand phenomena by isolating events and factors to arrive at meaningful statements based on the number of times a single variable can produce a similar result. These two systems of thought approach understanding from opposite directions, and if followed appropriately they can lead to a more complete understanding of natural phenomena. In the study of High Arctic marine mammals like the narwhal, both approaches are essential for understanding biology, ecology, and behavior.

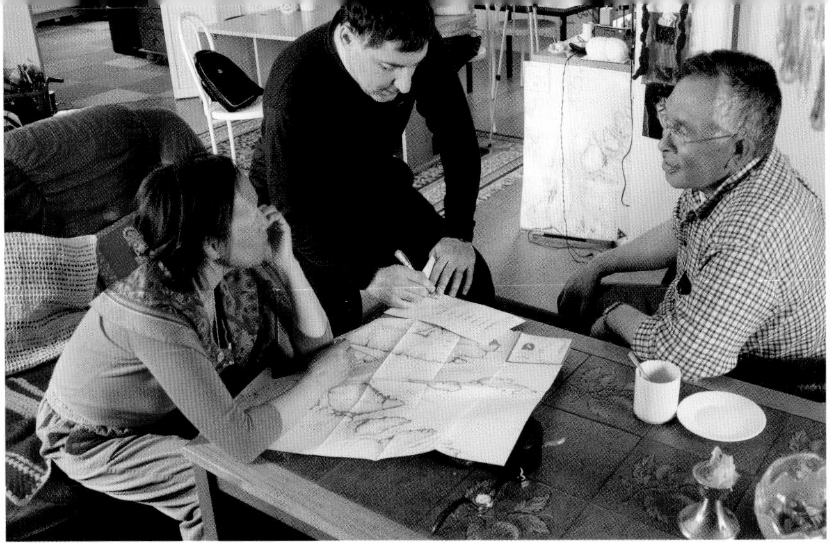

*9.3 **Narwhal Subspecies***
Lars Jeremiassen explains to Navaranna Sorensen and Dr. Nweeia distinct narwhal population groups on the northwestern High Arctic coast of Greenland. (photo: J. Meehan)

Our narwhal studies developed a three-dimensional "integrated knowledge model" to encompass the scientific method enhanced by the observations of Inuit elders and hunters as it related to narwhal tusk function. We devised a questionnaire covering anatomy, ecology, populations, distribution, and behavior. Asking both direct and more open-ended questions according to established methods of collecting traditional knowledge (Huntington 2000; Huntington et al. 2002) allowed hunters to share their experiences with the science team. These observations were then compared to scientific experiments designed to uncover aspects of tusk form and function. Some sample questions are highlighted below. Each question is presented in English, followed by versions in Inuktitut (in Canada) and Inughuit (in Greenland).

In gathering Inuit knowledge, these types of questions were asked:

1. What is your most memorable experience of a narwhal?

   ᑭᓱᒥᓪᓚ ᐃᖃᐅᒪᓯᔾᖃᓇᔾᖃᑉᐱᑦ ᕿᓚᓗᑭᕿᑦᑎᓪᓗᑎᑦ? ᒃᑭᕿᐅᑎᓕᑭᕿ ᐅᓯᓗᓗᖑᑕᓂᖃᐅ᙮

   Qilalukkat qernertat pillugit puigunaatsuunerpaaq eqqaamasat sunaava?

2. Do you notice that the tusk size relates to the size of the narwhal? Are there exceptions to this? If so, please describe them.

   ᐅᔾᔨᕈᓱᒃᓯᒪᕕᑦ ᕿᓚᓗᒐᐅᑉ ᐊᖏᓂᖏᓗᑦ ᑐᒐᖏᑦ ᒪᓕᒃᓯᒪᓱᖑᒪᖔᑕ? ᑕᐃᒪᓇ ᓂᕆᐅᓇᖅᓯᒪᕙ ᑕᐃᒪᐃᑲᔾᔪᒃᓂᖔᓄᑦ ᑕᐃᒪᑐᐸᑦ ᓇᓗᓇᐃᒃᑲᓐᓂᕈᓐᓇᐱᐅᒃ? ᒃᑭᕿᐅᑎᓕᑭᕿ ᐅᓯᓗᓗᖑᑕᓂᖃᐅ᙮

   Maluginiartarpiuk tuugaap angissusiata timaata angissusianut naleqqersuunne qarsinnaanersoq? tamanna ilaatigut allaassuseqartarpa? Allaassutsinik eqqaasaqarsinnaavit?

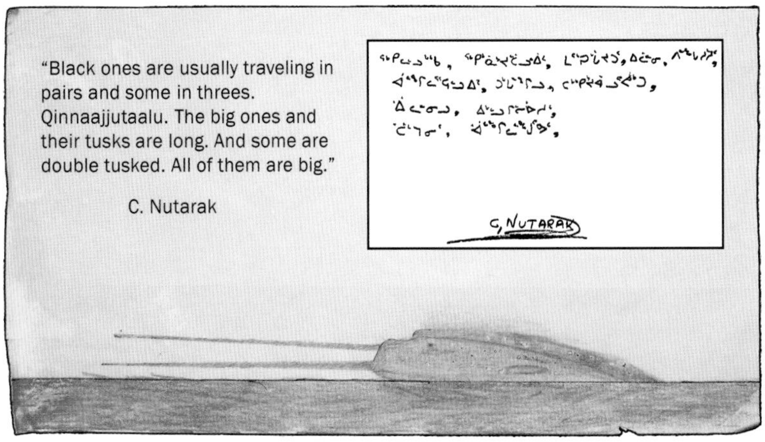
"Black ones are usually traveling in pairs and some in threes. Qinnaajjutaalu. The big ones and their tusks are long. And some are double tusked. All of them are big."
C. Nutarak
C. NUTARAK

*9.4 **Identifying Narwhal Anatomy***
Notes on narwhal anatomy from the journal of Cornelius Nutarak, 1924–2017, Pond Inlet elder and hunter. (photo: J. Meehan)

9.5 Hunter's Vigil
This graphic by James Houston illustrates a seal hunter waiting at the breathing hole for a seal. (Used by permission: Alice Houston)

3. How often do narwhal get trapped and die in forming pack ice? Is there any pattern to the weather or events that make it difficult for the narwhal to escape under such conditions?

   ᐊᓪᓚᖕᒍᐊᑦ ᐊᔪᖅᓯᐅᖅᑲᑲᑕᑉᐸᑉᓛᑦ ᓯᑯᓕᖅᑎᓪᓗᒍ? ᓯᓚᒧᑦ ᐊᓯᐊᒍᓪᓕᓐ#ᑦ ᐊᔪᕐᓇᖅᑐᖅᓯᑎᑕᐅᕙᑉᐸᑦ ᐊᓪᓚᖕᒍᐊᓄᑦ ᑕᐃᒪᓐᓇᒃ ᐊᑦᑕᓇᖅᑐᓂᑦ ᕿ$ᓇᓱᒃᑎᓪᓗᒋᑦ? ᒡᑭᕿᐅᑎᓕᑭᕿ ᐅᓯᑐᑐᖕᒍᑕᓂᖅᑲᐅ.

   Qanoq akulikitsigisumik qernertat imarnersamik sikusoorlutik toqusarpat? Silap qanoq innera aalajangersimasoq pissutaasarpa imaluunniit arlaatigut pisoqartarnera qernertanut qimaariarnissamik ajornakusoortitsisarpa?

What types of results and insights were gathered? Inuit told us there is an elaborate classification scheme for tusk size and shape that correlates with different populations, by sex of the animal, and by expression of the same tooth within the species. Narwhal tusks, just like human teeth, can vary in size and shape in different populations around the world. In humans we encounter the mongoloid dentition characteristic of Asian and indigenous American populations that is characterized by a "shoveling" on the backside of the upper front teeth and a characteristic bump on the biting surface, "the cusp of Carabelli," on the first molar. Similar differences are found in narwhal tusks, allowing Inuit to identify different populations.For example, male erupted tusks can appear shorter though wider in some northern populations, and longer and narrower in others. In Canadian populations the longer, narrower version of the tusk is associated with a darker-skinned narwhal, while the shorter, wider tusk is found on narwhal with more white spots on the dorsal or back surface and mostly white on the ventral or belly surface. Though most females do not express an erupted tusk, when they do they are typically narrower than the male tusk, with a spiraled morphology that is more tightly wound and with a cleaner appearance. Most male narwhal tusks have algae and diatoms covering much of their surface.

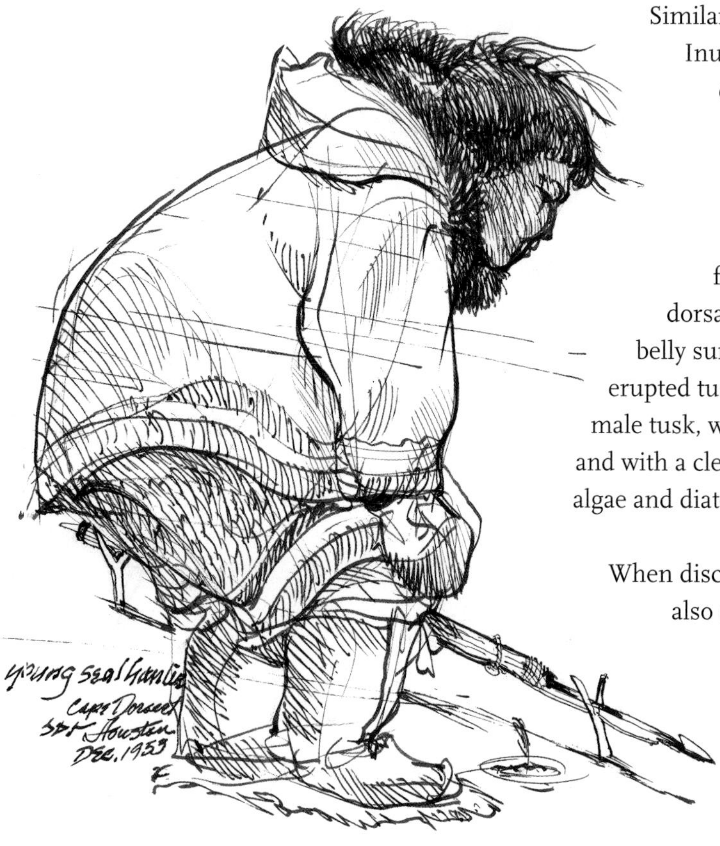

When discussing the anatomy of the narwhal body, Inuit are also able to distinguish between Canadian and Greenlandic animals by their body size, shape, and even behavior. They explain that Canadian narwhal are more narrow through the length of their body and taper toward the tail or fluke. Narwhals from Greenland, however, are more bulbous in the

anterior or front section and taper more narrowly before the tail. They describe Canadian narwhal as more curious, even gregarious, as opposed to the more shy and elusive narwhal from Greenland. Descriptions of narwhal tusk morphology are so specific that Inuit correlate the geographic locations where narwhals can be found with differing tusk expressions and body types. Narwhal having the shorter, wider tusks and more white skin markings would more commonly be found in Grise Fiord and East Greenland, according to elder Cornelius Nutarak, one of the most respected Inuit leaders to collect and record his observations in writing.

9.6 Narwhal Population Numbers Challenged
Pavia Nielsen from Uummannaq describes Greenland hunters' beliefs that narwhal population numbers are increasing despite scientific studies showing population decline. (photo: J. Meehan)

The topic of population numbers has been debated by Inuit hunters, who declare that narwhal numbers are larger than scientific government surveys that count animals in order to set quotas aimed at maintaining sustainable stocks. Inuit in both the High Arctic of Canada and Greenland have questioned such surveys because in many cases they limit the Inuit from taking what they consider a sustainable quota. Though figures in the past have placed the rough figure of 80,000 as a total population of Davis Strait narwhal, a more recent estimate from Fisheries and Oceans Canada has placed the world's population at 173,000. In 2007, this issue became such a debated topic between the Inuit of Greenland (known as Inughuit) and scientists that Narwhal Tusk Research funded hunter Pavia Nielsen, an outspoken and respected hunter and elder from Uummannaq in Greenland, to share his views at the Inuit Circumpolar Conference in Alaska.

Pond Inlet elder and mayor Charlie Inurak also described ice entrapments of narwhal in fast ice (*sikujjaujut*) and the conditions that cause ice to form too rapidly for narwhals to escape (*sikujjivik*). Though such events have occurred throughout history (Porsild 1918), they have been infrequent and largely unnoticed until recent years when more events have been reported. Typically, hundreds of whales are trapped in small areas of open water surrounded by encroaching ice and have no way to reach other breathing holes. Instead, they fight to maintain a shrinking hole, taking turns, until they drown or are frozen into the ice. The Inuit attribute some of these recent ice entrapments to climate change and seismic testing, loud sound bursts used to map sub-seafloor geology. The intense sound bursts are known to cause sea mammals to become disoriented and to shift their migration routes to quieter but less familiar territory.

9.7 Tusk Differences
*Charlie Inuarak from
Pond Inlet explains the
differences between
male and female tusks.
(photo: P. Peeters)*

Narwhal behavior is perhaps one of the most difficult areas for scientists to study. Windows of opportunity are rare, and methods of recording behavior are even more problematic. Once again, Inuit hunters have contributed important information not observed by schedule-bound scientists. Questionnaire responses from twelve hunters describe how adult males lead the spring and summer migrations; older males follow, and younger males flank the periphery as "scouts" to warn and protect the group. Many of the hunters also describe the difference in deep diving between males and females. Males with a tusk arch their bodies more during the deep dive, and sink slightly below the surface before such a dive. Females do not need to arch their bodies as they seldom express a tusk and thus have no need to compensate by arching their bodies before a deep dive.

Perhaps one of the most interesting observations that helped to inform science were Inuit comments on narwhal molting, the shedding of their outer skin. For many years scientists doubted that one of the most common reasons for migrating in summer into brackish inlets was for molting—the sloughing off of old dead skin—a behavior noted in published studies of the narwhal's closest relative, the beluga. However, three hunters described incidences where they observed narwhal molting during the summer, and from their descriptions, one can appreciate why the observation has not been observed by scientists. As a lead hunter from Qaanaaq (northwest Greenland), Rasmus Avike described, "I only saw this one time. I was paddling next to a narwhal when a thin gauze-like layer of white came off the whale and into the surrounding water. Within a short time, the thin white layer disappeared. I realized that this was the molting of the narwhal." For only three of sixty-three hunters to describe such an event, seeing it only once in their lifetimes, speaks to the difficulty in analyzing and collecting information during brief month-long studies by scientists.

Insights and observations of Inuit knowledge have also assisted the science of tusk anatomy, morphology, and function. This knowledge informs many aspects of narwhal population, distribution, migration, and behavior. The daily collection of knowledge for an Inuit hunter is careful and accurate, and relates directly to their ability to hunt and survive in one of the harshest environments on the planet. Such knowledge is invaluable to the process of science, which only affords a limited window of opportunity to collect information during scientific investigations.

*　*　*

Cornelius Nutarak explained narwhal population species differences identified by tusk form and body shape:

"There are those that we call *Qirnajuktat* blackish ones (mostly black), they are bull or male narwhal, stallions they are very big and are much longer than normal and they have long tusks. Then there are the regular narwhals, they are a bit smaller and their tusks are shorter than the bull narwhal. We do see double tusked narwhal too, but not always.

Then, there are narwhal that are shorter, they are male narwhal but they are stubby, even mature ones are not as big as the big bull ones I just spoke of, and their tusks are not as magnificent. Even the detailing of their tusks is not as elegant, the tusks go this way, like this and only in that direction. Every now and then the female narwhal have tusks too, and their tusks are not as wide as the male tusks and their tusks are marvelous, sometimes they can grow to be long tusks but narrower, and they are more beautiful tusks than the male ones. That's what I know."

(*Cornelius Nutarak, Pond Inlet, Narwhal Tusk Discoveries, p. 55*)

"The fully mature ones, those that appear the oldest, do not play as much, and their skin is much lighter."

CΔL ⊲ᐟᐱᒌᑫᕐᓂᐸᕐᓂᐊᓂᐊᓄᐃ ᐅᖅᐸᐅᔨᒌᖅᑕᖅᑖᕐ. CΔᑯᐊᐊ ᐃᕐᐁᐁᑐᐊᑉ, ᐃᑐᐊᐅᓂᖅᑐᑉ ᓪᐟᓗ, ᖅᐅᓂᑐᖅᑲᐸ᠊ᒐ᠊ᐅᐊᓄᐅᑉ ᒪᖅᒌᖅᕟ᠊ᑕ ᑕᑯᕐᐱᐅᓂᐎᒐ. CΔᑯᐊᐊ, ᓪᐟᓗ ᐃ᐀ᐟᑉᑐᐊᐅᑉ, ᖅᐱᐁᓂᖅᑕᐁᐊᕐᒪᐊᐃᑉᐊᑉ ᐈᐰᖅᓄᒌᐳ Cᐲᓂᖅᐁᐅᐱᐊᔫᒌᐱᓂᕐ ⊲ᐁᑭᓂᖅᐁᐅᕟᐅᒌᐱᓂ᠊ᓗᐊ. ⊲ᐃᕟᐱᐅᐱᕐᒪᑌᕆ CΔᑯᐊᐊ. ᒪᑯ᠊ᐊᐊᑐᐃ᐀ᐁᐃᑌ ᖅᐸᓗᐃᑐ᐀ᐁᐱᐺᔨᕐᖅᑐᖅᑐᕐ ᐃᑌᖅᐅᖅᑲᓄᒌᐊᐈᑯᑉᐁᐊᐊᓂᐊᓄ, ᓪᐟᓗ CΔᑯᑲᐃᐈᐱᓄᐆ ᒪᑯ᐀ᒌᐅᖅᑾ᠊ᑩᒌᐱᖅᑐᓂᕐ, ⊲᐀ᒪᐃᐅᐱᐰᕰᐟᔪᕐᒌ᠊ᑩᐱᓄ᠊ᓗ. CΔᑯᐊᐊ CΔᒪᑯᐈᐁᐱᑉᑿᖅᑌᒌᐸᐊᓂ. ᐃᑐᐊᐊᐃᑉ, CΔᑯᐊᐊ ᐃᑐᐱᐈᐱᒌ᠊ᐊᐊᕰᔨ᠊ᔫᕟ, ⊲᐀ᒪᐈᐁᐁᐺᕈᑯᐈᒌᐆᐁ᐀᐀ᐁᐁᑯᐱᕐ᠊ᔮᒫ᐀ᐁᑐᐁᐊᒪᐈ, Cᑯᐊᒌᐁᑰ ᒪᒌᑿᐁᐱᕗ ᖅᐅᓂᑐᖅᑲᐸ᠊ᒐᐊᐁᐃᑉ. CΔLᐊᐊ ᐃᑩᓪ ᖅᐅᐁ᐀ᒪᒌᖅᐺᐦᒌᑾᐁᐁᒫ᐀ᑉᐺᑯᐁᖅᑕᐺᑉ CΔLᐈᒌ᠊ᑩᐟ.

9.9 Narwhal Migration Routes
Pavia Nielsen describes changing narwhal navigation in Uummannaq. (photo: J. Meehan)

9.10 Narwhal Molting
Rasmus Avike describes narwhal response to hunters near the coastline off Qaanaaq in northwest Greenland. (photo: J. Meehan)

9.11 On His Own On The Ice
Kaviqanguak Kissuk from Qaanaaq is legendary for living extended periods on the ice by himself and being a keen observer of narwhal and Arctic wildlife. (photo: J. Meehan)

"Every summer, not once but many times do we see females with tusk. They are as numerous as the others but are rarely caught, these females with tusk."

ᐊᐅᔭᒡᒐᒥᑦᑎᐊᖅ ᐊᑕᐅᓯᐊᕐᔪᐊᖑᓐᓄᒐᓂ ᑕᐅᓇᖅᑲᑦᑕᑐᖅ ᐊᕐᓇᓂ ᑐᒑᓐᓂᒃ. ᐅᓄᖅᑐᐊᔪᖕᒥᒐᒻᒪᑕ ᑭᔮᓂ ᐱᔭᐅᒐᕋᐅᖕᒥᑎᐅᔭᓯᓂᖅᐅᖕᓱᑎᐅᐱᐊᓇᐄᕐᐱᐅ, ᑕᐄᑯᑕ ᐊᕐᓇᐄᒐ ᑐᒑᓐᓂᑦ.

(Jayko Peterloosie, Pond Inlet, Narwhal Tusk Discoveries, p. 87)

"The only thing I know of is the story my late father used to tell about how when they encountered difficulty with finding a route on the thinner ice, and as they tried to make their exit to the ocean, they used the smaller ones, the totally black ones, who were faster, to find a way. They used them to find them a way, on the thinner ice."

(Pavia Nielsen, Uummannaq, Narwhal Tusk Discoveries, p. 76)

"The responsible ones in the school of whales are often the old females [*arnatoqqat*], and we call them *ningiorsuit* [the female leaders]... guarding over the others. They call the young narwhals [*qernertaatsiaat*] as *oqajamaat* [the ones who inform others]... they may be spying. They stay at the water and hold their breath in a long time, placing themselves behind the others and watching over them. When the *qernertaatsiaat* emerge from the water, the others will disappear since they notice that a kayak is

following them. The narwhals are often very careful when they are being hunted... females and young narwhals. It is rare that they [females] have holes in the tusk. The females have no holes even when they are young or old. That's the difference.

According to what I have seen... the narwhals position themselves straight up. The one with the largest tusk is positioned in the middle. The ones with smaller ones were positioned a distance from the larger one, perhaps watching over the other ones. It is like that the others respect the larger one, while they are straightened up themselves toward the air. They are very nice to look at, some had large tusks. The one with the largest tusk was in the middle. It was very amusing, very funny."

(Rasmus Avike, Qaanaaq, Narwhal Tusk Discoveries, p. 84)

9.12 Returning To Camp
David Angnatsiak comes in off the spring ice floe near Pond Inlet. (photo: J. Mehan)

9.13 Narwhal Behavior
Albert Fleisher informed researchers about narwhal behavior during the mating season. (photo: J. Meehan)

"Yes, they have slaves down at the floe edge that I have seen. [They break their tusks] when they are chased by killer whales and when they are feeding in shallow waters."

(David Angnatsiak, Pond Inlet, Narwhal Tusk Discoveries, p. 79)

"I have, myself, perhaps around the end of the '80s, caught a very big whale that was shaped like a spring. It had a tusk that was about one meter long. Just like a spring. It was circular. Like this kind of spring. But I don't own it anymore."

(Alberth Fleischer, Uummannaq, Narwhal Tusk Discoveries, p. 83)

"There are two types of male narwhal that we see more north around Grise Fiord. One is a darker-skinned adult with a long tusk and one with a shorter tusk and wider at the base. This one has colored spots on its belly and more white color on the top."

(Jayko Alooloo, Pond Inlet, Narwhal Tusk Discoveries, p. 85)

Part 4

The Narwhal Future

"Global warming will reduce the area of the ice that is linked so closely to narwhal habitat. Narwhal ranges will probably contract to the north as ice cover reduces. How much ice is needed to maintain narwhal habitat? Narwhals clearly survived the conditions of the last interglacial 125 thousand years ago—a time of minimal ice, warmth, and high sea levels—and should survive them again. But, conditions of the last interglacial were not complicated by humans."

Ewan Fordyce, Chapter 6, this volume

Climate and the Changing Arctic

Mark C. Serreze

The Arctic is in large part defined by ice, collectively known as its cryosphere. This includes the floating sea ice cover of the Arctic Ocean, snow cover on land and sea ice, glaciers, ice caps and the Greenland Ice Sheet, lake ice, and permafrost. The undeniable fact is that the Arctic is beginning to lose its cryosphere. This transformation revolves around a critical number, namely, 32 degrees Fahrenheit or zero degrees Celsius, which is the freezing point of water. The date that air temperatures rise above the freezing point in spring now comes earlier than it used to. Summers are warmer, and the date at which temperatures dip below the freezing point comes later in autumn. Winter cold is not as strong as it used to be.

As recently as the 1980s, the climate of the Arctic was largely the climate that denizens of the North had always known and had adapted to. The rhythm of the seasons could be relied upon. But by the early 1990s, the Arctic began to stir. Evidence arose that the floating sea ice cover was beginning to recede, especially in late summer, accompanied by shifts in the circulation of the ocean. The scientific community noticed that some areas of the Arctic were warming, although others were cooling, attended by shifts in weather patterns. Areas of treeless, windswept tundra began to be taken over by shrubs. Permafrost—perennially frozen ground—was warming in some areas.

It had long been recognized that when global temperatures begin to rise, the impacts would be first observed and most pronounced in the Arctic, partly because of climate feedbacks associated with the loss of snow and ice that amplify the warming. However, for quite some time, it wasn't clear what was happening. While some of the emerging changes, notably the loss of summer sea ice, were broadly in line with what climate models were projecting as responses to increasing atmospheric greenhouse gas levels, others looked to be more easily explained as part of a natural climate cycle, reflecting shifts in the phase on the North Atlantic Oscillation and the Arctic Oscillation—patterns of atmospheric variability that have always been with us (Hurrell 1996; Thompson and Wallace 1998).

But the changes kept on coming, and it eventually became undeniable that a new Arctic was emerging. The new Arctic will be much warmer and likely free of summer sea ice well within this century, with effects on ecosystems and people that are now only starting to be understood. It seems clear that the impacts of Arctic change will not stay in the Arctic, but will reverberate

Previous spread:
10.0 Farming Returns to Greenland
Hay bales dot the lush pastures of Qassiarsuk, where Erik the Red settled in 985. Its meadows inspired the name he gave to Greenland "so that others would want to come and settle there." Today, as in Erik's time, farming has returned to Greenland following the Little Ice Age that doomed this first European settlement in North America.
(photo: W. Richard)

10.1 Rampant Jakobshavn Glacier
Climate change is having a massive effect on the Greenland Ice Sheet. The Jakobshavn Glacier at Ilulissat, which means "iceberg" in Greenlandic, is exporting so much ice from the Greenland Ice Sheet that it was designated a World Heritage Site in 2004. In recent years it has been discharging annually an amount of ice equivalent to the yearly water budget of a major US metropolitan region and has become a major attraction to climate scientists, journalists, and tourists.
(photo: W. Fitzhugh)

10.2 Declining Sea Ice Extent

September sea ice extent in millions of square kilometers from 1979 through 2015 along with the linear trend line. (illustration: NSIDC)

around the globe. This chapter describes some of the changes that have unfolded across the Arctic and Arctic Canada, in particular, and then takes a brief look at the future.

A Litany of Change: Sea Ice

The most visible manifestation of the changing Arctic is the loss of its sea ice, which is observed year round and is largest in late summer and early autumn. Predators such as polar bears, walrus, and narwhal are viewed as highly vulnerable to this loss. Polar bears and walruses use the sea ice as a platform for hunting. Of particular concern for narwhal is loss of sea ice in northern wintering grounds, such as Baffin Bay and Davis Strait. This is exacerbated by their strong site fidelity—despite changing conditions narwhal will continue returning to the same areas during migration (Laidre and Heide-Jørgensen 2005a; Laidre et al. 2008). Other immediate impacts of sea ice loss include increased coastal erosion and disruption of traditional hunting practices.

Arctic sea ice has historically ranged in extent from upwards of 15 million square kilometers in March to less than half that value in September, which is the end of the melt season. Apart from areas of ice locked to the shoreline, the ice cover is almost constantly in motion. This is due to the influence of winds on the upper surface of the sea ice cover and ocean currents. Cracks in the sea ice, known as leads, are the result of the deformation processes. Divergent (spreading) ice motion tends to form leads, while convergent motion can force one floe to ride over another, producing thicker deformed ice characterized by ridges and corresponding underwater keels. During winter, leads quickly refreeze to form areas of new, thin ice. Irregularly shaped openings in the ice, known as polynyas, can range from meters to many kilometers across. Polynyas can result from divergence, but processes such as tides and upwelling of warm ocean waters can also be involved. Large polynyas tend to form in the same place almost every year, a good example being the North Water

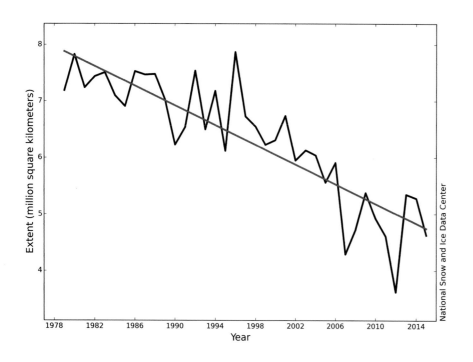

Polynia in northern Baffin Bay that provides a refuge for narwhal, beluga, walrus, and bowhead whales to feed and rest.

Our most consistent long-term record of sea ice extent comes from satellite sensors that detect the emission of microwaves from the surface. Microwave radiation has wavelengths in the centimeter scale. Different types of surfaces emit microwaves differently, and sea ice has a very characteristic signal. By putting together records from a series of satellite sensors, we have a daily record of Arctic sea ice extent going back to late 1978. Microwaves used to assess sea ice conditions are relatively unaffected by clouds and also provide information during the period of polar darkness (at the North Pole it is dark for six months of the year).

As assessed over the period 1979–2016, sea ice extent for the Arctic as a whole is dropping at about -3.2 percent per decade in January and about -3.5 percent per decade in February. These percentages are with respect to monthly averages over the period 1981 through 2010. The decline gets steeper from April through September. For September, which is the end of the melt season, the decline is a whopping -13.3 percent per decade. Other types of data show that the Arctic sea ice cover is also thinning.

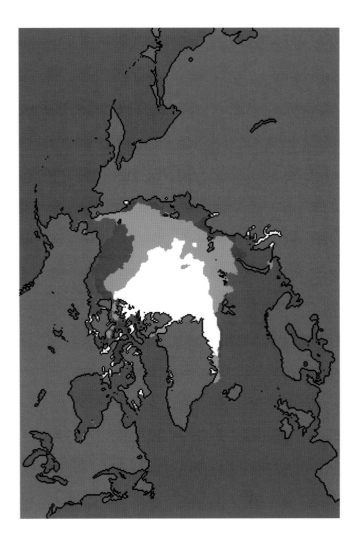

10.3 Sea Ice Reduction
September sea ice extent for 2012 (white areas), for 1998 (white and pink areas) and 1980 (white, pink, and red areas). (illustration: NSIDC)

The pronounced September trend in ice extent has gained the most attention, not just because it is the biggest, but because it is the best reflection of the overall health of the ice cover. Basically, after all of the autumn and winter ice growth has occurred, and after all of the spring and summer melt has taken place, what's left? That would be the ice extent in September. The trend is smaller in the winter months, because even as the Arctic warms up, it is still plenty cold enough for ice to form in winter, but that ice, while extensive, is fairly thin and is prone to melting out the following summer.

The downward trend for September has not been even. There are ups and downs from year to year, some of them quite pronounced. These largely reflect the natural variability in Arctic climate, especially the effects of variable summer weather patterns. The lowest monthly averaged September extent in the record occurred in 2012, at 3.6 million square kilometers. There was a big jump the next year, and then September extent was down again in 2014 and 2015, with the monthly average for 2016 ending up very close to 2015. But the overall trend is compelling and can be further illustrated by comparing the mapped extent for three years: 1980 (near the beginning of the record), 1998 (partway through the record), and 2012 (the record low year). The September average extent for 1980, of 7.8 million square kilometers, is approximately the area of the contiguous United States, minus Arizona. The extent for 2012, of 3.6 million square kilometers, is just 46 percent of the area recorded in 1980.

Air Temperature

Over the central Arctic Ocean and many land areas, winter temperatures of -30 to -40 C are common, and some areas can get colder. But the climate of the Arctic is far from uniform. Over the Atlantic side of the Arctic, moderated by ice-free waters of the northern North Atlantic, winter temperatures are much milder. Over the ice-covered parts of the Arctic Ocean, summer temperatures tend to stay close to the freezing point, but over Arctic lands, daytime summer highs of 15 C or even higher can be found. Temperatures across the Arctic have been rising for at least the past 50 years. In Canada, for example, surface air temperatures assessed over the period 1948–2012 increased up to 3°C in the northwestern part of the country to around 1°C warmer along the eastern coast.

Other areas have warmed even more, and the observed rise in air temperature for the Arctic as a whole is larger than for the Northern Hemisphere. This has a name—Arctic Amplification. Arctic Amplification has a number of causes that depend on both the season and region.

During the autumn and winter, Arctic warming has been especially pronounced along the coastal seas north of Eurasia and Alaska. These are the same areas that have seen the biggest summer and early autumn declines in sea ice extent. The link between the sea ice loss and Arctic Amplification relates to something called albedo feedback, albedo referring the reflectivity of a surface. As the climate has warmed, areas of dark, therefore low-albedo, open water have formed earlier in spring and summer than they used to, and these dark areas (much darker than white sea ice) readily absorb the sun's energy. When the sun sets in autumn, much of this heat that was gained in the top 20 m or so of the ocean through spring and summer is then released back to the atmosphere, keeping the atmosphere warm (Serreze et al. 2009). In the Barents Sea in winter, on the Atlantic side of the Arctic, there is a very prominent area of warming that results not from albedo feedback, but from warm ocean waters coming into the region from the south that inhibits winter ice formation. When winter ice covers a region, it effectively separates the fairly warm ocean from the colder atmosphere. Remove the sea ice and that ocean heat can now warm the atmosphere. This is what is happening in the Barents Sea in winter.

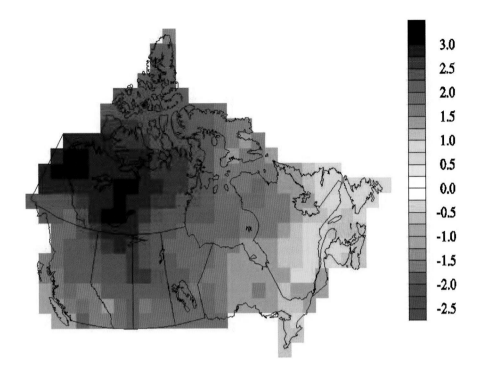

10.4 Change in Surface Air Temperature Across Canada, 1948–2012 (illustration: NSIDC)

Albedo feedback also explains part of the Arctic Amplification in spring over land areas: there has been a trend toward less bright springtime snow cover, meaning that darker underlying surfaces are exposed, readily absorbing the sun's energy and furthering the warming. Arctic temperature changes in summer have been rather small over the ocean. When sea ice is melting the temperature right at the surface is pegged to the melting point of water, so the air immediately above the surface just can't budge much. This does not mean that it isn't warming over the Arctic Ocean—it is just that the extra energy is being used to melt more ice rather than raise the air temperature. Also, the rise in summer air temperature isn't especially big over open water areas because much of the solar energy is being used to raise the heat content of the upper ocean. Come autumn, this heat is then released back up to the atmosphere, contributing to Arctic Amplification.

Another contributor to Arctic Amplification is temperature inversions that limit mixing and keep the heat focused near the surface. When there is an inversion, air temperature increases rather than decreases with height. Temperature inversions are almost ubiquitous in the Arctic during winter. Such inversions can also trap pollutants near the surface, resulting in poor air quality in parts of the Arctic. Changes in cloud cover and water vapor also play a role—clouds and water vapor absorb longwave radiation emitted by the surface, and then redirect some of it back downward (Kay and Gettleman 2009; Serreze et al. 2012). Changes in atmospheric circulation are also involved—for example, an extreme warm event over the Arctic Ocean in November of 2016 was in part due to a pattern of atmospheric circulation drawing lots of heat into the region. Finally, there is something called the Planck effect (Pithan and Mauritsen 2014). While too complicated to delve into here, the Planck effect says that in a cold region like the Arctic, balancing the "radiative forcing" associated with the increase in atmospheric carbon dioxide requires a bigger temperature change than in areas that are already warmer.

Precipitation and the Water Cycle

Precipitation over much of the Arctic is low or modest. Some areas, notably the Queen Elizabeth Islands of Canada, are classified as polar desert, with a total precipitation of less than 20 cm per year. This is primarily because the cold conditions limit the amount of water vapor that the atmosphere can hold, so there is little that can be condensed to form precipitation. Over such polar desert regions, and, more broadly for Arctic land areas as a whole away from Atlantic and Pacific influences, there is a general summer maximum in precipitation, corresponding to the higher temperatures and hence higher water vapor content in the atmosphere. The highest precipitation amounts are found over the Atlantic side of the Arctic, which in large part reflect ample open water, warmer conditions, and the influence of the North Atlantic cyclone track. Precipitation here tends to peak during the cold season because this is when the North Atlantic storm track is most active. Areas on the Pacific side of the Arctic are influenced by what is known as the East Asian storm track and also have a winter precipitation maximum.

Assessing variability and trends in Arctic precipitation is notoriously difficult—there are relatively few sites where precipitation is monitored, and blowing snow is hard to measure. But annual precipitation is known to have generally increased across Canada, especially across the northern part of that nation. For example, at the High Arctic station Eureka in central Ellesmere Island, annual precipitation over the period 1950–2007 appears to have increased by at least 40 percent (Zhang et al. 2011). At least locally, Arctic precipitation seems to be responding to the loss of sea ice. By provid-ing a new moisture source and warmer air, open water in the Barents and Kara seas seem to have fostered increased autumn precipitation over northern Eurasia (Wegmann et al. 2015).

Most of the precipitation that falls in autumn and winter is stored as snow. Subsequent melt of this snowpack results in a strong pulse of river discharge to the Arctic Ocean in late spring and early summer. The Arctic Ocean is rather small as oceans go, containing only about one percent of the global ocean volume, yet it receives about 10 percent of the global river discharge. The river discharge helps to maintain a fairly fresh ocean surface layer, which makes it easy for sea ice to form in winter and, as the oceanic equiva-lent of the Arctic temperature inversions just discussed, keeps heat from the underlying warmer layer of the Arctic Ocean (derived from the inflow of waters from the Atlantic) from mixing upward. The bulk of this river discharge is contributed by a small number of large rivers, the four biggest being the Ob, Yenisey, and Lena in Russia and the Mackenzie in North America, which originates in Canada. Since the onset of reliable records in the middle 1930s, discharge to the Arctic Ocean aggregated for the biggest Eurasian rivers has shown a general increase. Changes over North America, for which records are only available from the middle of the 1970s onward, also show more discharge, although as with Eurasia, there is a lot of variability and the pattern is different for different rivers (Peterson et al. 2002; Dery et al. 2016). The increased discharge can only be readily explained by an increase in net precipitation (an excess of precipitation over evaporation). Higher air temperatures also imply greater evaporation, but the increase in precipitation seems to be winning (Zhang et al. 2013).

Snow Cover

Depending on latitude and region, snow covers Arctic lands for 30 or more weeks of the year. Because precipitation tends to be modest or low for Arctic areas away from Atlantic and Pacific influences, the snowpack is generally fairly shallow. For example, over Arctic Canada, an April snow depth of between 30–60 cm can be considered typical. Of course, much greater depths can be found in areas of drifting. Because snow is an excellent insulator, it provides protection for many species against the extreme winter cold. Snow is also critical to people who live and work in the Arctic because it greatly aids in transportation by snow machine and sled.

With the rise in air temperatures, Arctic snow cover is on the decline. Satellite data show a substantial reduction in Northern Hemisphere snow cover during spring and early summer, and at this time much of the snow is isolated to the Arctic regions. The rate of loss of June snow cover extent between 1979 and 2011 has been measured at a remarkable –17.8 percent per decade (Derksen and Brown 2012). Because the snow is melting earlier, the seasonal pulse in river discharge to the Arctic Ocean is also creeping earlier into spring. Over the Russian Arctic coastal lands, there seems to have been an increase in rain-on-snow (ROS) events during autumn and winter. This has been linked to sea ice loss in the Barents and Kara Seas: all of the open water makes the coastal areas warmer and also provides a moisture source for precipitation. Two major winter rain-on-snow events on the Yamal Peninsula, one in 2006 and another in 2013, led to a massive die-off of reindeer. The problem is that after it rains, the temperature drops, forming a hard ice crust, which interferes with foraging. The 2013 event led to the death of 61,000 reindeer out of a population on the Yamal Peninsula of 275,000 animals (Forbes at al. 2016).

*10.5 Glacier Mass
Reduction 1989–2011*
*Mean annual (bars) and
cumulative (heavy line)
climatic mass balance
from 1989 to 2011 based
on all available annual
measurements from Arctic
glaciers reported to the
World Glacier Monitoring
Service by January 2013.
(from Sharp et al. 2013)*

Glacial Ice

The health of a glacier, ice cap, or ice sheet depends on its mass balance.
Winter snowfall adds to its mass. Summertime melt and water runoff
reduces it. If there is more winter mass gain than summer loss, the glacier,
ice cap, or ice sheet grows. If there is more summer melt than winter gain, it
shrinks.

Directly monitoring mass balance from field measurements is costly and
often logistically difficult, but the picture that has emerged from both
these direct measurements and other ways of getting at mass balance from
aircraft and satellite data reveals a worldwide loss of ice mass. One can
always find the odd glacier that is advancing, but these are the exceptions
that prove the rule. In the Canadian Arctic, mass balances have been directly
monitored for the Devon Ice Cap, Meighan Ice Cap, Melville South Ice Cap,
and the White Glacier. Consistent with results from other Arctic glaciers, as
assessed over the period 1980 through 2010, all four have had negative
average annual mass balances (AMS 2016). While precipitation seems to
have increased across Canada, this is overwhelmed by the effects of
greater summer warmth.

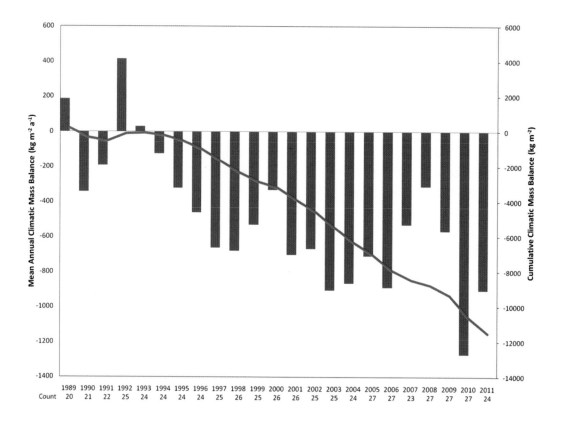

142

Ice core data point to acceleration of ice cap melt rates over the last few decades across the entire Canadian Arctic (Fisher et al. 2012). However, reflecting variable climate conditions, annual balances are also quite variable. For example, for the 2013/2014 balance year (the most recent data available), the White Glacier had a strongly negative balance while the small Meighan Ice Cap actually gained a little mass (AMS 2016). Some Canadian ice caps have exhibited a remarkable shrinkage in their areal coverage. For example, two small ice caps on the Hazen Plateau of northeastern Ellesmere Island that covered 7.48 square kilometers and 2.93 square kilometers (based on 1959 aerial photography), had shrunk to only five percent of their former areas by 2016 (Serreze et al. 2017).

A number of methods using satellite and aircraft data have been used to assess the mass balance of the Greenland Ice Sheet. There is no doubt that the mass balance of the ice sheet has turned negative, meaning that it is contributing to rising sea level, assisted, in turn, by mass losses from glaciers and ice caps around the world and the Antarctic Ice Sheet. Mass losses from the Greenland Ice Sheet are due to both the calving of icebergs into the ocean and surface runoff in summer, the latter now appearing to play the dominant role. The mass losses for Greenland are larger than for the Antarctic Ice Sheet, and mass losses from Greenland appear to have accelerated (Shepherd et al. 2012).

Permafrost

Much of the Arctic land area is underlain by permafrost. Temperatures measured in boreholes point to a general warming of permafrost over the past several decades, and in some areas near its southern limit, the permafrost is thawing. Permafrost also appears to be warming faster than expected in some areas. Permafrost thaw can have dramatic influences on the landscape, causing bucking and slumping of the ground, buildings, roads, and infrastructure, including pipelines. Much of the northern part of the Alaska pipeline that carries crude oil from the fields at Prudhoe Bay down to the southern coast at Valdez is built atop permafrost that is known to be warming. Recent work, looking across Russia, Alaska, and Canada, has focused on how permafrost alters the hydrology through the degradation of ice wedges. Ice wedges form when winter freeze causes cracks to open in the ground, which then fill with water in summer from melting snow. Then the water refreezes in winter, but because the water expands when turning to ice, the cracks widen. Through repeated winter freeze and summer thaw cycles, ice wedges eventually form that can extend ten or fifteen meters deep. Some are thousands of years old. But now, in the warming Arctic climate, these wedges are starting to melt out, greatly altering the landscape (Liljedahl et al. 2016).

The Future

What will the Arctic look like in the year 2050? It will certainly be much warmer. Whatever summer ice remains will hang out north of the Canadian Arctic Archipelago. This is because the average pattern of winds tends to push ice up against the coast, where it can thicken through ridging. This area may become a refuge for marine mammals like polar bears that depend on the sea ice. As discussed elsewhere in this volume, narwhal are also vulnerable to sea ice loss, and this is exacerbated by their strong site fidelity. But it appears that narwhal also have some flexibility when it comes to sea ice and habitat selection (Laidre and Heide-Jørgensen 2005a; Laidre et al. 2008).

Walruses are widely distributed across the Arctic. They give birth on sea ice and use the ice as a haul-out platform for feeding (on mollusks and other prey), and for protection from storms and predators. In such areas as the Alaskan coast, the summer sea ice now regularly retreats well beyond the shallow continental shelf, making it impossible to feed so the walruses are obliged to haul out on land. Since walruses can haul out on land, loss of the sea ice by itself will not result in their extinction. However, fewer animals could likely be supported (Kovacs et al. 2015).

Loss of the sea ice cover will affect traditional hunting practices. Also of concern is coastal erosion. A good part of the Arctic coast is comprised of frozen sediments or permafrost. It used to be that when a summer storm came through, the presence of sea ice would limit wave action. Now, with much less summer ice, winds have a long fetch over open water, resulting in larger waves and mechanical erosion. Because the permafrost is warmer, and the ocean waters are also warmer than they used to be, the waves also result in thermal erosion because they hasten thaw of the permafrost. Erosion is endangering coastal communities. As one example, in August 2016, the residents of the village of Shismaref, Alaska, voted to relocate to safer ground.

With much less sea ice by 2050, the Arctic is likely to be busier. Oil and natural gas resources along the continental shelves will be easier to access. The period since 2007 has already intermittently seen late summer opening of both the Northern Sea Route, along the coast of Eurasia, and the Northwest Passage, through the channels of the Canadian Arctic Archipelago. There are several Northwest Passage routes. The one that has most commonly opened is the southern route, also known as Amundsen's route. With less sea ice, prospects for Arctic shipping increase. However, much depends on economics. Whether there is a rush to tap the Arctic's riches depends on the price of oil and natural gas, and for many years to come, the Northern Sea

Route and Northwest Passage will only be open on a seasonal basis. Expansion of the Suez and Panama canals to handle bigger ships must also be considered. Effects of increasing shipping and other activities on Arctic wildlife are unclear.

With more water vapor in the atmosphere, precipitation in 2050 will be higher than today. As has already been observed over other parts of the world, there will likely be more extreme precipitation events, with the potential for flooding and erosion. Rain-on-snow events will be more common; as has already been seen, this can pose difficulties to reindeer and other terrestrial herbivores (Forbes et al. 2016). However, the snow season will be shorter, with snow forming later in autumn, and melting out earlier in spring. Vegetation will have changed, with areas of treeless, windswept tundra taken over by shrubs. Over large areas, near-surface permafrost will have thawed; in areas where permafrost is presently isolated (e.g., confined to north-facing slopes), it will have largely disappeared.

A wild card with global implications is the permafrost carbon feedback (Schaefer et al. 2011). There is a great deal of carbon stored in Arctic lands in frozen soils. The concern is that as the Arctic warms and permafrost thaws, soil microbes will become active, resulting in a release of some of this carbon back to the atmosphere as either carbon dioxide or methane, hence raising the atmosphere's concentration of greenhouse gases. When the permafrost carbon feedback starts, how strong will it be? Estimates exist, but the answers are not yet at hand. Another wild card revolves around the extent to which Arctic Amplification will affect jet stream patterns, contributing to amplified weather patterns whereby, for example, Chicago is in a deep freeze while at the same time, Alaska experiences abnormal warmth (Francis and Vavrus 2012; Barnes 2013). Whether such effects have yet emerged, and how strong they are or will be in the future in comparison with other drivers of climate variability, such as El Nino, is currently a matter of vibrant scientific debate. By contrast, it seems quite certain that the Greenland Ice Sheet, along with Arctic ice caps and glaciers, will continue to lose mass, contributing to sea level rise. This is something that should concern all of us.

10.6 The Future of the Arctic?
This photo of the Russian icebreaker Kapitan Khlebnikov *was taken north of Wrangel island looking toward the North Pole on July 13, 2007, a record minimum summer ice year.*
(photo: W. Fitzhugh)

Narwhals and the Global Mercury Issue

Rune Dietz and Christian Sonne

Mercury biomagnifies in the Arctic ecosystem, where high-trophic marine species such as seabirds, seals, whales, and polar bears obtain the highest mercury (Hg) loads (Dietz et al. 1996). This contamination has human health implications, since resident Inuit populations are dependent upon these animals as part of their aboriginal subsistence diet. In certain Arctic or Subarctic areas (e.g., Greenland and the Faroe Islands), human populations are exposed to daily intake of Hg (and persistent organic pollutants) that exceed the threshold level for negative effects on children's neurodevelopment (Dewailly and Weihe 2003).

In the Faroe Islands local health authorities recommended that the pilot whale (*Globicephala melas*) was not suitable for human consumption (Hansen et al. 2009). Mercury levels in toothed whale meat is much higher than in polar bears and seals because these animals excrete mercury through their fur (Dietz et al. 2013). Toothed whales in northeastern Canada and northwest Greenland are primarily hunted during the summer; hence, the Inuit are exposed to mercury mostly during the open-water season (Greaves et al. 2012).

In the Greenland Arctic bordering the Northwater region of northern Baffin Bay the seasonal Hg influx from the meat of hunted game is estimated based on the Hunters Lists of Game (Piniarneq 2016) and average Hg loads in muscle tissue from published and unpublished contaminant studies. The major influx comes between June and October, with narwhals being responsible for the majority (72.7 percent) of Hg influx. The dietary importance of the narwhal is enhanced by the prestige attached to hunters capable of consistently harpooning narwhals from a kayak (the only allowable practice). Since historic times the tusk of the narwhal has been regarded as a valued trade object; in the Middle Ages its tusks were worth more than ten times the value of gold.

In a recent assessment under the Arctic Monitoring and Assessment Programme (AMAP) the mercury loads for Arctic marine mammals were evaluated (Dietz et al. in prep). In general, most marine mammal species and various regions showed low Hg exposure, with the majority of concentrations in risk categories "below any known effect" or "low risk." However, some high-trophic species exceeded this general pattern, including polar bears, certain toothed whales including pilot whale, narwhals, and belugas (*Delphinapterus leucas*), and hooded seals (*Cystophora cristata*). Adult narwhals from the Qaanaaq region bordering the Greenland

Northwater had 6.7 and 13.3 percent of the population within the "severe risk" and "high risk" Hg categories. These levels were not found among narwhals from the Greenland East Coast around Ittoqqortoormiit. Adult belugas from Hendrickson Island had 1.2 and 3.3 percent of the population within the "severe risk" and "high risk" Hg categories, and juvenile belugas from the same region had 5.4 percent "high risk." However, belugas from southern Hudson Bay did not have any animals in the two high-risk groups. The examinations of narwhals revealed liver Hg concentrations (0.4-32 µg g-1 ww) from the Northwater region with similar histological changes in

liver and kidney to those found in other studies of Arctic mammals (Sonne et al. 2013).

The high concentration of mercury in game animals is not a new finding. Dietary advice in Canada and other Arctic countries are handled by health authorities where narwhals and other marine mammals are an important part of the diet, such as in Canada, Greenland, and the Faroe Islands. Such advice encourages people to eat more terrestrial food and more food from lower trophic levels. Passage of the Minamata Convention undoubtedly will reduce the long-distance transport of mercury from other parts of the world in the same way as the Stockholm Convention reduced organic

pollutants. Finally, there are many beneficial effects of vitamins, micronutrients, and fatty acids found in the Arctic marine diet. Narwhals have high concentrations of vitamin D and selenium in their skin (*maqtaaq*). Climate warming will bring many changes, but Inuit have survived thousands of years in the Arctic so it is likely they will weather the challenges of the future, together with narwhals.

10.7 Mercury Contamination
Seasonal Hg load in the hunted game of Avanersuaq based on average hunt from 1994 to 2014 (Piniarneq 2016) and average Hg loads in muscle tissue from contaminant studies in Greenland. (photo: Rune Dietz).

10.8 Shrinking Ice
Melting Arctic sea ice is confining
walrus foraging closer to land
due to their need for periodic
haul-outs. (photo: G. Williams)

As Goes the Arctic...

Luc Bas

The record-low level of winter Arctic Ocean sea ice occurring in January 2017 should be ringing all alarm bells. Evidence of the recent warming of the Arctic is documented by records of increasing temperatures, melting glaciers, sea ice, and permafrost—and by rising sea levels. Global temperatures are expected to increase further during the 21st century. In the Arctic, this warming is expected to be substantially greater than the global average. During the coming century average annual temperatures are projected to rise by 3 to 7° C, with the greatest warming occurring in the winter months. Precipitation is projected to increase by roughly 20 percent; sea ice is expected to continue to decline significantly, reflecting less solar radiation and further accelerating regional and global warming: and the area of Arctic land covered by snow is expected to decrease by 10 to 20 percent.

The resulting changes in the environment will present risks across the Arctic. The large reduction in summer sea ice threatens the future of several ice-dependent species while increasing marine access by ship to resources and population centers. Changes will be gradual because of the complexity of the Earth's climatic system, but major surprises are possible if the climate evolves differently. Ocean currents in the North Atlantic might undergo major changes with wide-ranging consequences for global climate.

Many Arctic animals such as polar bears, seals, walruses, and seabirds rely on the sea's biological productivity and on the presence of sea ice, both of which are highly dependent on climatic condition. Changes in sea-surface temperatures or currents could have a strong effect on Arctic marine fish stocks, which are an important food source for the world and play a vital role in the local and regional economies. Rising temperatures could have both positive and negative effects on the aquaculture of salmon and trout, which is a major industry in the Arctic. A decline in certain types of vegetation and unseasonably warm winters with rain-on-snow events would affect animals ranging from lemmings to reindeer. In turn, predators like foxes or birds of prey and human communities that depend on these animals would be affected. Freshwater ecosystems, such as rivers, lakes, and wetlands are home to a variety of animals that would be affected by increases in water temperature, thawing permafrost, and ice cover breaking up earlier in spring.

The impacts of the changing climate in the Arctic are already being widely observed and felt. They provide an early indication for the rest of the world of the significance of climate change that will ultimately affect global climate, sea level, biodiversity, and many aspects of social and economic systems. Climate change in the Arctic deserves and requires urgent attention by decision-makers worldwide.

10.9 Caribou Crashes
Unseasonably warm weather produces freezing rain-on-snow (ROS) events that have devastating impacts on caribou herds and people that depend on them. (photo: S. Loring)

Narwhal: An Uncertain Future

Steven H. Ferguson and David S. Lee

What makes narwhal especially remarkable is their ability to navigate and to live in a marine environment that is associated with sea ice. Like beluga and bowhead whales, narwhal are intimately habituated to sea ice. All three whales have lost the dorsal fin that would impede movement through ice.

Yet this environment poses significant risk to the survival of the species. Some of the very traits that have allowed the narwhal to thrive in the Arctic —their amazing diving capacity (feeding) and directional biosonar for detecting prey items at long distances—may not afford the same advantages as the environment changes and sea ice retreats northward. The deep-diving narwhal gets most of its seasonal food in winter in waters that are 95 percent ice-covered—a feat that appears exclusive to this species. If sea ice diminishes, these exclusive feeding opportunities and presumed shelter from predators such as killer whales may also diminish.

We have already witnessed a number of ecosystem changes in other areas. For example, there has been a substantial shift in the marine food web where the ice-associated Arctic cod (*Boreogadus saida*) has declined in the diet of marine mammals in place of more pelagic fish, such as the Subarctic capelin (*Mallotus villosus*), as shown in the accompanying figure (Marcoux et al. 2012b; Watt et al. 2015c; Brown et al. 2014, 2017).

Further, it is not known how increasing human activities such as shipping, oil and gas exploration, and fisheries will impact the relatively undisturbed acoustic environment and access to resources that narwhal have enjoyed up to now. Therefore, some degree of uncertainty about its future is not surprising, due to the nature of the rapid changes in the Arctic as a result of global warming.

The narwhal's environment includes the open water and sea ice in the eastern Canadian Arctic Archipelago and Greenland. If the nature of marine environment and especially sea ice continues to change, most of the habitat that narwhal have historically inhabited will be altered. Reductions in sea ice extent or duration of ice cover present both direct and indirect effects on narwhal. An example of an indirect effect is that sea ice that once kept killer whales (*Orcinus orca*) from accessing the region in summer will be removed. Likely, the impact on narwhal from killer whale predation will vary with the presence of sea ice during calving and early nursing when young are less capable of escaping killer whales. The potential effects of increased killer whale access to narwhal are largely unknown.

Another indirect effect is the seasonal and long-term changes

10.10 Ecological Shifts

Cumberland Sound feeding habits of predators before (top) and after (bottom) capelin invasion. All of the predators have largely lost their unique and different feeding niches and now concentrate on the same food (Yurkowski et. al.).

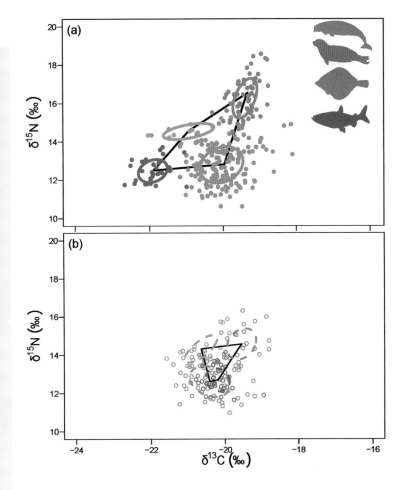

in the primary productivity of the marine food web, which may compel changes in the type of prey that narwhal consume. The complex interactions of components of the food web remain poorly understood, and the consequences of a shift from a sea-ice Subarctic ecosystem to a more open-water ecosystem is unknown. If some key ice-adapted species begin to diminish, narwhal behavior and distribution may also change as a result of changes in prey distribution and biological functions of the Arctic ecosystem. Another potential problem for narwhal is the appearance of new diseases or parasites as temperate species expand their distribution northward. As new species extend their range into the Arctic due to more suitable climatic conditions, they may bring diseases such as phocine distemper, brucella, and morbillivirus.

Although narwhal have experienced periods of warming in

the past (such as in the Middle Weichselian, 30–50,000 years ago) that included considerable changes in sea ice, temperature, and precipitation, the magnitude and diversity of anthropogenic stressors represent significant new threats. Some activities are already impacting narwhal. Shipping activity for the Baffinland Iron Mine in North Baffin Island has caused changes in the behavior of

narwhal in Eclipse Sound. Ship-based ecotourism of the Arctic has also increased and will likely continue to increase because of opportunities to observe the Arctic environment and its wildlife. It is expected that further reductions in sea ice will make shipping through the Arctic more attractive. With increased shipping, other threats to narwhal such as ship strikes, oil spills, and noise

10.11 Periscoping Narwhals
Based on new research of tusk sensory function, such behavior may be linked to the narwhal's ability to detect atmospheric conditions. (photo: G. Williams)

Some new areas of concern are the effects of ocean acidification and the presence of microplastics that can be ingested and bio-accumulated. These threats and global climate change highlight the importance of monitoring and understanding narwhal and their habitat requirements.

disturbance also increase. Contaminants represent another threat to narwhal. Contaminants can accumulate over time and become more abundant further up the food web, meaning that higher trophic level species, such as narwhal, that live long lives are at greater risk of toxic problems affecting reproduction and nervous system functioning. Contaminants typically arrive in the Arctic through air and water transport from southern latitudes. But glacial melting in the Canadian archipelago and Greenland could also result in a release of previously trapped contaminants such as mercury.

At present there is no evidence that contaminants are causing problems to narwhal health. However, their closest biological cousin—the beluga in the Saint Lawrence estuary—have been exposed to contaminants for many decades and continue to show no population recovery.

Oil and gas exploration remains one of the most immediate potential threats. Inuit have recently opposed exploration using seismic testing in the offshore waters of Baffin Bay because of the potential impact on marine mammals, especially narwhal.

The narwhal's home range is remote, large in spatial scale, and encompasses minimal and dispersed human infrastructure on which to base research efforts. However, Inuit elders and hunters are providing natural history observations and detailed environmental knowledge. For example, interviews with elders in Pond Inlet suggested that when noise disturbance is minimal, narwhals traveled in close proximity to the floe-edge (as close as five metres). They have also observed changes in narwhal migratory routes through Eclipse Sound. The long-term information derived from monitoring and Inuit observations provides a baseline on which changes can be measured.

Further, new techniques and technologies are constantly being developed to detect and track environmental and biological changes. For example, modern chemical techniques, such as stable isotopes, fatty acids, highly branched isoprenoids, genetic analysis, and newer techniques in development can be used with the archived collections of narwhal samples that have been collected by community-based monitoring. Results include knowledge of narwhal diet variation among social groups, between sexes, among age classes, and with other species across seasons. This information provides a better understanding of seasonal habitat use, for example, which can be used to delineate and to protect critical narwhal habitat. Combining techniques, such as

chemical signals and genetics, can reveal social networks within narwhal populations and assist in providing information necessary to understand how they may or may not be able to adapt to changing environmental conditions. Monitoring and research activities will be key activities to provide an understanding of changes in narwhal and narwhal populations. Increased knowledge of the life cycle needs of narwhal and the interactions between predators, competitors, and prey species will be critical to understand resilience and habitat requirements.

Ultimately, any solutions to mitigate the impacts of rapid changes that are occurring in the Arctic would be costly and short-term. Whether the species can respond by shifting distribution northward, allowing for a continued breeding population is unknown. Shifts in distribution are challenging

to predict and the reasons for such changes may be due to both indirect and direct effects of global climate change.

What can be done to safeguard the narwhal's habitat? Greenland halibut are likely the key winter food for narwhal and for their requisites for life processes is key. These areas include the offshore deep coral beds in Baffin Bay should be protected from excessive trawling by commercial fishing. Similarly, hydrocarbon exploration and extraction from these same waters should be limited, until impacts from these activities on narwhal are better understood. Finally, ecotourism and shipping in areas inhabited by narwhal nursery groups in July-August should follow best practices that limit such activity. Unless we begin to implement policies and to change our behavior to address global climate change, the future of narwhal will remain insecure.

10.12 *Projected Arctic Sea Ice Decline*

This figure shows projected and hindcasted September sea ice extent for climate models participating in the Intergovernmental Panel on Climate Change 5th Assessment, along with observations (black line). The projections are for four scenarios of greenhouse-gas concentrations for the future (starting in 2006) that relate to the radiative forcing at the top of the atmosphere that could occur at the year 2100. The shading indicates the one standard deviation range in the hindcasts and projections. (credit: J. Stroeve and A. Barrett, NSIDC)

The Last Ice Area

Clive Tesar

Nothing says climate change like a polar bear clinging to a remnant of sea ice. But beneath and around that sea ice is a sea of other life dependent to some extent on the ice cover. The ice is a source of nutrients, as ice algae form the base of a food web. It is also a resting, breeding, and feeding platform, and a protective shield from the incursions of pelagic predators.

For some time, World Wildlife Fund (WWF) has been looking at projections of melting Arctic sea ice, and watching the sea ice beat those early projections,

declining in extent by about 11 percent per decade when at its lowest ebb. We've been promoting mitigation of climate change as the primary response, knowing that unless we apply the brakes to the rate of change, the sea ice will effectively disappear in the summer. Yet even as nations, businesses, and individuals begin to apply those brakes to change, the effects of the greenhouse gas already in the air will linger on for decades, and the Arctic will keep melting.

This requires a secondary response, one that can be more

immediately effective in preserving life associated with sea ice. That response is to limit or remove other ecosystem-level stressors in the parts of the summer sea ice projected to remain the longest, the place where sea ice will be most resilient. WWF has relied on the efforts of sea ice modellers and has also commissioned its own modelling to attempt to refine the picture. All of the credible published sources agree: the area most likely to retain summer sea ice in the decades to come stretches from the Canadian High Arctic Islands across the top of Greenland. The ice ends up there because of two forces operating on the ice pack: it is pushed off the coast of Russia by the transpolar drift and circulated by the Beaufort Gyre.

This is not to say that there will not be locally important pockets of ice in other parts of the Arctic in years to come.

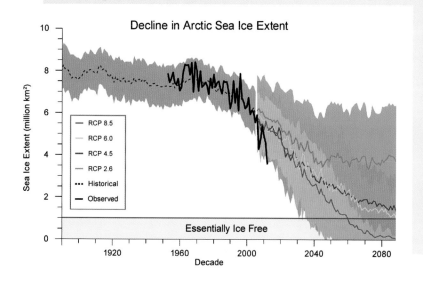

154

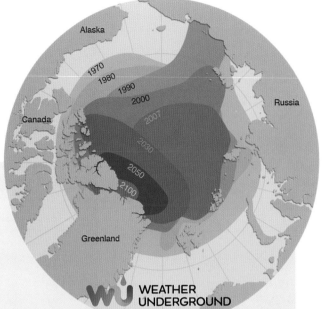

10.13 Arctic Ice Reduction Map
Past reductions are based on observations; future ones are based on average of model projections. Data from NOAA sources. (credit: Weather Underground)

Those will occur, and should also be afforded protection from other stressors. However, the Last Ice Area, that is, the main body of ice in national waters that are also the shallower, more productive waters, will be the responsibility of Canada and Greenland.

WWF has been talking since 2012 to people in the Canadian territory of Nunavut and to people in Greenland. We have encouraged them to discuss the future of this area, as it will become increasingly important to them, as a source of food and a cultural resource. We have also supported research in the area, helping to gather both scientific and traditional knowledge about its current and future importance.

The Last Ice Area will also be important internationally as a reservoir of sea ice for ice-dependent life. Inuit in the region have recently decided to engage in discussing the future of part of this area, through the

Pikialasorsuaq Commission. This body set up by the Inuit Circumpolar Council is consulting people in the region on management of the North Water polynya, an important feature that helps keep ice-dependent animals alive through the Arctic winter. The Canadian government has also recently announced that it will "with Indigenous and Northern partners, explore how to support and protect the future of the Arctic Ocean's 'last ice area' where summer ice remains each year." To recognize the global importance of the area, WWF is also promoting the possibility of establishing a World Heritage Site there, a suggestion first put forward by the Arctic Council.

With all of these measures taken together, and with the support of local people and international institutions, we hope to secure the future of the narwhal, and a whole sea-ice ecosystem that surrounds and sustains it.

10.14 The Future of the Bear
As Arctic ice recedes many questions emerge. How will polar bears respond as their ice habitat shrinks? Extinction? Readaptation to land? Hybridization with grizzlies in the west? Coexisting with black bears in the East? (photo: W. Richard)

Arctic Change, Resource Extraction, and Inuit Communities in Nunavut

Noor Johnson

In 2014 two projects related to resource development moved forward in the North Baffin region of Nunavut Territory. In June, the National Energy Board of Canada granted a permit to a consortium of companies to begin a five-year seismic-testing program in Baffin Bay. The goal of the seismic project was to develop better information about offshore resource potential; maps generated through the project could then be sold to oil and gas companies. During community consultations, Inuit residents who routinely travel, hunt, and fish in the nearshore waters of Baffin Bay voiced strong concerns about the potential impact of the testing on marine mammals. When the seismic permit was granted despite their recorded concerns and objections, representatives of the small hamlet of Clyde River (known in Inuktitut as Kangiqtugaapik) launched a legal strategy aimed at halting the testing. Supported by Greenpeace, they submitted a request for judicial review to the federal Court of Appeal stating that the government had failed to adequately consult them prior to issuing the permit.

Meanwhile, in September of 2014, the Baffinland Iron Mine began operations at Mary River, approximately 150 kilometers south of Pond Inlet (Mittimatalik). The following summer, the mine sent its first shipment of iron ore from a port in Milne Inlet directly past the community of Pond Inlet on its way to European markets. The company anticipated an annual shipment of 3.5 million tons of

11.1 A New Generation
Times, technology, and climate are changing, but language, cultural traditions, and subsistence practices still define Inuit culture, even as economic development expands. Dominic Kublu and others like him are comfortable with change but want assurance their their land, animals, and environment are protected. (photo: W. Richard)

11.2 Public Meeting Notice
Poster announcing a community meeting to discuss an expanded shipping season for Baffinland Iron Mine. (photo: N. Johnson)

11.3 Protesting Seismic Testing
Demonstrators support Clyde River outside the Canadian Court of Appeal in Toronto in April, 2015. (photo: N. Johnson)

ore during the open-water season from mid-July to mid-October. Since the shipments began, residents have raised concerns about the impacts of shipping on marine mammals; they have noticed fewer narwhal in Milne Inlet during key migration and calving periods, and believe that the presence of daily ships during summer months is one of the main factors (personal interviews 2015). Residents also note other changes that may be affecting narwhal, including more tourist ships, changes in the timing of the formation of sea ice, and an increase in orca whale (an apex predator known to hunt narwhal and other marine mammals) in the region.

Arctic residents are often described as being on the "frontlines" of climate change. Indeed, the Arctic is warming at more than twice the global average, and retreating sea ice and melting permafrost are causing diverse changes to marine, coastal, and terrestrial ecosystems and community infrastructure. Similarly, recent media coverage of the Arctic correlates with increased investments in mining and offshore exploration—and with sea ice retreat. As I describe in this chapter, however, interest in Arctic resources by outside groups stretches back hundreds of years. Inuit living in the Baffin region, drawing on this longer view, experience climate change as the most recent manifestation of a larger suite of changes whose roots are primarily social rather than environmental.

Arctic Resource Extraction in Historical Perspective

Although there has been much discussion of the role of sea-ice retreat in driving a rush to Arctic resources, nation states and resource companies have been interested in Arctic resources for hundreds of years. Martin Frobisher's Northwest Passage expeditions of 1576–78 during the Elizabethan period was the first post-Norse European venture to seek resources—in this case, gold—from the North American Arctic. Whalers and fur traders were the first to extract resources on a wide scale from the Canadian Arctic. In the mid-to-late 1800s, as whale stocks in the Atlantic Ocean dwindled due to overharvesting, whalers began to visit Baffin Island, eventually establishing several outposts at which Inuit would gather to look for employment or engage in seasonal trade (Eber 1989). When the bowhead whale population was severely depleted from overharvesting, economic interest shifted to fox fur pelts. By the early 1920s, Hudson's Bay Company trading posts had replaced whaling stations as the primary point of contact with Europeans in the Canadian Arctic (Damas 2002).

Around this time, petroleum products gradually replaced whale oil as a source of fuel. The first major northern oil discovery came in 1920, with a successful strike in what is now Norman Wells in the Northwest Territories;

in the 1950s and 60s, oil exploration, including seismic testing, exploratory drilling, and moderate production, was concentrated in the High Arctic islands and the Mackenzie Delta and Beaufort Sea in the western Canadian Arctic. Inuvialuit communities—the name preferred by Inuit living in western Canada—were on the frontlines of this resource-exploration boom, but without any recognized rights to benefit from potential discoveries nor any way of participating in decision-making about whether to pursue development. In the 1970s, a federal inquiry into a pipeline proposal, known as the "Berger Inquiry"—named after Justice Thomas Berger, who oversaw the commission—concluded that development in the Mackenzie Delta should be put on hold for at least a decade until Inuit and First Nations communities had settled land claims with the government of Canada.

In Canada, land claim agreements—modern treaties that were negotiated between the federal government and representatives of indigenous peoples—set parameters around the kinds of benefits that Inuit can expect from resource extraction. For decades, Inuit were subject to a top-down colonial model of governance in which decisions were made on their behalf by *qallunaat* (white, non-Inuit) bureaucrats, often with devastating impacts on Inuit well-being. This era began in earnest in the 1950s with policies that formally settled Inuit into year-round communities. One of the most harmful policies sent Inuit

11.4 a,b Frobisher's Mines Martin Frobisher's Northwest Passage voyages of 1576–78 brought back to England tons of "gold ore" excavated from this mine trench on Kodlunarn Island in Frobisher Bay, southeastern Baffin Island. Returning from their third voyage, they learned the rock was worthless. Although the investors went bankrupt, priceless knowledge was gained about Arctic geography and the Inuit. (photos: W. Fitzhugh)

children to residential schools hundreds of miles away from home, where they were taught a curriculum in a foreign language with no relevance to life in the Arctic. Although the experiences of those who attended these schools were not monolithic, many suffered physical, sexual, and emotional abuse (Truth and Reconciliation Commission 2015). Sending this generation away to school also caused major disruptions to family and social life, both in their absence as well as upon their return.

In spite of the harm inflicted by the policy of sending Inuit to residential schools, graduates of these schools became the leaders who negotiated land claims, drawing on the formal bureaucratic and English-language skills they gained in the classroom. One of their goals was to make sure that Inuit would be able to make decisions about policies that would affect their lives, including those related to education, health, resource management, and development. For example, land claim agreements created co-management boards that are required to use both Inuit and scientific knowledge; these include impact review boards that are charged with assessing proposed development projects. Land claim agreements also established corporations responsible for negotiating impact and benefit agreements with resource development companies, which can include requirements for education and workforce training, preferential hiring for Inuit, as well as subcontracting to Inuit-owned companies for goods and services.

In Nunavut, organizations that negotiated the land claim agreement have evolved to take on responsibilities related to oversight. Nunavut Tunngavik Incorporated (NTI) is the territorial organization for Nunavut; Qikiqtani Inuit Association (QIA) is a regional organization representing 13 communities from the Baffin region, including Pond Inlet and Clyde River. These institutions are charged with engaging both the federal government and the territorial government of Nunavut to better serve Inuit in the region. The Nunavut Land Claims Agreement (NLCA) also established four co-management boards that draw on both scientific and Inuit knowledge for decision-making; these include The Nunavut Impact Review Board (NIRB), the Nunavut Wildlife Management Board (NWMB), the Nunavut Water Board (NWB), and the Nunavut Planning Commission (NPC). Another organization, the Nunavut Marine Council (NMC), was created in 2012, drawing from the four existing co-management boards. NMC's mandate is to increase public awareness of and engagement in marine issues. The seismic-testing project did not undergo review by NIRB or NWMB because the offshore is not part of the Nunavut Land Claims agreement; in contrast, the Baffinland Iron Mine project went through extensive review.

Inuit leaders and community members have different views of resource development. Many active hunters and harvesters have deep concerns about potential impact of offshore oil and gas exploration and development on marine mammals. They point to the significant risks of operating in an environment where ice is prevalent for most of the year. Those who are more open to resource development emphasize the need for jobs at the community level. The environmental impact statement for the Baffinland Iron Mine suggested that the project would yield a 30 percent increase in jobs in the Baffin region over its 33-year projected lifespan (George 2011). While local opinion about the mine was mixed, the regional land claim organization, the Qikiqtani Inuit Association (QIA), negotiated an impact and benefit agreement that included a 25 percent minimum hiring quota for Inuit as well as significant financial commitment from the company for investment in education. Approval of the mine by territorial authorities and the QIA rested largely on its promise of employment and training opportunities. In contrast, the seismic-testing program in Baffin Bay had no clear link to job creation, apart from a few seasonal jobs for marine mammal monitors onboard the seismic ships.

Economic benefits from non-renewable resource development rarely persist once the resource is exhausted. A study of the social benefits of two lead-zinc mines that operated in Nunavut for decades suggested that benefits in terms of jobs and education did not last beyond the lifetime of the mines (Bowes-Lyon et al. 2009). Still, given limited options and a history of investment in extractive industry, many Inuit leaders support resource development as a mechanism for job creation. In Greenland and Nunavut, there is an additional link between resource development and sovereignty. In 2009 Greenland gained control of resource development as part of self-government, a step toward full independence from Denmark. Greenlandic politicians have emphasized the role of non-renewable resource development in providing the economic foundation for further devolution. Similarly, Nunavut would like to gain greater independence from the federal government, but to do so, it will need to reduce reliance on transfer payments to support regional government functions (Cameron and Campbell 2009).

Community and Household Economies

While there are differences in opinion about non-renewable resource development, there is widespread recognition among Inuit of the potential risks to fragile marine and coastal ecosystems from offshore activities. Marine-mammal hunting has always been central to Inuit livelihoods, even as these livelihoods have become more diversified due to broader economic changes and government policies. Today, families continue to harvest wild foods, called "country food," which are important both nutritionally and culturally.

11.5 Subsistence Hunting
A father and son walk together near their hunting camp. Subsistence hunting for seals, walrus, caribou, and birds makes an important contribution to the diet of Arctic residents.
(photo: N. Johnson)

In spite of its importance, however, country food is not equally distributed among households. Modern hunting practices involve the use of rifles, ammunition, snowmobiles, boats, and ATVs, all of which require income to maintain. A European ban on seal skin products, introduced in 1983 after lobbying by environmental organizations, led to a significant drop in the price that hunters receive for sale of seal skins. As a result, wage labor, rather than income from selling seal skins, began to play an increasingly important role in supporting hunting activities (Wenzel 1991).

Today, many younger Inuit find it difficult to gain both the income and the skills needed to become successful hunters. These skills are traditionally transmitted within a family context in which a grandparent or parent directly mentored a younger family member. Formal education that takes students

away from time on the land, loss of specialized terminology in native languages, and demographic growth leading to a larger elder-to-youth ratio have made environmental knowledge transmission more challenging (Pearce et al. 2011). Schools and community organizations run land-based programs to try to maintain some kind of connection for younger generations, but it has become more difficult for most youth to gain the experience and confidence needed to become proficient hunters (Pearce et al. 2011). The interdependence of wage income and subsistence activities for Inuit has led to the adoption of the term "mixed" economy; another widely used term is "social" economy, which includes the role of formal and informal community institutions in addressing social and economic needs (Abele and Southcott 2016).

Although country food plays an important role for both nutrition and culture, store-bought food is also critical to household food security. In every northern community, the grocery store is a central hub of activity where shoppers can buy many of the same products sold in stores in cities like Ottawa and Montreal, albeit with a more limited selection and at significantly

11.6 Resupplying Baffin
*The "sea lift" ship arrives
in late summer after
the sea ice melts, bringing
needed supplies.
(photo: N. Johnson)*

11.7 Northern Store
*As subsistence hunting
declines due to the high cost
of hunting equipment and
the need for wage employ-
ment, communities increasingly depend on expensive
food and goods shipped in
by sea and air. The Northern
Store in Clyde River is the
hamlet's only grocery and
general supply store.
(photo: N. Johnson)*

higher prices. In 2016, the average price for a liter of milk in Baffin communities was \$4.10 compared to the Canadian average of \$2.46, while a loaf of whole wheat bread cost \$4.21 compared to \$3.04 national average (Nunavut Bureau of Statistics 2016). The average cost of groceries for a family of four in Nunavut is \$19,760 per year, while almost half of Inuit adults earn less than \$20,000 annually (Council of Canadian Academies 2014).

Given the high costs associated with hunting and purchasing store-bought food, it is perhaps unsurprising that food insecurity—a lack of access to an acceptable amount of healthy food—is a problem in Nunavut. In 2012, 56 percent of adults in Nunavut reported experiencing food insecurity; while 27 percent of adults in Inuit Nunangat (the four Inuit land claims regions of Canada) experienced hunger because they could not afford to buy enough food (Arriagada 2017).

Another indicator of social and economic inequity at the community level is the significant gap in available housing. More than half of Nunavut residents (52 percent) live in subsidized housing (which Canadians refer to as "social" housing); nearly 40 percent of those in subsidized housing are dealing with overcrowding (Audla 2016). Overcrowded housing has been linked to numerous health problems, including higher prevalence of tuberculosis, asthma, and respiratory infections. Inuit associate a range of problems with crowded houses including difficulty sleeping, feelings of anger, and increased social conflict (Tester 2009). In spite of significant investments in housing infrastructure, the problem persists; in 2016 the Nunavut Housing Corporation estimated that eight communities, including Pond Inlet, needed 35 to 40 percent more public housing units than were currently available (Rohner 2016).

11.8 Tourists From The World

Tourist cruising has become a new industry in the Arctic. Here an expedition team from The World *explores King Christiansund at the southern tip of Greenland. (photo: W. Fitzhugh)*

High costs of housing, infrastructure, heating, and food in northern communities are exacerbated by high rates of unemployment and under-employment and a scarcity of employment opportunities in smaller community centers. Although the official unemployment rate in 2016 for Inuit adults age 15 and older was 18.2 percent, this number masks the uneven distribution and seasonal nature of employment in the territory. Jobs in government and education, the largest employment sector (54.2 percent of jobs), are concentrated in the territorial capital, Iqaluit, and in larger communities where some government offices are headquartered. Construction jobs have provided a boon in smaller communities like Clyde River in recent years, but these jobs are seasonal and short-term in nature. One woman in her 20s from Clyde River described using her experience and training in construction to get a job in heavy equipment operation at Baffinland. With a 21-year life expectancy for the mine, the job seemed much more secure than her previous employment; she said of the mine: "It's bringing in job opportunities for people with experience; we won't get much other work here" (personal interview 2015).

Other sectors have the potential to diversify the northern economy. While still a small part of the economy, tourism is growing: between 2005 and 2015 the number of passenger vessels in Nunavut increased from 11 to 40, a nearly four-fold increase (Gregoire 2016). In 2016 ten tourist ships called into Pond Inlet, alone, including the 1,000-plus passenger cruise ship, the *Crystal Serenity*, the first large cruise ship to successfully transit the Northwest Passage. Although thick sea ice remains an impediment to

wide-scale use of the Northwest Passage for shipping, models suggest that this will change significantly by mid-century, with increasing numbers of ships expected as the sea ice retreats (Smith and Stephenson 2013).

While ship-based tourism creates some opportunities, for example, for artists to sell their products, it also poses challenges, including increased pollution and marine litter. Additionally, only a small amount of money relative to the high cost of these cruises ends up staying in communities—$692 compared to an average ticket cost of $17,000 per passenger (Nunavut Tourism 2016). In contrast, land-based travel, including business travel and tourism, generates more income and employment opportunities through spending on lodging, meals, and guiding or outfitting services. Limited infrastructure and facilities pose a challenge for communities interested in promoting land-based tourism, however. In Clyde River, the Ilisaqsivik Society, a community health and wellness organization, addressed this problem by investing in a new hotel, which was developed as a social enterprise, with profits reinvested in the Society (Johnson 2016).

11.9 Bountiful Fishery
The cod and halibut fishery, carried out from the ice edge or boats in spring, is an important source of cash income as well as a subsistence resource for Greenland and Baffin Inuit. (photo: W. Richard)

The fisheries sector also has a strong potential for growth in Nunavut in the coming years; in 2015 the sector grew by 14 percent. With a market value of more than $86 million, fisheries employ around 370 Nunavut residents (Conference Board of Canada 2015). One of the barriers to expansion has been a lack of baseline information about fish stocks. Recent investments by the Canadian and Nunavut governments are supporting research on fish stocks for inshore and offshore fisheries. Environmental organizations like WWF are also focusing on small-scale fisheries as an alternative to oil and gas exploration for job development in the Canadian Arctic.

Clearly, building a base for sustainable economic development in the Arctic will require infrastructure investment on a broad scale. In 2011 the Inuit Circumpolar Council, an organization that represents Inuit in international decision-making forums including the Arctic Council, released a statement of principles for resource development that emphasized the importance of placing human needs, including food security, at the center of development.

The document highlighted the importance of infrastructure, stating: "healthy communities in the Arctic require the establishment, maintenance and improvement of core infrastructure needs, including housing, education, health care, and social service delivery infrastructure, and core transportation and communications networks" (ICC 2011).

Natan Obed, the President of Inuit Tapiriit Kanatami, the national Inuit organization of Canada, has recently noted that economic diversification in the Canadian Arctic will require investment in infrastructure, including traditional infrastructure such as port facilities and docks, as well as digital and communications infrastructure that communities in southern Canada take for granted (Obed 2017). A 2011 report highlighted the "growing gap" between communications infrastructure in southern and Arctic Canada, documentry shortage of affordable bandwidth, frequent network outages, and inadequate geographic coverage (Imaituk, 2011). "We have to diversify," Obed stated, "A lot of it is going to be led by equity within this digital age, and not expecting us to succeed without having the foundation of infrastructure that all other Canadians are eligible for" (Obed 2017).

Building Capacity for Community Involvement in Resource Development Decision-Making

Despite a recent slump in commodity prices for iron and other precious metals, economic predictions suggest that Nunavut's economy will grow in the coming years, largely due to mining development (Conference Board of Canada 2015). There is much less clarity about the future of offshore oil and gas development in the region. Oil companies have withdrawn from the Alaskan and Western Canadian offshore, regions where the presence of resources is much more clearly established, due to a slump in global prices as well as public pressure to keep Arctic oil in the ground. Although companies may still pursue offshore oil and gas in the North American Arctic, at a minimum, the timeline for these efforts has been significantly delayed.

The future of the seismic-testing project in Baffin Bay is also unclear. In August of 2015, the Court of Appeal issued a decision denying Clyde River's request for judicial review based on the conclusion that the government had adequately consulted with Baffin communities. Clyde River appealed the decision to the Supreme Court of Canada, which heard the case in November of 2016; the court's decision is pending. Meanwhile, the process has brought major international media attention to the hamlet's efforts to halt seismic testing. Clyde River residents initiated a social media campaign called "Unite

Against Seismic Testing." Their Facebook page features pictures of Inuit enjoying the land and eating country food, alongside quotes like this one, posted by Teema Palluq from Clyde River:

> I grew up learning how to hunt from my father and I'm teaching my son and his son how to be hunters. Hunting from the ocean is our way of life, it is where we get our food. Nothing can replace our food, or traditions, or those memories made when we hunt. Leave the ocean as it has always been and should always be.

In both Pond Inlet and Clyde River, community organizations are evolving to support capacity-building for local involvement in knowledge production and decision-making. This includes supporting locally initiated research projects, documenting local environmental observations in community-based monitoring programs, and developing new tools to make research and monitoring information more accessible at the community level. For example, in Clyde River, the Ittaq Heritage and Research Centre is developing an atlas to support access to research results and to develop geospatial visualization of relevant knowledge products. The impetus for the atlas lay partly in the need for better information at the community level to equip residents with information that would support their efforts to stop seismic testing (Johnson et al. 2016). Residents of both communities have partnered with academic researchers to develop community-based sea ice monitoring programs that provide information to support safe travel. In Pond Inlet, the SmartICE (Sea-ice Monitoring And Real-Time Information for Coastal Environments) project uses Inuit knowledge, sensors, and satellite imagery to provide

*11.10 **Hydrocarbon Addiction***
The Arctic, like the rest of the world, has become addicted to hydrocarbon for engines, heating, and electricity. Greenland (shown here) has the potential for hydropower from melting glaciers, but everywhere the cost of developing sustainable power is prohibitive without subsidies.
(photo: W. Richard)

167

information about sea-ice thickness; the information is used by both community members and industry to help inform decisions about coastal on-ice travel and shipping (Bell et al. 2014).

The significance of these projects goes beyond just providing important information; for residents, they also represent a movement to reclaim ownership over research practices so that they can be more involved in making decisions about the future in all areas of life, including sustainable development. As a resident of Pond Inlet explained:

> Inuit have stepped up and want to take ownership of research and monitoring. All this needs to be Inuit based, community based, and Inuit oriented... We need to be ready, we need to be prepared, and we need to take our own steps. I look forward to what the future holds because I think more and more will evolve from this (personal interview, 2015).

The concerns expressed by residents of Clyde River and Pond Inlet about the impacts of resource development and increased offshore activity on narwhal and other marine resources are both new and not new. They reflect the quickening of change related to the impacts of climate change, as well as a longstanding economic interest in Arctic resources on the part of nation states and private companies that ebbs and flows with global market forces. While acknowledging the need for jobs and the integration of local economies with global markets, Inuit also seek to maintain their connections to the marine environment through hunting and travel on sea ice and open water. Narwhal are particularly important for subsistence and maintaining Inuit cultural values. Increasingly, communities are looking for ways to strengthen their ability to participate in decision-making that could threaten these important connections.

11.11 Cod-Fishing in Ilulissat
Despite huge outflows of glacier ice and cold melt-water from Jakobshaven Glacier, warming seawater temperatures have resulted in a northward expansion of codfish along the West Greenland coast. Cod and halibut are major staples for the West Greenland subsistence and market fisheries and are now the major source of food for sled dogs. (photo: W. Richard)

Drowning in Noise

Christopher W. Clark

A century ago in the early part of the twentieth century, a grain of sand in the hourglass of this continent and a few lifetimes in a narwhal's world, these "unicorns of the sea" roamed the waters of Baffin Bay and Davis Strait without fear of seismic explosions from ships exploring for fossil fuels beneath the sea floor or the growing roar from commercial ship traffic. Around this same time the commercial slaughter of bowhead whales ended and the Arctic entered a period of acoustic tranquility. In those earlier years, whales could hear the calls of other whales and answer in turn to communicate about such things as where they were and what they were doing. They could hunt for Greenland halibut, Arctic cod, and squid under the familiar, normally quiet conditions of their acoustic environment. Whales that were calves and teenagers during the Great War knew the sounds of that quiet ocean, could listen to the subtle roar of the Labrador current, and grew up to understand the tell-tale signs of winter ice and summer calms, the opportunities for feeding, the chances of finding a mate, and giving birth.

Those days are gone now; the ancient quiet lost beneath the crescendo of noise that portends the arrival of human progress, a rising tide of noise that drowns the calls and songs of whales, that bleaches their quilted world of sound into acoustic whiteness, and dissolves their exquisite listening into a din of nothingness. What is the message other than to say the barn is burning brightly, and that we are getting better at knowing how brightly and at what temperature and when it will be destroyed? Is there something here other than an exercise in self-distraction, something other than another lost revelation? Can we, will we, can I do something about this?

Each of the extant marine mammals endemic to the Arctic has remarkable adaptations that provide distinct advantages for living in what we perceive to be an extremely harsh environment. Many of these adaptations are associated with auditory perception and sound production. That is to say, Arctic whales possess exceptional and exquisite bioacoustic abilities; all of which underscore the adaptive significance of listening to and producing sound for survival.

Imagine living in a place where the temperature is between -1 and 5° Celsius (that means, the ocean is the warmest place to live), and where for much of the year there is little to no sunlight. These are two fundamental characteristics of the Arctic's marine environment. Whales migrate and forage in complete darkness often within dynamic, massive fields of ice that extend for many hundreds of square miles. We know that

11.12 Noise Pollution Record

A sound spectrogram showing 32 explosions recorded at a distance of < 3000 km from a survey ship that was using a seismic airgun array to prospect for hydrocarbon deposits beneath the seafloor. This spectrogram is similar to a musical score: time runs along the bottom from left to right, pitch (frequency) is lower at the bottom and higher at the top, and the loudness of the sound is indicated by color and brightness. As a human listening to this acoustic scene at such a great distance, one would hear a regularly repeated crescendo-decrescendo of noise lasting many seconds and rising and falling every 10-11 seconds. (credit: C. Clark)

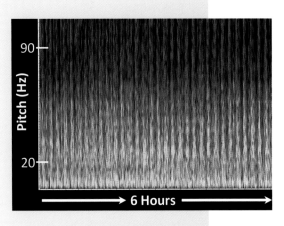

whales, even adult bowheads, will get trapped and die in ice, so there is clearly a selective advantage from specialized attributes that enable animals to sense such threats. We also know that all three species of Arctic whales—belugas, bowheads and narwhals—appear to prefer ice over open water: they will retreat into the ice when threatened, and will selectively hunt in ice.

All Arctic whales use passive and active acoustics for life's basic functions: communicating, detecting predators, foraging, and navigating. Thus for example, they can navigate by passively attending to the sounds of ice grinding, cracking, sliding, and exploding; or by actively listening to the reverberations and echoes of their calls and echolocation clicks off ocean features. We know from acoustic research in the Arctic that there are subtle differences in the acoustic environments

of multi year ice, young ice, and open water, as well as all myriad combinations of these conditions. As a simple exercise, try walking down a hallway or into a room in which doors are open or closed. Do this with your eyes shut and while listening intently. You will hear subtle differences between door-open and door-closed conditions. These passive acoustic contrasts are analogous to what a whale might experience in the darkness of the Arctic winter while listening for breaks in the ice in which to breathe. Another benefit from passive listening is gained from discriminating between acoustic features that are reflections of an area's bathymetric characteristics, which in turn are associated with foraging opportunities.

Our present understandings of Arctic whales are a rich collection of knowledge gathered by American Natives who have lived in the Arctic for millennia and by relatively recent observa-

tions obtained through the modern, scientific paradigm. My small contributions to this basis of understanding are through the scientific route, but I well remember a powerful experience, which was profound and humbling, when an Inupiat elder shared his knowledge. I had gained permission to visit his hunting camp on the frozen Arctic ice during the spring hunt off Barrow, Alaska. His crew had just landed a bowhead, and I was hoping to receive his permission to recover the whale's inner ears for a scientific colleague so that she could better understand bowhead hearing abilities. He patiently listened to my overly exited and too-fast explanation of my request. When I finally stopped speaking, he looked directly into my eyes. Speaking slowly and deliberately, this is what he said: "The ears of the whale are sacred, because the ears are the entrance to its soul." I was stunned by the import of this simply revelation. After a long moment of silence, I asked if he would like to listen to the sounds of whales and seals that I had recorded from under the ice. He listened intently. His eyes glistened as he nodded his head slowly, and then one by one he identified every voice in that wild underwater chorus. He knew them all! He stood up slowly, and I knew that the meeting was over. We walked out of his tent. I headed toward my snow machine. He headed toward his *umiaq*, and as I watched, he took a paddle from the boat, walked over to the ice edge, placed the broad edge of the paddle into the water and its butt end against the back of his jaw, just below his ear. He waved at me to come over, holding the paddle up as if to say, "Now you try it!" I mimicked his use of the paddle

and was immediately rewarded with a symphony of Arctic voices. No hydrophone, no cable, no batteries, no recorder: just a wooden paddle and a chorus of life beneath the ice.

Today, the Arctic's naturally quiet acoustic environment is under siege from the growing threat of noise from civilization's advancing progress. There is no ambiguity about the reality of this rising tide of anthropogenic din. Yes, there are and will be disagreements as to how much and how fast and what is biologically tolerable and what is not; but those are only debatable waypoints along a continuum of threats that are unambiguously increasing in density and distribution. There is no ambiguity regarding the exquisite uniqueness of Arctic marine-mammal bioacoustic capabilities, most details of which remain to be discovered. Yes, there will continue to be scientific revelations about how well

they hear and how remarkably they call, sing, and echolocate; and those are beautiful waypoints along a continuum of discoveries that will further demonstrate life's remarkable and seemingly endless inventiveness and capacity. But pause for a moment and think about the implications of these two, star-crossed trajectories. Back away as best you can from the temptation to slip into the vortices of reductionism and determinism, and simply consider the overall situation... the Arctic environment is changing radically, both physically and biologically; temperature, ice, primary productivity, life. We are moving expeditiously to take advantage of these opportunities. Will we take into consideration the lost opportunities for the life that's already there? What happens when Arctic life has nowhere to go?

Rethinking Human Development

Pamela Peeters

Canadian diver Joe McInnis had a special relationship with the Arctic. It all started in 1970, when he began diving beneath the ice to learn about the Arctic Ocean. Over the next thirteen years, Joe made some 500 dives in the Northwest Passage and the first dives at the North Pole. His relationship with the Arctic brought him much more than scientific results: he says it taught him "leadership and things that really matter." Today, his focus has shifted: he is urging humanity to reassess its relationship with the Arctic and the planet as a whole.

Testimonials like these, combined with images of crumbling ice caps and emaciated polar bears, have made Arctic climate change front-page news. "Turning down the thermostat" of earth by reducing carbon dioxide emissions is part of the debate, but this tends to divert attention from the real problem: the urgent need for a new approach to human development. Humans must develop new ways to deal with the long-term effects of our outdated Industrial Age economic model.

With four and a half billion years of wisdom and expertise in systems thinking, Earth may be its own best advocate. "Looking to Genes for the Secret to Happiness" (New York Times, August 2013) cited research by Steve Cole of the University of California, Los Angeles, that altruistic people produce higher levels of antibodies and that this benefits their health and the reproduction of their genes. Cole concludes that human gene expression is most likely driven by an evolutionary strategy for goodness. Let's hope so.

I hope as well that a charismatic animal like the narwhal will encourage people to reflect on the impact human lifestyles have on the Arctic. Perhaps then we will be inspired to begin restoring the earth's ecosystems and developing a new consciousness for planetary sustainability.

11.13 A Sustainable Arctic?
Pamela Peeters interviewing Joe McInnis, a Canadian Arctic diving pioneer who has devoted much of his life to the preservation of Arctic landscapes, animals, and cultures. (photo: M. Nweeia)

Now is the Time

Melanie Lancaster and Brandon Laforest

The narwhal, sometimes referred to as "the unicorn of the sea," is one of Earth's most mysterious mammals, partly because it spends most of its life in and around pack ice and is accessible to humans only for brief periods during its migratory cycle. Its strong association with sea ice makes it one of the Arctic marine mammals most vulnerable to climate change. Although the narwhal populations now is fairly high, its vulnerability and iconic status as an ice-adapted species has made it one of the World Wildlife Fund's priorities for focused conservation action across the Arctic.

The full implications of climate change on narwhals are not yet fully understood. We know that changes to the Arctic food web are already happening and that less sea ice will open up Arctic waters to more southern species, some of which may compete with narwhals for food and habitat,

or more worryingly, view narwhals themselves as prey. For example orcas, an open-water species and a summer predator of narwhals, have been appearing in parts of the Arctic that they were previously unable to access because their large dorsal fins prevented them from moving through closely packed sea ice.

Less summer sea ice in the Arctic also means greater access for industrial development. Accelerating oil and gas exploration, mining, and shipping in Arctic waters all pose serious threats to Arctic biodiversity, narwhals included. Oil spills could have devastating, long-term effects on Arctic ecosystems. Underwater noise produced by shipping and mineral exploration in narwhal habitats and migration pathways is likely to disturb or even displace narwhals and affect their ability to find food and navigate using echolocation.

Inuit peoples in Canada and Greenland are concerned about the effect on narwhals of increased pressure for industrial development. Inuit possess deep traditional knowledge of narwhal, which have been integral to their survival for millennia and remain vital to the wellbeing of families and communities. The narwhal skin/blubber interface, called *maqtaaq*, is eaten both raw and boiled, and is a significant source of vitamin C, and the narwhal's tusk, made of ivory, is one of the few source of income for Inuit hunters and carvers in some communities.

World Wildlife Fund works to conserve narwhals and their Arctic environment in a number of ways. We have Arctic offices in Greenland (Nuuk) and Canada (Iqaluit and Inuvik). We advocate for informed decision-making and policy setting by governments, including direct action to reduce greenhouse gas emissions. We also work

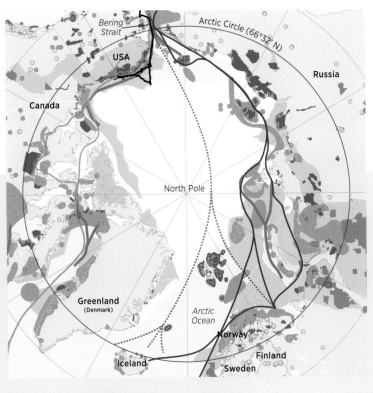

THERE GOES THE NEIGHBORHOOD

As the melting Arctic opens for business, industry is increasingly encroaching on critical habitats. Here's a look at the places where wildlife and humans are colliding.

— Route of the USCGC *Healy,* July 2015

Critical Bird and Mammal Habitat

▓ Audubon and BirdLife International Circumpolar Global Important Bird Areas/Alaska State and Continental IBAs

▒ Areas identified as being of heightened ecological significance to birds by the Arctic Monitoring and Assessment Programme and the Institute of Marine Research

— Marine mammal migration corridors

Human Activity

Shipping

— Northern Sea Route
— Northwest Passage*
····· Potential trans-Arctic route

Oil and Gas

▓ Production areas
▒ Petroleum basins/provinces in which production is occurring
● Major oil spills
▒ Areas with a 50% or greater chance of holding significant reserves of undiscovered oil and gas

Mineral Mining

○ Producing mines
● Potential mines in exploration/development

(First full transit by an unescorted cargo ship occurred in 2014.)

toward minimizing the effects of industry by ensuring responsible planning by companies that takes into account the needs of Arctic wildlife and indigenous communities. We advocate for the protection of sensitive marine habitats such as narwhal calving grounds, feeding areas, and seasonal migration routes.

Sound decision-making requires comprehensive knowledge about narwhals. At WWF we promote the use of science and traditional knowledge in decision-making. We are proud

to be a long-time participant in the only narwhal tracking initiative in Canada, providing funding and field support in partnership with the Canadian government and local communities. Using GPS tags, researchers track individual narwhals to obtain data on the timing of and pathways for migrations, feeding areas, and calving grounds. Although challenging, these research projects take scientists and WWF staff to some remote and beautiful corners of the Arctic, where we have been fortunate enough to join tagging field

camps, including one just outside of the community of Pond Inlet, Nunavut. One of the most beautiful sights in the world is waking up at three o'clock in the morning with the sun on the horizon and peering out of a tent to see hundreds of narwhals swimming by.

With such an uncertain future ahead, now is the time to support research and implement conservation efforts in collaboration with the Inuit to ensure a future for these majestic mammals as they respond to the changing Arctic environment.

11.14 Arctic Development
Projected impacts in the Arctic region include shipping, oil and mineral exploitation, tourism, fishing, and national defense—all with potentially negative effects on human and animal residents as well as land and sea environments. (credit: Greeninfo Network)

Out of the Arctic, Into the Smithsonian: Making the Narwhal Exhibition

Laura Donnelly-Smith

It's almost spooky inside the Smithsonian's Museum Support Center in Suitland, Maryland—shadowy and silent, except for the ever-present humming of the ventilation system maintaining a precise temperature and humidity. Lights are kept low or off until they're needed, to protect the specimens stored here. Inside this football-field-length "pod" (one of five), massive metal shelves reach nearly to the ceiling. And here, in the area reserved for the whale collection, are row upon row of ribs, vertebrae, skulls the size of cars, and other whale parts. As the content development team for a new exhibition on narwhals at the National Museum of Natural History, we've come here to see the fabled narwhal tusk up close.

Pushed up against a wall, metal storage containers that look like big filing cabinets hold the tusks. Marine mammal collection manager Charley Potter opens drawers to reveal meticulously labeled specimens of varying lengths and thicknesses, many numbered to match corresponding skulls stored nearby. There are also casts—exact replicas of actual tusks—that we can handle, to feel their heft. They conjure images of the unicorns narwhals helped inspire, and raise lots of questions: What does that tusk do? How did it evolve? And why are narwhals still so mysterious?

Much of what many people believe about narwhals is rooted in myth. Common misconceptions include the idea that narwhals are violent, and that they use their tusks to spear prey. Narwhals are frequently, and erroneously, cited as mythical creatures, or as a species that once lived, but is now extinct.

12.1 Modern Inuksuk
One of the highlights of the Smithsonian exhibition is a contribution made by Abraham Ruben: his modern interpretation of an inuksuk, *the traditional Inuit stone construction used for way finding and to signify important events or concepts in the Arctic countryside. (photo: Abraham Ruben)*

12.2 The Narwhal Collection
Marine mammal collection manager Charley Potter and exhibit designer Kim Moeller with a narwhal skull and tusk at the Smithsonian Museum Support Center in Suitland. (photo: C. Solhan)

12.3 Super-Narwhal
Fascination with the narwhal among the young has been fueled by narwhal-themed web programs, advertisements, and children's books like Super-Narwhal and Jelly-Jolt, *illustrated by Ben Clanton and published by Tundra Books. (courtesy of Tundra Books)*

Why a Narwhal Exhibit? Why Now?

Beginning in 2015, the National Museum of Natural History began exploring the possibility of building an exhibition about narwhals. We learned that not only are narwhals deeply fascinating in their own right, but that there is still a lot that's unknown about these animals—a world of questions, yet unanswered. Recent research into tusk sensitivity and narwhal genomics is driving new scientific interest in an animal that, in the past, was compelling mostly for its mythological connections.

While the world narwhal population is currently stable at around 180,000 individuals, climate change in the Arctic may pose the narwhal's biggest threat. Scientists, policymakers, and native communities are keen to understand what these dramatic environmental changes will mean in the long term. Between 2015 and 2017, the United States served a two-year chairmanship of the Arctic Council, an intra-governmental body that promotes cooperation on issues affecting Arctic states and ecosystems. Spotlighting the narwhal and its environment during the same timeframe allowed the National Museum of Natural History to further its mission to demystify science for the public and use our collections to help educate visitors about how they can be responsible stewards of our planet and its life. We saw this charismatic whale as a useful entry point into a deeper exploration of Arctic climate change, people, and ecosystems.

We also saw the potential for great fun. We wanted to build on narwhals' unusual pop-culture cachet. Blame or thank the catchy "narwhal song" from a 2015 cell-phone commercial that went viral, but narwhals' cool factor seems pretty undeniable.

First Things First

Every exhibition at the Smithsonian begins with proposal. *Narwhal* came from curator Dr. William Fitzhugh and research associate Dr. Martin Nweeia, who are experts in Arctic cultures and narwhal tusk research, respectively. After a vetting process involving multiple museum departments, that proposal was accepted and the emphasis shifted to developing an exhibition.

Each exhibition has its own core team: the people who take it from concept to reality. In addition to Fitzhugh, Nweeia, and content curator Dr. Marianne Marcoux, a research scientist with Fisheries and Oceans Canada, the *Narwhal* team included project manager and exhibit developer Christyna Solhan, designer Kim Moeller, educators Trish Mace and Jennifer Collins, fabricator Jonathan Zastrow, and me: writer Laura Donnelly-Smith. An extended team of reviewers and advisers from both the Museum and other institutions provided ongoing advice, feedback, and reality checks.

Work on the exhibition began in spring 2015. The core team considered the assets we had and brainstormed the stories we wanted to tell. The next step was a "data dump"—the curators wrote up short content briefs on topics like narwhal biology, people in the Arctic, and mammalian tooth structure (we all learned, early on, that the narwhal's tusk is an extended tooth!). We also visited the museum Support Center to see the tusks, skulls, and anthropological objects we might include.

We carefully considered the physical space we'd have, and what needed to fit there. The gallery designated for *Narwhal* is a long, thin rectangle. Exhibit designer Kim Moeller knew she needed to leave plenty of room for the star of the show: a 13.5-foot, life-sized model of a male narwhal with a six-foot tusk. Moeller also wanted to highlight breathtaking panoramas of the Arctic, so she designed several gently curving walls within the gallery to feature large-scale land-scape images, plus maps created by Smithso-

12.4 Ethnography Collections
Bill Fitzhugh assesses a sinew bow and harpoons to determine if the pieces need conservation before inclusion in the Narwhal exhibition. (photo: C. Solhan)

12.5 Planning the Exhibition
Pond Inlet residents and exhibit team members meet for discussion about the Inuit life section of the exhibition. Included here (left to right) are Martin Nweeia, Charlie Inuarak, Enookie Inuarak, Laura Donnelly-Smith, Christyna Solhan, Nicole Webster, and Bill Fitzhugh. (photo: P. Peeters)

nian cartographer Dan Cole. And then there were the tusks—including two that belonged to a remarkable, rare, double-tusked skull—all requiring specially built cases to keep them safe.

Guenschel case: 1829mm [72" (6')] w x 762mm [30" d] x 2134mm [84" h (7')]

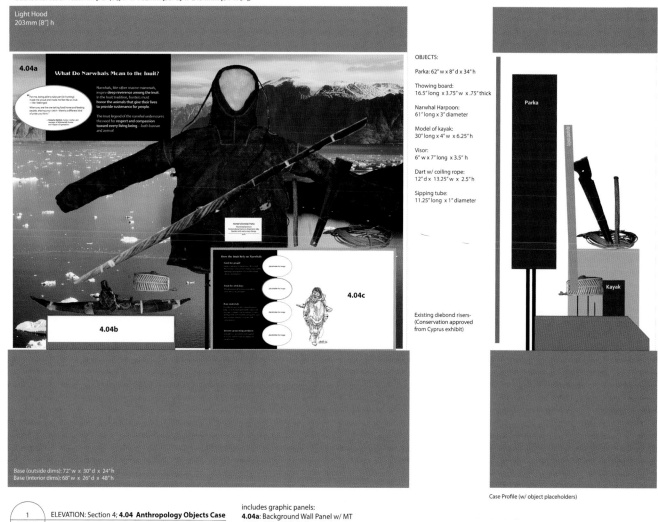

1 / EX-00-00 — ELEVATION: Section 4; **4.04 Anthropology Objects Case**

includes graphic panels:
4.04a: Background Wall Panel w/ MT
4.04b: Object labels (beveled riser)
4.04c: Riser panel w/ subtext/object labels

Case Profile (w/ object placeholders)

12.6 Exhibition Graphics

After script development, the exhibit entered an intense period of architectural design that brought together text, objects, and graphics into an integrated whole as shown in this elevation view.
(illustration: K. Moeller)

"Each hall has challenges of space, size, and budget, as well as the conservation requirements for the objects," Moeller explained. "It's not just about making things pretty—I have to know what my defining elements are to make it all work."

Our advisers—including marine mammal specialists, narwhal genetics experts, liaisons to Inuit (indigenous Arctic) communities, and climate-change scientists—weighed in with advice and concerns as we developed the exhibition outline. Project manager and exhibit developer Christyna Solhan was in charge of incorporating their comments.

"It's a challenge to integrate the many perspectives from our reviewers," she said. "But ultimately, the result is a stronger exhibit that really benefits from the collaborative, holistic process."

Welcome to Pond Inlet

From the earliest days of developing *Narwhal*, the team knew we wanted the deep involvement of the Inuit—the people who know the animal best. The challenges posed by the Arctic's remoteness and unpredictable storms mean that scientists can only spend a few weeks in the field, studying narwhals during good summer weather. But the Inuit are there year-round and have been hunting narwhals for subsistence and observing their behavior for many generations.

Content curator Martin Nweeia introduced the team to Pond Inlet, an Inuit community of about 1,600 people on the northeastern edge of Baffin Island in Nunavut, Canada. Nweeia had visited Pond Inlet many times for field research and had developed close relationships with numerous Inuit elders, hunters, and other community members.

Solhan and I set up phone interviews with some of these community members to learn more about their lives and the narwhal's significance in them. But first, we tried to immerse ourselves in the content we'd be discussing. We read about narwhal biology, the subsistence hunt, traditional and modern Inuit culture, and Arctic weather patterns in sources ranging from peer-reviewed scientific papers to university theses to anthropological sources like personal journals.

Setting up time to talk to the Pond Inlet residents posed some unique challenges. While many residents have government or private-sector jobs, most men (and some women) still hunt for subsistence. So when conditions are right, they drop everything and go out on the land, sometimes for weeks at a time. But when they were in town, our Inuit collaborators were always willing to answer our questions.

"We were matching up this aggressive exhibition development schedule with the realities of people's private lives," Solhan recalled. "Everyone was so generous with their time."

During our phone calls to the Arctic, I made an intensive effort to spent more time listening than I did talking. I tried to be especially conscious of not paraphrasing what I thought the community members were suggesting when they paused during our conversation. I wanted to make sure all had the time and space to tell their stories at their own pace.

12.7 *Meeting the Director*
Enookie Inuarak, Martin
Nweeia, Charlie Inuarak,
and Pamela Peeters
meeting with NMNH
director, Kirk Johnson.
(photo: P. Peeters)

To avoid the pitfall of "mythicizing" or insensitively portraying Inuit culture, core team members had a debriefing with Smithsonian anthropologist Stephen Loring, in which we discussed appropriate language usage for the exhibition text. A word like "village," for example, sounds innocuous. But it can carry unintended connotations of primitiveness or underdevelopment. That's why "community" is a better choice when writing about indigenous people's homes.

Throughout exhibition development, our Pond Inlet collaborators weighed in on our content, providing critiques and suggestions. One particular highlight was a visit from two Pond Inlet residents to the Museum—elder, hunter, and Pond Inlet mayor Charlie Inuarak, and his son, hunter Enookie Inuarak. The Inuaraks spent several hours with the exhibition team talking about their community, their observations of narwhal behavior, and how contemporary media, particularly documentary filmmakers, have portrayed the Inuit—both accurately and inaccurately. They cited films about seals and polar bears that led to stronger hunting regulations, which had a negative outcome on Inuit subsistence.

"When documentaries aren't in line with reality, it affects people up North," Enookie Inuarak told us. "When there's too much pressure from the outside, it affects families in the North."

What Happens in the Arctic...

...doesn't stay in the Arctic. Climate change in the North has far-reaching, global effects on animals; food stability for humans; weather patterns; shipping; travel; and energy production, as well as geopolitical relationships. The *Narwhal* exhibition team wanted to keep this message at the front of our visitors' minds. We thought that Arctic climate change should have its own section of the gallery, alongside narwhal biology, Inuit knowledge, and the art and myth of narwhals and unicorns.

But some of our experienced colleagues from the exhibitions and education departments at the Museum disagreed. Several cited research about climate-change education, reminding us that often the public "tunes out" talk of climate change or global warming because the topic is so widespread in the news media. In addition, the statistics are uniformly grim, which can lead to feelings of hopelessness, despair, and "shutting down," rather than the discussions of innovation for change that we wanted to inspire. The advisory team expressed concern that some visitors might just skip a climate-change section in *Narwhal*.

So the team decided to work the climate-change message throughout the exhibition, instead of segregating it in one part of the gallery. Designer Kim Moeller created a Climate Connection logo to brand this content. In writing these labels, I tried to tie the climate content very closely to how it affected narwhals—which were, of course, the main reason most people would be coming to the exhibition in the first place.

The team's educators, Trish Mace and Jennifer Collins, helped make sure the Climate Connection labels were effective at conveying challenging information. Educators use prior knowledge and data from past visitor surveys and in-hall observations to help shape exhibit text and messages.

"Educators provide the visitors' perspective, and have the capacity to understand content and goals and audiences," Collins said. "We find effective strategies to make connections."

Science in Progress

Narwhals look like creatures out of a fairy tale. The team counted on this "wow" factor to bring our visitors in through the gallery door. But once they're inside, it's our job to make sure they gain a deeper understanding of this very real animal and its environment.

For example, the team wanted our visitors to leave *Narwhal* knowing that research on this elusive whale is ongoing. Recent discoveries have shed light on multiple tusk functions, but there is much more to be discovered. That's where our "In the Field" and "How Do We Know?" exhibition labels come in. These labels highlight current, ongoing research projects and the people who make them happen.

Those people include scientists like Dr. Cortney Watt, who studies the narwhal diet, and Inuit hunter James Simonee, who noticed an increase in shipping traffic near Pond Inlet and developed a research question about contaminants in marine life. Now he's working with the University of Waterloo in Ontario, Canada, to collect fish samples that can be analyzed for various heavy metals.

A video featuring images and words from the Inuit highlights their observations and traditional knowledge about narwhals, which have amplified and furthered scientific research. The goal is to show visitors that traditional knowledge is vital to scientific understanding about many different species in the Arctic.

"There's a critical partnership between the locals and the scientists in the Arctic—you can't separate them," Collins explains. "We couldn't do science in the Arctic without the active participation of the Inuit community." The exhibit uses a soundscape of narwhal vocalizations, ice cracking, and howling wind to immerse visitors into the experience of living and working close to the North Pole. Touchable objects, featured quotes from Pond Inlet residents, and those large-scale panoramic shots of the landscape all provide entry points for visitors, appealing to those with different interests and learning styles.

"A measure of our success will be if people come out of Narwhal with a better understanding of the complexities of the Arctic and the animals and people who live there," Solhan said.

Putting it All Together

The *Narwhal* exhibition houses objects ranging from tiny narwhal-ivory carvings and tools made by Inuit artisans up to narwhal skulls and nine-foot-long tusks. Museum conservators assessed each of these items to ensure it was stable enough to be displayed. Most items from the anthropological collections require special cases that contain a desiccant—a substance that absorbs the moisture that can damage objects.

Fabricator Jon Zastrow and the exhibit production team built three new cases for the exhibition, while modifying three existing cases to display Inuit-made objects like a hunting visor, parka, and narwhal-ivory tube for sipping melted water. Graphics, lighting, and audio-visual specialists printed the panels, designed and installed the exhibition lighting, and perfected the video and soundscape presentations.

Zastrow said one of the biggest challenges was the logistics of installation. "It's a lot of structure for a small gallery, and there was a tight time frame. We had to build everything before the install started. We had to stage

12.9 and 12.10
Carved Narwhal
Tusk

This tusk, one of two Abraham has carved, was exhibited in a special Ruben exhibition at the National Museum of the American Indian in 2012. The twisting ivory strands carry entwined figures from Inuit and Nordic culture and history. This carving is also exhibited in the narwhal exhibition.
(photos: Kipling Gallery)

everything. There's a lot of logistics," Zastrow explained. "In terms of objects, the skull case was a challenge. You want these skulls to essentially float in midair—and look good doing it."

An *inuksuk* is a cairn (a human-made rock stack) traditionally built by the Inuit to aid with navigation in the Arctic. The *Narwhal* exhibit features renowned Inuit artist Abraham Anghik Ruben's interpretation of a traditional *inuksuk*. Ruben's sculpture is carved out of soapstone with a white alabaster base and features depictions of Inuit spirits, sea ice, and animals of the sea and land.

The sculpture, which weighs about 1,200 pounds—around the weight of a young narwhal—required a specially constructed pallet base to allow installers to move it smoothly into place while also supporting its weight. The fabrication team built the base out of a high-quality fire-retardant plywood. A cover fits over the pallet to provide a finished look. The exhibition also includes another of Ruben's pieces: an ivory narwhal tusk carved with images from Inuit mythology.

The life-sized narwhal model in the center of the gallery took a trip on a truck within a specially designed, padded carrying case from its original home at the Dr. Samuel D. Harris National Museum of Dentistry in Baltimore to the National Mall. Once it arrived, the museum's installation team hung the hollow fiberglass model from the lighting grid within the *Narwhal* gallery. Thin wires stabilized the model and kept it from swaying in air currents and from building vibrations.

Collins and other museum educators trained a new cohort of volunteers specifically for *Narwhal*. Within the gallery, the volunteers answer questions and engage in dialogue with visitors, but also provide interesting hands-on activities with tusk casts, skulls, and anthropological objects from the Museum's teaching collection.

All told, it took 28 months from the *Narwhal* exhibition kick-off meeting
until the day the exhibition opened for the public—about twice as long
as the narwhal gestational period. When the team first visited the Museum
Support Center to see narwhal tusks (most of us for the first time ever)
we didn't yet realize how closely connected this animal is to sea ice, to the
lives of the Inuit, and to the rest of the Arctic. The continued, complex
environmental changes underway in this region will bring uncertainty in the
future. We hope the *Narwhal* exhibition opens our visitors' eyes to the
interconnectedness of Arctic ecosystems, marine mammals, and the people
who rely upon them.

"The new Arctic will be much warmer and likely free of summer

sea ice well within this century, with effects on ecosystems

and people that are now only starting to be understood. It seems

clear that the impacts of Arctic change will not stay in the Arctic,

but will reverberate around the globe."

Contributors

David Angnatsiak is an extreme hunter from Pond Inlet, a Ranger serving as sergeant and master corporal. He has assisted with search and rescue, and regarded as a master marksman. His expertise on the ice and land has assisted, narwhal tagging teams, and sample collections completed under this scientific investigation.

Luc Bas is the current European Regional Director of International Union for the Conservation of Nature (IUCN). He was the European Director of The Climate Group in Brussels working with business and government to reach more ambitious EU climate policies and prepare for a true energy transition. He also was an advisor to the Belgium and Flemish Government and on the Expert Panel for the Organization for Economic Co-Operation and Development.

Sandra Black is a wildlife and zoo veterinarian with years of experience working with a large variety of species. She is also a clinical associate professor in the Department of Ecosystem and Public Health at the Faculty of Veterinary Medicine, University of Calgary, Canada. Mentored by Jack Orr, she has provided veterinary support to narwhal and beluga tagging projects since 2004. Her current research includes assessing the physiological effects of capture on narwhals, as well as investigating measures of health and chronic stress in narwhal over the past several decades.

Barbara Drake Boehm is the Paul and Jill Rudduck Senior Curator at the Met Cloisters in New York City and a specialist in the field of medieval goldsmiths' work and manuscript illumination. In 2013, she was curator of the exhibition *Search for the Unicorn* (2013). Among her acclaimed exhibitions for The Metropolitan Museum of Art, the most recent is *Jerusalem 1000-1400: Every People Under Heaven*, co-curated with Melanie Holcomb. Dr. Boehm received her undergraduate degree from Wellesley College and her Master's and Ph.D. from the Institute of Fine Arts, New York University.

David J. Bohaska is a museum specialist in the Department of Paleobiology, Smithsonian Institution, specializing in fossil marine mammals. His interest in paleontology began with a grade school trip to Calvert Cliffs, Maryland, famous as a source of Miocene marine mammals. For a period he served as registrar at the Calvert Marine Museum in Solomons, Maryland. He has collected fossils on the coastal plain from Delaware to Georgia, regularly attends fossil fairs and festivals, and lectures to avocational enthusiasts. These amateur contacts have greatly enlarged the Smithsonian's fossil marine

13.1 The Long Journey
Inuit artist, Samuel Shooyook created this petroglyph image on an outcropping of Qaqqiat Point, Arctic Bay, evoking the millennia-old partnership between Inuit and narwhal. (photo: M. Nweeia)

mammal collection. The fossil *Bohaskaia monodontoides* in the narwhal exhibition was named in his honor in 2012.

Christopher W. Clark, an engineer and biologist, is the founding Director and Imogene Johnson Senior Scientist for the Bioacoustics Research Program at Cornell University's Lab of Ornithology and Department of Neurobiology and Behavior. The mission of the Bioacoustics Research Program is to collect and interpret sounds in nature by developing and applying innovative technologies across multiple ecological scales to inspire and inform conservation of wildlife and habitats. When asked what he does, his answer is simple: "I listen to this singing planet!" Most recently Chris has devoted considerable effort to scientific advocacy through documentary films (Racing Extinction http://racingextinction.com/ and Sonic Sea, http://www.sonicsea.org/), as well as many outreach programs.

Rune Dietz is a biology professor at Aarhus University, Institute for Bioscience and the Arctic Center in Aarhus, Denmark. He has 35 years of experience working with marine mammals and contaminants in the Arctic including many years of work on narwhal tagging in Greenland and Canada as well as genetic and contaminants work. Rune has worked for the Arctic Monitoring and Assessment Program from its beginning and has been involved as a national key expert and lead country expert.

Daniel L. Distel received his B.S. in Biology from Cook College, Rutgers University and his Ph.D. in Marine Biology from Scripps Institution of Oceanography, University of California San Diego. He held research appointments at Woods Hole Oceanographic Institution, Scripps Institution of Oceanography, UCSD, and Harvard University, Cambridge, Massachusetts and was an Associate Professor in the School of Marine Science and the Department of Biochemistry, Microbiology and Molecular Biology at the University of Maine, Orono. At present, he is the Director of the Ocean Genome Legacy Center at Northeastern University and a professor in the Department of Marine and Environmental Science.

Frederick Eichmiller is a vice president and science officer at Delta Dental of Wisconsin, Stevens Point, Wisconsin. He is a graduate of the University of Minnesota with degrees in dentistry and mechanical engineering. He served for eight years as chief clinical research scientist and twelve years as managing director of the American Dental Association Foundation's Volpe Research Center, a dental research enterprise operated by the American Dental Association's Foundation. He has published an array of academic papers and has thirteen patents reflecting research on dental restorative materials and other topics. He serves on numerous panels and committees for the National Institutes of Health, the International Standards Organization, and the American National Standards Institute.

Steve Ferguson works as a marine mammal research scientist with Fisheries and Oceans Canada at Freshwater Institute Science Laboratory, Winnipeg, Manitoba. He is responsible for the population health of marine mammals in the Canadian Arctic. His research investigates how global warming and human economic development in the Arctic affects the ecology of marine mammals and ways to mitigate potential problems. The goal is to conserve the region's diversity of marine mammals and their immediate environment. Knowing more about the Arctic food web and animal foraging behavior helps us understand variation in marine mammal food and its relation to Inuit traditional lifestyle. Such projects include incorporation of community-based monitoring to better understand changes occurring in the circumpolar Arctic. His research focuses on eastern Canadian Arctic species, including killer whales, ringed seals, and bowhead whales with an emphasis on predation.

Frank Fish is a Professor of Biology at West Chester University of Pennsylvania, where he has been on the faculty since 1980. He received a B.A. in Biology from the State University of New York in Oswego in 1975. He completed a Ph.D. in 1980 in zoology at Michigan State University, where he studied the energetics and biomechanics of swimming in the muskrat. Recent projects have included examination of the evolution of swimming modes in aquatic mammals, energetics and maneuverability of aquatic animals, hydrodynamic design and flexibility of biological control surfaces, and analysis of animal swimming for biomimetic AUV design. His narwhal research investigates the design parameters of narwhal flukes and physical and functional differences between the flukes of male and female narwhals in relation to their diving and feeding behaviors.

William W. Fitzhugh is Arctic Curator and Director of the Smithsonian Institution's Arctic Studies Center in the National Museum of Natural History in Washington, D.C. and Visiting Professor at Dartmouth College. He has conducted anthropological and archaeological research throughout the circumpolar. The narwhal exhibition and book is the latest in a series of Smithsonian exhibitions that include Bering Sea Eskimos, the Ainu of Japan, cultures of Siberia and Alaska, Vikings, Genghis Khan, and ancient Bering Sea Eskimo art. His most recent books are *Maine to Greenland: Exploring the Maritime Far Northeast* and *Bark and Skin Boats of Northern Eurasia*, to appear in 2018.

R. Ewan Fordyce is a Professor of Paleontology at the University of Otago, New Zealand and a research associate in paleobiology and vertebrate zoology at the Smithsonian's National Museum of Natural History. His research focuses mainly on the evolution and structure of fossil whales and dolphins. He graduated from University of Canterbury, New Zealand and was a Smithsonian postdoctoral fellow in 1979. He is a Hutton Medalist, a Fellow of the Royal Society of New Zealand, and senior editor of the *Journal of the Royal Society of New Zealand*.

Pedro A. F. Galante earned a BS in molecular science (2003) and a Ph.D. in biochemistry and molecular biology (2007) from University of Sao Paulo, Brazil. Galante moved to Harvard University for postdoctoral training in bioinformatics (2008). In 2011 he became senior researcher at Hospital Sirio-Libanes (Sao Paulo, Brazil) where his research has focused on the study of genomic variation and post-transcriptional variation in humans and other vertebrates. Galante has authored over 60 peer-reviewed publications.

Baojun Beryl Gao is the founder and board director of CloudHealth Genomics Ltd. and CloudHealth Medical Group Ltd. She is also the Head of Longevity and Health Research Institution at Shanghai Jiaotong University. She received her undergraduate degree in management from Fudan University, China, and her MBA from Massey University, New Zealand. Madam Gao has devoted her life to promoting public health in China, and the public health industries globally, including climate change and wildlife preservation efforts.

Henry P. Huntington is science director for the Arctic projects of Pew Charitable Trust. He earned his masters and doctoral degrees in polar studies at the University of Cambridge. Huntington's research includes studies of subsistence hunting in northern Alaska, documenting traditional ecological knowledge of beluga and bowhead whales, examining Iñupiat Eskimo and Inuit knowledge and use of sea ice, and assessing the impacts of climate change on Arctic communities and marine mammals. He was co-chair of a U.S. National Academy of Sciences committee on emerging research questions in the Arctic and served on a Council of Canadian Academies panel on food security issues. In addition to academic and popular articles, as well as two books, Huntington has traveled widely in the Arctic by dog team, boat, and snowmobile.

Jason G. Jin is the founder and CEO of CloudHealth Genomics Ltd. and CloudHealth Medical Group Ltd. Jin is also an adjunct professor at Shanghai Institutes of Biological Sciences, Chinese Academy of Sciences, Fudan University, and Shanghai Jiaotong University. He received Ph.D. and post-doctoral training in biology from University of California, San Diego, an M.D. from the School of Medicine, Fudan University in Shanghai and an MBA from Rutgers University.

Noor Johnson is a cultural anthropologist whose research focuses on environmental governance and Indigenous knowledge in the Arctic. Currently she is a research scientist with the National Snow and Ice Data Center at the University of Colorado in Boulder. She received her BA from Brown University, an MA from American University, and a PhD in international development anthropology from McGill University. From 2015-2016 she investigated economic development in the Canadian Arctic as a Fulbright Arctic Initiative Scholar. Previously she served as a science policy advisor at the Smithsonian Institution in Washington, D.C. and has worked for non-profit organizations.

Jeremy Johnson has been the Project Manager for the Vertebrate Genomics Group at the Broad Institute of MIT and Harvard for over 10 years. In that time, he's worked on many of the higher profile vertebrate genome projects, including dog, elephant, anolis lizard and coelacanth. More recently he has played a key role in the 200 Mammals Genome Project, collecting samples, sequencing and generating genome assemblies from over 150 different mammalian species, including the narwhal.

Elinor K. Karlsson, PhD leads the 200 Mammals Genome Project, an international effort to compare the genomes of hundreds of different mammalian genomes, and investigate evolution by looking at how DNA changes between species. She also founded Darwin's Dogs, a citizen science project that invites dog owners to participate directly in research exploring the genetic basis of dog behavior, as well as diseases such as OCD and cancer. Dr. Karlsson is the director of the Vertebrate Genomics Group at the Broad Institute of MIT and Harvard, and assistant professor in bioinformatics and integrative biology at the University of Massachusetts Medical School.

Winston Patrick Kuo is the chief technology officer and head of business development for CloudHealth Genomics, focusing on big-data guided precision medicine. Prior to industry, Kuo was assistant professor in the Department of Developmental Biology at Harvard School of Dental Medicine and director and founder of the Harvard Clinical and Translational Science Laboratory for Innovative Translational Technologies at Harvard Medical School. Kuo is a computational biologist with interests in craniofacial and evolutionary biology. He has researched such diverse topics as Darwin's Finches, mouse craniofacial structure, and understanding sensory aspects of the narwhal tusk.

Brandon Laforest lives in Iqaluit, Nunavut, and is the senior specialist for Arctic species and ecosystems for World Wildlife Fund-Canada. Brandon holds a bachelor's degree in wildlife biology from Guelph University and a Guelph master's in animal nutrition and metabolism. He is currently completing his PhD in environmental studies at York University on climate change aspects of the feeding behavior of the southern Hudson Bay polar bears. He has also worked with Cree communities along the shores of southeastern Hudson Bay and James Bay, and with zoos, to incorporate traditional ecological knowledge into his analysis of polar bear food web dynamics. Brandon now manages WWF-Canada's work on all priority Arctic species, including narwhal.

Melanie Lancaster is a senior specialist for Arctic species with the World Wildlife Fund's Arctic program. Melanie is a conservation biologist with expertise in program management and research into and management of the multitude of threats facing species and their habitats. Melanie works with the WWF national offices to coordinate and implement conservation strategies for WWF priority Arctic species—polar bears, walruses, beluga and bowhead whales, narwhals, and caribou/reindeer. Most recently, her work has focused on some of Australia's most endangered species. She has a science degree with a PhD in conservation biology and genetics of Antarctic fur seals.

David S. Lee is a wildlife biologist with Nunavut Tunngavik Incorporated (NTI) in Rankin Inlet, Nunavut, Canada. NTI represents the Inuit of Nunavut and is responsible for implementing the Nunavut Agreement. David received a PhD in geography from McGill University, studying social and ecological dynamics of Inuit narwhal hunting in northern Baffin Island. In addition to conducting research, David contributes regularly to Nunavut's wildlife co-management programs.

Lucila Ohno-Machado received her medical degree from the University of São Paulo and her doctoral degree in medical information sciences and computer science from Stanford. She is associate dean for informatics and technology and the founding chair of the Health System Department of Biomedical Informatics at UCSD, where she leads a faculty with backgrounds in medicine, nursing, informatics, and computer science. Prior to her current position, she served at Brigham and Women's Hospital, Harvard Medical School, and at the MIT Division of Health Sciences and Technology. She serves as editor-in-chief for the *Journal of the American Medical Informatics Association*.

Marianne Marcoux has been a marine mammal research scientist since 2014 with Fisheries and Oceans Canada based at the Freshwater Institute Laboratory, Winnipeg, Manitoba. Marianne's interest in marine mammals started when she was 13, after she won a trip to Mingan Island, Quebec, and saw her first humpback, minke, and finback whales. Her research focuses on narwhals and belugas in the Canadian Arctic. Specifically, she uses passive acoustic monitoring and aerial photography to gain insight into the ecology and population biology of these species. She is also interested in the impacts of increased Arctic shipping traffic on the behavior, physiological stress, acoustic communication, and reproductive success of narwhals and beluga.

Pavia Nielsen has served as chairman of KNAPK, Kalaallit Nunaanni Aalisartut Piniartullu Kattuffiat, the Association of Fishers and Hunters in Greenland, was a member of the parliament of Greenland, and was a municipal councilor and congregation representative in Uummannaq municipality. He was decorated with honors by both Danish and Greenlandic governments, including the Order of the Dannebrog from Denmark. Under an NSF Grant with Martin Nweeia he delivered an address on narwhal quotas and hunting practices to the 2006 Inuit Circumpolar Conference.

Kooneeloosee (Cornelius) Nutarak Sr, was born on Jan. 1, 1924 in Piniraq near Clyde River, on Baffin Island and lived most of his life in Pond Inlet before passing away on January 15th 2007. Considered as the guardian of Inuit Culture, he was named as member of the Order of Canada in 2006, and in 1999, The Inuit Heritage Trust named gave him the Elder's Recognition Award for assisting other Nunavummiut in understanding their own culture. Interview content combined with his notes on the behavior, migration, distribution and anatomy of the narwhal were included as part of the Inuit knowledge used in this article and study to guide and assist scientific studies on tusk function.

Martin T. Nweeia is Lecturer at the Harvard School of Dental Medicine and clinical assistant professor at Case Western Reserve University School of Dental Medicine where he received his doctorates of dental surgery and medicine. He is content curator for the exhibit *Narwhal: Revealing an Arctic Legend* and a research associate in the Marine Mammal Program at the Smithsonian Institution where he previously received fellowships in physical anthropology and vertebrate zoology. As a National Science Foundation scientist, he is principal investigator for Narwhal Tusk Discoveries, the Narwhal Genome Initiative, and Narwhal HoloLens and has led five and collaborated on 11 High Arctic expeditions investigating narwhal tusk sensory function. Nweeia was honored by an Explorer's Club Lowell Thomas Award in 2017.

Jack R. Orr is the Arctic project leader for Fisheries and Oceans Canada. He has been a marine mammal research technician in Arctic Research Division since 2000. His work has focused largely on population stock assessment of Arctic cetaceans (belugas and narwhals), including hunter kill biological sampling, population census surveys, and studies of movement and habitat use using satellite tracking and time-depth recording. For the past thirty years Jack has been developing and perfecting field techniques related to the capture, handling and tagging of belugas and narwhals from eastern Russia to Svalbard.

David H. Pashley is a retired regents professor of oral biology at the College of Dental Medicine and professor of physiology and endocrinology at the School of Medicine, Georgia Health Sciences University in Augusta, Georgia. Dr. Pashley graduated from Portland State University and received his DMD from the University of Oregon. He has received NIH research grants for more than forty years and has authored or coauthored more than 750 papers in dozens of journals. Besides his doctorate in dentistry, he has a PhD in physiology from the University of Rochester. His area of expertise in the physiology of dentine and dentine sensitivity has made him a key player in the study of narwhal tusk physiology and function.

Ryan Paterson is a graduate student at the Canadian Museum of Nature in Ottawa researching the evolution of aquatic mammals. He received a bachelor's degree at the University of Toronto where he studied biology. He explored the archaeological cultural history of Ontario before beginning his studies on the evolutionary history of mammals that returned to the sea.

Pamela Peeters is an environmental economist and sustainability strategist consulting with companies globally and developing educational programs for youth with her Eco-Hero program, now established in five countries. After completing a post-graduate research fellowship at Columbia University, she launched the "Our Planet" television series, the "Sustainable Planet" film festival, and "Sustainability Week" productions in New York and Brussels. An author, filmmaker, and educator, she was on the marketing team of U.S. partnerships for the UNESCO decade of Sustainable Development, and in 2008 she prepared the state visit of the Prince of Belgium to India.

Vladimir Pitulko is senior archaeology research associate at the Institute for the History of Material Culture, Russian Academy of Sciences in St. Petersburg. He studied at Leningrad State University (now St. Petersburg State U.) and began his early fieldwork with Nikolai Dikov in Chukotka and Kamchatka. He has served as field engineer for cultural and archaeological landmarks and was a junior associate at the Russian Ethnographic Museum. Following his PhD on Russian Arctic archaeology he held a research post at the Smithsonian's Arctic Studies Center. His research on the 8000 BP Zhokhov Island village and the 27,000 BP Upper Paleolithic Yana RHS sites have revolutionized thinking about early human cultures in the High Arctic.

Joy S. Gaylinn Reidenberg is professor of anatomy at the Center for Anatomy and Functional Morphology, Icahn School of Medicine at Mount Sinai, New York. She studies the anatomy of whales (including dolphins and porpoises) and other animals adapted to environmental extremes. Studying such "natural experiments" helps uncover basic biomechanical relationships that affect all animals, including humans. She also presents animal anatomy and science education to the public through television documentaries, including *Inside Nature's Giants* (featuring anatomy and evolution of large animals including fin and sperm whales) and *Sex in the Wild* (featuring reproductive biology of animals including dolphin.)

Natalia Rybczynski is a palaeobiologist and research associate with the Canadian Museum of Nature and adjunct research professor at Carleton University. Her research focuses on the Neogene Age (21–3 million years ago) fossil record of the Arctic. She has led expeditions resulting in the discovery of new fossils including, *Puijila* (an ancient "missing link" in the lineage that includes modern seals, walruses and sea lions) and a High Arctic giant camel. In 2015 she was recognized by *Canadian Geographic* as one of Canada's top modern-day explorers.

Mark C. Serreze is director of the National Snow and Ice Data Center and professor of geography at the University of Colorado in Boulder. His Arctic research includes atmosphere-sea ice interactions, synoptic climatology, boundary layer problems, numerical weather prediction, and climate change. His efforts over the past decade have increasingly focused on trying to make sense of the rapid environmental changes being observed in the Arctic.

Laura Donnelly-Smith is a writer and editor in the exhibitions department at the Smithsonian National Museum of Natural History. Prior to coming to Natural History, she spent a decade writing about higher education and science for various publications and organizations. During the past year she has worked with curators, narwhal experts, Inuit hunters, and graphic designers to craft the themes and exhibit script for the exhibition *Narwhal: Revealing an Arctic Legend*.

Christian Sonne is professor at Aarhus University, Denmark in veterinary ecotoxicology and wildlife health with degrees in veterinary medicine and wildlife population health. Since 1997 he has specialized in biological effects from exposure to environmental chemicals, diseases, and climate change in a variety of species including predatory mammals, raptorial birds, sea birds, fish, and humans. His work includes internal and reproductive biology; research on skeletal, immune, and endocrine systems; modelling, blood biochemistry, and infectious diseases. His research frequently takes him to Greenland and northern Canada where he has studied birds and terrestrial and sea mammals including polar bears and narwhals.

Clive Tesar of World Wildlife Fund grew up in Canada's Northwest Territories and spent ten years traveling the Canadian Arctic as a reporter, producer and host for the Canadian Broadcasting Corporation. Prior to joining WWF, he worked throughout the Arctic as a communications consultant for NGOs, indigenous peoples' organizations and governments. Clive has a masters degree in environmental education and communications. In addition to leading WWF Arctic communications and helping manage relations with stakeholders and other organizations, Clive leads the Last Ice Area project. He lives in Canada, but is frequently found in other parts of the Arctic.

Alexander J. Trachtenberg earned his BA in science from the University of North Florida and his MSc in biology from the University of Massachusetts in Boston. Currently, he is the president and board director of the nonprofit StART (Stem-cells for Assisted Reproductive Technologies) for Families, Inc. Previously, he was the primary research assistant in a translation medicine lab at Harvard Medical School.

Cortney A. Watt is research scientist with Fisheries and Oceans Canada, Freshwater Institute Sciences Laboratory, Winnipeg, Manitoba, who studies Arctic marine mammals. Her special interest in researching how narwhals and belugas are changing their distribution and foraging behavior in response to changes in climate. Her PhD research at the University of Manitoba focused on narwhal diet and dive behavior in the world's three narwhal populations.

George W. Wenzel is professor of geography and adjunct professor of anthropology at McGill University. He has conducted long-term ethnographic research in Nunavut and Nunavik in Canada and in West Greenland. His current research is on the ecology and economy of Inuit hunting in relation to food security and wildlife management issues. His recent publications discuss changes in the role of Inuit subsistence hunting and resource use in Nunavut's Qikiqtaaluk Region.

Kristin H. Westdal is a marine biologist who has been researching Canadian Arctic beluga, narwhal, and killer whales for the past fifteen years. She has a masters of environmental science from the University of Manitoba and is researching environmental and biological factors affecting beluga movements in Hudson Bay for a PhD. Currently she is working with Oceans North Canada on conservation programs for narwhal and beluga.

John Wilken was a Bentson Scholar in aquatic biology at the University of California, Santa Barbara. Awarded the prestigious Explorers Badge from the Eagle Scouts, John assisted the narwhal genetic sample collection for the Smithsonian Institution and supported the Narwhal Tusk Discoveries Expedition in Pond Inlet, Nunavut, 2015. As a science educator, John shares his passion for ocean life with students and visitors at the Pennington Marine Science Center and UCSB's REEF facility.

Acknowledgments

Thank you to the many hunters and elders who graciously gave their time and energy to fieldwork that was completed under NSF grants 0739858, 0839989, 0922052 and 1025981 from the Division of Integrative and Organismal Systems, and grants 0630561, 0646872, 0701534, 0756708 and 1551190 from the Office of Polar Research. Noteworthy contributions were made by David Agnatsiak, Cornelius Nutarak, Elisapee Ootova, Jake Anaviapik, Joseph Inuk, Jayko Alooloo, James Simonee, Natasha Mablik, Paniloo Sangya, Charlie and Enookie Inuarak from Pond Inlet, and Philippa Ootoowak, archivist at the Pond Inlet Library and Archives Society.

Thanks also to Bruce Donoff, Dean of the Harvard School of Dental Medicine; Dr. Kenneth Chance, Dean, Case Western Reserve University School of Dental Medicine; James Mead, Curator Emeritus of the Marine Mammal Program, Smithsonian Institution, for his ongoing perceptive guidance; Dr. Peter Hauschka, Harvard School of Dental Medicine and Boston Children's Hospital, for his assistance with the fabrication of floating laboratories; Mike Manyak of the Explorers Club, World Center for Exploration; Peter Ewins, Director of the Endangered Species Program, WWF-Canada; Mary Ellen Thomas, Senior Research Officer at the Nunavut Research Institute's Arctic College; Jason Akearok, Executive Director of the Nunavut Wildlife Management Board; Jobie Tukkiapik, Director of Makivik Corporation; and Fisheries and Oceans Canada, particularly Jack Orr, Arctic Project Lead, and his assembled teams of assistants, without whom none of the advances in this tusk research would have been possible.

We thank the University of Copenhagen Zoological Museum, Grass-Telefactor, the Forsyth Institute, the Canadian Museum of Nature, AstroNova, Inc. (formerly Astro-Med, Inc.), Midmark International, and organizations that donated considerable time, effort and equipment needed to complete the tusk sensory research.

For the analyses and interpretation of electrocardiogram data, we thank physician Michael Parker and Shahin Tahery, Senior Technician and Trainer at Midmark International. For extensive library searches of foreign and obscure published accounts of the narwhal, our thanks to Mary Sears at the Ernst Mayr Library of the Harvard Museum of Comparative Zoology; Keiko Meshida, Rare Books Collection, Vertebrate Zoology Library, Smithsonian Institution; and David Osterber at Countway Library, Harvard Medical School.

We thank the following individuals for their assistance and collaboration: Judy Chupasko and Mark Omura, Division of Mammals, Harvard Museum of Comparative Zoology, for their support and supplies in collecting anatomical specimens; Greg Marshall and Mehdi Baktiara of National Geographic Society; Evelyn Flynn and Lisa Marie Leclerc, Boston Children's Hospital; Joseph Paradiso, Medialab, Massachusetts Institute of Technology; Leslie Parr, San Jose State University, and her graduate evolutionary biology class who assisted with the Inuit Traditional Knowledge questionnaire and provided valuable insights into the evolutionary origin of cetacean teeth as related to the narwhal; Francis Thackeray, University of the Witwatersrand, Johannesburg; Ari Shapiro, Massachusetts Institute of Technology; Keith Yip and Judy St. Leger, SeaWorld San Diego; Allison Tuttle and Tracy Romano at Mystic Aquarium: Anthony Giuseppetti, National Institute of Standards and Technology; the late Donald Ortner, Biological Anthropologist, Smithsonian Institution; Jeremy Johnson, Project Coordinator at Broad Institute; Kevin Hand, illustrator; Ethan Tyler, illustrator; Glenn Williams, photographer; Adam Ravetch, film maker; marine mammal scientist Paul Brody; John Castle, Chairman and CEO of Castle Harlan Corporation; the late Martin Bergman, former director of the Polar Continental Shelf Project; and research assistants Katherine Tiisler, Nancy Stabley, Janet Kurland, Judy Moran and Benjamin Gray Jr. from Narwhal Tusk Research and Discoveries.

Funding for field research and laboratory analysis was provided by grants from The Neural Systems Cluster of the Division of Integrative Organismal Systems at the National Science Foundation, Harvard Schools of Medicine and Dental Medicine, Harvard Museum of Comparative Zoology, World Wildlife Fund, National Geographic Exploration Fund, Explorer's Fund Pearlman Grants, and the Smithsonian Institution. Support for the collection, translation, and interpretation of Inuit traditional knowledge was provided by grants from the Office of Polar Programs, NSF.

This book and the Smithsonian exhibition of the same title required assistance from a host of individuals. The exhibition was organized by a Core Team led by Christyna Solhan, whose mastery of coordination and attention to detail made the two-year preparation process efficient and enjoyable. Besides Christyna, the Core Team members included writer-researcher Laura Donnelly-Smith, educators Trish Mace and Jennifer Collins, picture researcher Caitlin Gillis, narwhal biologist Marianne Marcoux, designer Kim Moeller, narwhal tusk researcher Martin Nweeia, exhibition curator William W. Fitzhugh, and fabrication specialist Jon Zastrow. Much of the Core Team's work also appears in this book as does the advice and consultations with a much larger advisory panel of narwhal-related researchers, museum whale biologists (including James Mead and Charlie Potter), and cetacean paleontologists Nick Pyenson and David Bohaska. Others included Frederick Eichmiller, Ewan Fordyce, Winston Kuo, Lee Weight, Daniel Schrag, Mark Serreze, Steve Ferguson, Shari Gearheard, Glenn Williams, David Angnatsiak, Jayko Alooloo, Rune Dietz, Martin Nweeia, Marianne Marcoux, and William Fitzhugh. We especially thank Assistant Director of Exhibitions Kara Blond, Chief of Exhibition Development, and Project Manager Junko Chinen, and the rest of the exhibit staff for strong support throughout the project. A generous grant from the exhibition budget made it possible for us to publish this book. Ryan Lavery organized media outreach, and the education department directed by Shari Werb developed supporting programs with assistance from Jennifer Collins and her team.

This book involved many of the above-mentioned people and offices. Martin and I especially thank our chapter and sidebar authors, who took on the difficult task of writing articles suitable for a wide audience on very short notice and were generous in offering their own photographs and illustrations. Others who contributed photographs were Martin Nweeia, Joseph Meehan, Gretchen Freund, Isabelle Groc, Pamela Peeters, Clint Wright, Cortney Watt, Glenn Williams, Wilfred Richard, Henrik Saxgren, Norman Hallendy, Eric and Stephen Loring, Robin Ohern, Alice Houston, Cornelius Nutarak, and Bettina Ovgaard (see credits for others). Several institutions were also generous in supplying illustrations, including the Metropolitan Museum of Art, the Royal Danish Collection, the Musée National du Moyen Âge, the Smithsonian's National Anthropological Archives, the New York Jewish Theological Seminary, U.S. National Snow and Ice Data Center, National Oceanographic and Atmospheric Administration, National Air and Space Administration, and the Nunavut Legislative Assembly, Canada. Kim Moeller, Dan Cole, and David Lee provided cartographic maps; Marcia Bakry drew illustrations; Maggie Dittemore provided library services; Gina Rappaport and Daisy Njoku contributed National Anthropological Archive images; Kevin Hand produced several anatomical and other illustrations; and Mary Parrish and Carl Buell gave access to their artful paleontological reconstructions.

The assembly of the book fell to a small production team that worked closely and efficiently to produce the book in record time. Douglas Harp, Susan Reynolds, and Jennifer Fisher of Harp and Company Graphic Design of Hanover, New Hampshire, performed the herculean task of designing and editing. Letitia O'Connor performed proof-reading

miracles, and Scribe assembled the index. Administrative support was
provided by Diana Zarick of the Smithsonian Office of Contracting,
Nancy Shorey assisted by Margaret Litten at the Smithsonian Arctic Studies
Center, and Judith Moran in Martin Nweeia's office. Illustration acquisition
was accomplished by Martin Nweeia and Caitlin Gillis. Publication was
by International Polar Institute Press, directed by Peter Mittenthal, working
with New England University Press for distribution.

We close where we began this note. This book and the narwhal exhibit could
never have been done without years of support and collaboration offered
to researchers, laboratory scientists, artists, photographers, and many others
by members of several northern communities, especially Pond Inlet and
Arctic Bay in Canada, and Uummannaq and Qaannaq in Greenland. Many
Inuit and non-Inuit northern residents of these and other communities
were also involved, and some of these people have since passed on. Their
contributions are remembered and celebrated here along with others who
carry on narwhal traditions. We thank you all. We hope that *Narwhal:
Revealing an Arctic Legend* in its exhibition, book, and web formats will
inspire more exciting work on this amazing Arctic whale.

We are especially grateful to James Mead, Curator Emeritus in the Marine
Mammal Program, Division of Mammals, Department of Vertebrate Zoology
at the Smithsonian Institution and Igor Krupnik, Curator in the Division
of the Arctic Studies Center, Department of Anthropology, Smithsonian
Institution for providing scholarly reviews of submitted manuscripts.

References

Abele, F., and C. Southcott, eds. 2016. *Care, cooperation, and activism in Canada's northern social economy*. Edmonton: University of Alberta Press.

American Meteorological Society (AMS): State of the climate in 2015. 2016. J. S. Blunden and D. S. Arndt (eds.), Special Supplement to the *Bulletin of the American Meteorological Society* 97: 275.

Armitage, D. 2005. Community-based narwhal management in Nunavut, Canada: change, uncertainty, and adaptation. *Geography* 18(8): 715–731.

Arriagada, P. 2017. Insights on Canadian society food insecurity among Inuit living in Inuit Nunangat. *Statistics Canada: Insights on Canadian Society*. http://www5.statcan.gc.ca/olc-cel/olc.action?objId=75-006-X201700114774&objType=47&lang=en&limit=0

Asselin, N. C., S. H. Ferguson, P. R. Richard, and D. G. Barber. 2012. Results of narwhal (*Monodon monoceros*) aerial surveys in northern Hudson Bay, August 2011. Canadian Scientific Advisory Secretariat, Department of Fisheries and Oceans. *Science Advisory Report* 037: iii + 23 p.

Audla, T. 2016. Nunavut is facing a severe housing crisis. Nunavut Housing Corporation's presentation to the Standing Senate Committee on Aboriginal Peoples. March 23, 2016.

Auger-Méthé, M., M. Marcoux, and H. Whitehead. 2010. Nicks and notches of the dorsal ridge: promising mark types for the photo-identification of narwhals. *Marine Mammal Science* 26: 663–678.

Aureli, F., C. M. Schaffner, C. Boesch, S. K. Bearder, J. Call, C. A. Chapman, R. Connor, A. D. Fiore, R. I. Dunbar, S., P. Henzi, K. Holekamp. 2008. Fission-fusion dynamics: new research frameworks. *Current Anthropology* 49(4): 627–654.

Bamforth, Stephen. 2010. On Gesner, Marvels and Unicorns. *Nottingham French Studies* 49(3): 110–145.

Barnes, L. G. 1984. Fossil odontocetes (Mammalia: Cetacea) from the Almejas Formation, Isla Cedros, Mexico. *PaleoBios* 42: 1–46.

Barnes, L. G., and T. A. Demere. 1991. A new beluga-like monodontid (Mammalia: Cetacea) from the Late Miocene San Mateo Formation at Oceanside, California. *Journal of Vertebrate Paleontology* 11 (3, Supplement): 15A

13.2 Aerial of Uummannaq, Greenland
(photo: W. Richard)

Barnes, E. A. 2013. Revisiting the evidence linking Arctic amplification to extreme weather in middle latitudes. *Geophysical Research Letters 40*, http://doi: 10.1002/grl.50880.

Bell, T., R. Briggs, Bachmayer, R., and Li, S. 2014. Augmenting Inuit knowledge for safe sea-ice travel — the SmartICE information system. In Bell et al., *Oceans '14 Conference Proceedings, September 14–19*: 1–9. St. John's, Government of Newfoundland and Labrador.

Berkes, F. 1995. Indigenous knowledge and resource management systems: a native Canadian case study. In *James Bay, Property rights in a social and ecological context: Case studies and design applications*, eds. Susan Hanna and Mohan Munasinghe, 99–109. Washington, D.C.: Beiher International Institute of Ecological Economics and the World Bank.

———— 1999. *Sacred ecology: traditional ecological knowledge and resource management*. Philadelphia: Taylor & Francis.

Best, George. 1578. *A true discourse of the late voyages of discoverie, for the finding of a passage to Cathaya, by the northwest, under the conduct of Martin Frobisher*. London: Bynnyman.

Best, R. C., and H. D. Fisher. 1974. Seasonal breeding of the narwhal (*Monodon monoceros L.*) *Canadian Journal of Zoology* 52: 429–431.

Best, R. C. 1981. The tusk of the narwhal: interpretation of its function. *Canadian Journal of Zoology* 59: 2386–2393.

Boas, Franz. 1904. The folklore of the Eskimo. *Journal of American Folklore* 17: 1–13.

Bogoslavskaya, L. 2003. The bowhead whale of Chukotka: integration and scientific and traditional knowledge. In *Indigenous ways to the present; native whaling in the western Arctic*, ed. A.P. McCartney, 209–253. Studies on Whaling No. 6. Edmonton: Canadian Circumpolar Institute.

Bolshiyanov, D. Y., and V. M. Makeyev. 1995. *Severnaya Zemlya Archipelago: glaciation and environmental history*. St Petersburg: Gidrometeoizdat.

Bowes-Lyon, L.-M., J. P. Richards, and T. M. McGee. 2009. Socio-economic impacts of the Nanisivik and Polaris Mines, Nunavut, Canada. In *Mining, Society, and a Sustainable World*, ed. Jeremy Richards, 371–396. Heidelberg: Springer.

Bracco, Silvia, et al. "Characterization of Elephant and Mammoth Ivory by Solid State NMR." *Periodico di Mineralogia* 82.2 (2013): 239-250.

Brännström M. 1962. The elicitation of pain in human dentin and pulp by chemical stimuli. *Archives of Oral Biology* 7: 59–62.

Brännström M. 1986. The hydrodynamic theory of dentinal pain: sensation in preparations, caries, and the dentinal crack syndrome. *Journal of Endodentistry 12(10)*: 453–457.

Broadbent, N. D. 1996. Toward an integration of the human and natural sciences in Arctic research. In *Climate and man in the Arctic*. Proceedings from a Danish Polar Center Symposium, 12–17. Copenhagen: Danish Polar Institute.

Brown, T. A., C. Alexander, D. J. Yurkowski, S. H. Ferguson, and S. T. Belt. 2014. Identifying variable sea ice carbon contributions to the Arctic ecosystem: A case study using highly branched isoprenoid lipid biomarkers in Cumberland Sound ringed seals. *Limnological Oceanogrraphy* 59(5): 1581–1589.

Brown, T. A., E. Chrystal, S. H. Ferguson, D. J. Yurkowski, C. Watt, N. E. Hussey, and S. T. Belt. 2017. Coupled changes between the H-Print biomarker and δ15N indicates a variable sea ice carbon contribution to the diet of Cumberland Sound beluga whales. *Limnology and Oceonagraphy*. In press.

Budge, S. M., S. J. Iverson, and H. N. Koopman. 2006. Studying trophic ecology in marine ecosystems using fatty acids: a primer on analysis and interpretation. *Marine Mammal Science* 22(4): 759–801.

Caesar, Julius. 1952. *The Gallic Wars Pars II (De Bello Gallico)*, trans. H. J. Edwards, 350–352. London and Cambridge: Charles Scribner's Sons.

Cameron, K., and A. Campbell. 2009. The Devolution of natural resources and Nunavut's constitutional status. *Journal of Canadian Studies* 43(2): 198–219.

Chen, Zhuo, X. Shixia, K. Zhou, and Y. Guang. 2011. Whale phylogeny and rapid radiation events revealed using novel retroposed elements and their flanking sequences. *BMC Evolutionary Biology* 11:314. DOI: 10.1186/1471-2148-11-314.

Clark, D. A., D. S. Lee, M. M. R. Freeman, and S. G. Clark. 2008. Polar bear conservation in Canada: defining the policy problems. *Arctic* 61(4): 347–360.

Conference Board of Canada. 2015. Territorial Outlook: Summer 2015. Ottawa, ON.

Contadini, Anna. 2003. A bestiary tale: text and image of the Unicorn in the *Kitab na't al-Hayawan*. (British Library, Or. 2784), *Muqarnas*, vol. 20: 17–33.

Cosens, S. E., and L. P. Dueck. 1986. Responses of migrating narwhal and beluga to icebreaker traffic at the Admiralty Inlet ice-edge, N.W.T. in 1986. In *Port and ocean engineering under Arctic conditions*, eds. W. M. Sackinger and M. O. Jeffries, vol. 2: 39–54. Fairbanks: University of Alaska.

———— 1990. Spring sightings of narwhal and beluga calves in Lancaster Sound, N.W.T. *Arctic* 43: 127–128.

———— 1991. Group size and activity patterns of belugas (*Delphinapterus leucas*) and narwhals (*Monodon monoceros*) during spring migration in Lancaster Sound. *Canadian Journal of Zoology* 69: 1630–1635.

Council of Canadian Academies. 2014. Aboriginal food security in northern Canada: an assessment of the state of knowledge. http://doi:org/10.1162/LEON_r_00884=

Damas, D. 2002. *Arctic migrants, Arctic villagers: the transformation of Inuit settlements in the Central Arctic*. Montreal & Kingston: McGill-Queen's University Press.

Deméré, T. A., M. R. McGowen, A. Berta, and J. Gatesy. 2008. Morphological and molecular evidence for a stepwise evolutionary transition from teeth to baleen in mysticete whales. *Systematic Biology* 57(1): 15–37.

Department of Fisheries and Oceans Canada (DFO). 2012. *Advice on total allowable landed catch for the Baffin Bay narwhal population*. Science Advisory Secretariat, Science Advisory Report 2012/021. Ottawa: Department of Fisheries and Oceans.

———— 2015. *Abundance estimates of narwhal stocks in the Canadian High Arctic in 2013*. Science Advisory Secretariat, Science Advisory Report 2015/046. Ottawa: Department of Fisheries and Oceans.

Derksen, C., and R. Brown. 2012. Spring snow cover extent reductions in the 2008-2012 period exceeding climate model projections. *Geophysical Research Letters* 39, DOI: 10.1029/2012GL053387.

Dery, S. J., T. A. Stadnyk, M. K. McDonald, and B. Gauli-Sharma. 2016. Recent trends in river discharge across Northern Canada. *Hydrology and Earth System Sciences.* DOI: 10.5194/hess-2016-461.

Dewailly, E., and P. Weihe. 2003. Chapter 9, The effects of Arctic pollution on population health. In *AMAP assessment 2002: Human health in the Arctic,* 95–105. Arctic Monitoring and Assessment Program.

DFO (See Department of Fisheries and Oceans Canada)

Dietz, R., F. Rigét, and P. Johansen. 1996. Lead, cadmium, mercury and selenium in Greenland marine animals. *Science of the Total Environment* 186 (1-2): 67–93.

Dietz, R., M. P. Heide-Jørgensen, P. R. Richard, and M. Acquarone. 2001. Summer and fall movements of narwhals (*Monodon monoceros*) from northeastern Baffin Island towards northern Davis Strait. *Arctic* 54: 244–261.

Dietz, R., A. D. Shapiro, M. Bakhtiari, J. Orr, P. L. Tyack, P. Richard, I. G. Eskesen, and G. Marshall. 2007. Upside-down swimming behaviour of free-ranging narwhals. *BMC Ecology* 7(1): 14.

Dietz, R., M. P. Heide-Jørgensen, P. Richard, J. Orr, K. Laidre, and H. C. Schmidt. 2008. Movements of narwhals (*Monodon monoceros*) from Admiralty Inlet monitored by satellite telemetry. *Polar Biology* 31(11): 1295–1306.

Dietz, R., P. M. Outridge, and K. A. Hobson. 2009. Anthropogenic contribution to mercury levels in present-day Arctic animals — a review. *The Science of the Total Environment* 407: 6120–6131.

Dietz, R., E. W. Born, F. F. Rigét, A. Aubail, C. Sonne, R. C. Drimmei, and N. Basu. 2011. Temporal trends and future predictions of mercury concentrations in Northwest Greenland Polar Bear (*Ursus maritimus*) hair. *Environmental Science & Technology* 45: 1458–1465.

Dietz, R., N. Basu, B. Braune, T. O'Hara, R. Letcher, T. Scheuhammer, C. Sonne, M. Andersen, C. Andreasen, D. Andriashek, G. Asmund, A. Aubail, H. Baagøe, E. W. Born, H. M. Chan, A. E. Derocher, P. Grandjean, K. Knott, M. Kirkegaard, A. Krey, N. Lunn, F. Messier, M. Obbard, M. T. Olsen, S. Ostertag, F. Peacock, A. Renzoni, F. F. Rigét, J. U. Skaare, G. Stern, I. Stirling, M. Taylor, Ø. Wiig, S. Wilson, and J. Aars. 2013. What are the toxicological effects of mercury in Arctic biota? *Science of the Total Environment* 12/2012; 443: 775–790. http://dx.doi.org/10.1016/j.scitotenv.2012.11.04

Dietz, R., A. Mosbech, and I. Eulaers. 2017a. Fangstdyr ved Nordvandet og den globale kviksølvforurening. *Tidsskriftet Grønland* 1/2017: 26-36.

Dietz, R., J. P. Desforges, I. Eulaers, R. J. Letcher, C. Sonne, S. Wilson, E. Andersen-Ranberg, B. D. Barst, N. Basu, J. O. Bustnes, J. Bytingsvik, T. M. Ciesielski, P. E. Drevnick, G. W. Gabrielsen, A. Haarr, K. Hylland, B. M. Jenssen, M. Levin, M. A. McKinney, D. D. G. Muir, J. Provencher, J. Staffansson, and S. Tartu S, In Prep. An assessment of the biological effects of organohalogen and mercury exposure in Arctic wildlife and fish. AMAP, 2017. AMAP Assessment 2017b. *Arctic Monitoring and Assessment Programme* (AMAP), Oslo, Norway.

Doniol-Valcroze, T., J. F. Gosselin, D. Pike, J. Lawson, N. Asselin, K. Hedges, and S. H. Ferguson. 2015. Abundance estimates of narwhal stocks in the Canadian High Arctic in 2013. DFO Canadian Science Advisory Secretariat Research Document 2015/060.

Dowlsey, M., and G. Wenzel. 2008. The time of the most polar bears: A co-management conflict in Nunavut. *Arctic* 61(2): 177–189.

Eales, N. B. 1950. The skull of the foetal narwhal, *Monodon Monocerus,* L. *Philosophical Transactions of the Royal Society of London. Series B. Biological Sciences.* 235(621): 1–33.

Eber, D. 1989. *When the whalers were up north: Inuit memories from the Eastern Arctic.* Montreal & Kingston: McGill-Queen's University Press.

Ettinghausen, Richard. 1950. *The Unicorn.* Washington: Smithsonian Institution.

Finley, K. J., R. A. Davis, and H. B. Silverman. 1979. *Aspects of the Narwhal Hunt in the Eastern Canadian Arctic.* International Whaling Commission.

Finley, K. J., and E. J. Gibb. 1982. Summer diet of the narwhal (*Monodon monoceros*) in Pond Inlet, northern Baffin Island. *Canadian Journal of Zoology* 60: 3353–3363.

Finley, K. J., G. W. Miller, R. A. Davis, and C. R. Greene. 1990. Reactions of belugas, *Delphinapterus leucas,* and narwhals, *Monodon monoceros,* to ice-breaking ships in the Canadian High Arctic. *Canadian Journal of Fisheries and Aquatic Sciences* 224: 97–117.

Fisher, D., J. Zheng, D. Burgess, C. Zdanowicz, C. Kinnard, M. Sharp, and J. Bourgeois. 2012. Recent melt rates of Canadian Arctic ice caps are the highest in four millennia. In *Global and Planetary Change* 84-85, March 12, http://doi: 10.1016/j.gloplacha.2011.06.005.

Foote, A. D., Y. Liu, G. W. C. Thomas, T. Vina , J. Alföldi, J. Deng, S. Dugan, C. E. van Elk, M. E. Hunter, V. Joshi, Z. Khan, C. Kovar, S. L. Lee, K. Lindblad-Toh, A. Mancia, R. Nielsen, X. Qin, J. Qu, B. J. Raney, N. Vijay, J. B. W. Wolf, M. W. Hahn, D. M. Muzny, K. C. Worley, M. T. P. Gilbert. 2015. Convergent evolution of the genomes of marine mammals. *Nature Genetics* 47(3): 272–275.

Forbes, B. C., T. Kumpula, N. Meschtyb, R. Laptander, M. Macias-Fauria, P. Zetterberg, M. Verdonen, A. Skarin, K.-Y. Kim, L. N. Boisvert, J. C. Stroeve, and A. Bartsch. 2016. Sea ice, rain-on-snow and tundra reindeer nomadism in Arctic Russia. *Biological Letters* 12, 20160466, http://dx.doi.org/10.1098/rsbl.2016.0466.

Ford, J. K. B., and H. D. Fisher. 1978. Underwater acoustic signals of the narwhal (*Monodon monoceros*). *Canadian Journal of Zoology* 56: 552–560.

Ford, J., and D. Martinez, eds. 2000. Invited feature: traditional ecological knowledge, ecosystem science, and environmental management. *Ecological Adaptations* 10(5): 1249–1250.

Ford, J. K. B., and G. M. Ellis. 2006. Selective foraging by fish-eating killer whales *Orcinus orca* in British Columbia. *Marine Ecology Progress Series* 316: 185–199.

Francis, J. A., and S. J. Vavrus. 2012. Evidence linking Arctic amplification to extreme weather in mid-latitudes. *Geophysical Research Letters* 39, L06801, http://doi: 10.1029/2012GL051000.

Furgal, C., and R. Laing. 2012. A synthesis and critical review of the traditional ecological knowledge literature on narwhal (*Monodon monocerus*) in the Eastern Canadian Arctic. Canadian Science Advisory Secretariat, Research Document 2011/131. Ottawa: Government of Canada.

Gaborit-Chopin, Danielle. 1991. *Le Trésor de Saint-Denis* (Exhibition Catalog). Paris: Musée du Louvre, no. 68: 310–311.

Garde, E., M. P. Heide-Jørgensen, S. H. Hansen, G. Nachman, and M. C. Forchhammer. 2007. Age-specific growth and remarkable longevity in narwhals (*Monodon monoceros*) from west Greenland as estimated by aspartic acid racemization. *Journal of Mammalogy* 88(1): 49–58.

Gaston, A. J., P. A. Smith, and J. F. Provencher. 2012. Discontinuous change in ice cover in Hudson Bay in the 1990s and some consequences for marine birds and their prey. *ICES Journal of Marine Science* 69: 1218–1225.

Gearheard, S. F., L. K. Holm, H. Huntington, J. M. Leavitt, A. R. Mahoney, M. Opie, T. Oshima, and J. Sanguya. 2013. *The Meaning of Ice: People and Sea Ice in Three Arctic Communities*. Hanover, NH: International Polar Institute Press.

George, J. 2011. Mary River mine promises jobs, jobs and more jobs for Nunavut. *Nunatsiaq News Online*. April 11. http://www.nunatsiaqonline.ca/stories/article/110455_mary_river_mine_promises_jobs_and_more_jobs.

Gingerich, P. D., M. ul Haq, I. S. Zalmout, I. H. Khan, and M. S. Malkani. 2001. Origin of whales from early artiodactyls: hands and feet of Eocene Protocetidae from Pakistan. *Science* 293(5538): 2239–2242.

Gonzalez, N. 2001. Inuit Traditional Ecological Knowledge of the Hudson Bay Narwhal (Tuugaalik) Population. Unpublished Manuscript, report prepared for Fisheries and Oceans Canada, Iqaluit, NU. 26 p.

Gotfredsen, Lise. 1999. *The Unicorn*. New York: Abbeville Press.

Greaves, A. K., R. J. Letcher, C. Sonne, R. Dietz, and E. W. Born. 2012. Tissue-specific concentrations and patterns of perfluoroalkyl carboxylates and sulfonates in East Greenland polar bears. *Environmental science and technology* 46 (21): 11575–11583.

Gregoire, L. 2016. Nunavut sets out plan to manage increased cruise ship tourism. *Nunatsiaq News* Online. June 8. http://www.nunatsiaqonline.ca/stories/article/65674.

Gronnow, Bjarne. 1994. Qeqertasussuk: the archeology of a frozen Sarqaq site in Disko Bugt, West Greenland. In Threads of Arctic Prehistory: Papers in Honor of William E. Taylor, Jr. D. Morrison and J.-L. Pilon, eds. *Archaeological Survey of Canada Mercury Series Paper* 149: 197–238. Ottawa: Canadian Museum of Civilization.

Hansen, J. C., J. Van Oostdam, A. Gilman, J. Ø. Odland, A. Vaktskjold, and A. Dudarev. 2009. In AMAP Assessment Report 2009: *Human health in the Arctic. Arctic Monitoring and Assessment Programme* (AMAP), Oslo: xiv+256 pp.

Harington, C. R. 1977. Marine mammals in the Champlain Sea and the Great Lakes. *Annals of the New York Academy of Sciences* 288(1): 508–537.

Hay, K. A. 1984. The life history of the narwhal (*Monodon monoceros L.*) in the Eastern Canadian Arctic. PhD dissertation. 280 pp. Institute of Oceanography. Montreal: McGill University.

Heide-Jørgensen, M. P., and R. R. Reeves. 1993. Description of an anomalous monodontid skull from West Greenland: A possible hybrid? *Marine Mammal Science* 9(3): 258–268.

Heide-Jørgensen, M. P., R. Dietz, K. L. Laidre, and P. Richard. 2002. Autumn movements, home ranges and winter density of narwhals (*Monodon monoceros*) tagged in Tremblay Sound, Baffin Island. *Polar Biology* 25: 331–341.

Heide-Jørgensen, M. P., R. Dietz, K. L. Laidre, P. Richard, J. Orr, and H. C. Schmidt. 2003. The migratory behaviour of narwhals (*Monodon monoceros*). *Canadian Journal of Zoology* 81(8): 1298–1305.

Heide-Jørgensen, M. P., K. L. Laidre, M. L. Burt, D. L. Borchers, T. A, Marques, R. G. Hansen, M. Rasmussen, and S. Fossette. 2010. Abundance of narwhals (*Monodon monoceros*) on the hunting grounds in Greenland. *Journal of Mammalogy* 91(5): 1135–1151.

Heide-Jørgensen, M. P., and E. Garde. 2011. Fetal growth of narwhals (*Monodon monoceros*). *Marine Mammal Science* 27(3): 659–664.

Heide-Jørgensen, M. P., P. R. Richard, R. Dietz, and K. L. Laidre. 2013a. A metapopulation model for Canadian and West Greenland narwhals. *Animal Conservation* 16(3): 331–343.

Heide-Jørgensen, M. P., R. G. Hansen, K. H. Westdal, R. R. Reeves, and A. Mosbech. 2013b. Narwhals and seismic exploration: Is seismic noise increasing the risk of ice entrapments? *Biological Conservation* 158: 50–54.

Heide-Jørgensen, M. P., N. H. Nielsen, R. G. Hansen, and S. B. Blackwell. 2014. Stomach temperature of narwhals (*Monodon monoceros*) during feeding events. *Animal Biotelemetry* 2: 9.

Higdon, J. W., and S. H. Ferguson. 2009. Loss of Arctic sea ice causing punctuated change in sightings of killer whales (*Orcinus orca*) over the past century. *Ecological Applications* 19(5): 1365–1375.

Huntington, H. P. 1992. *Wildlife management and subsistence hunting in Alaska*. London: Belhaven Press.

——— 1998. Observations on the utility of the semi-directive interview for documenting traditional ecological knowledge. *Arctic* 51: 237–242.

——— 2000. Using traditional ecological knowledge in science: methods and applications. *Ecological applications* 10 (5), 1270–1274.

———— 2005. We dance around in a ring and suppose: Academic engagement with traditional knowledge. *Arctic Anthropology* 42(1): 29–32.

———— 2011. The local perspective. *Nature* 478: 182–183.

Huntington, H. P., S. Gearheard, A. R. Mahoney, and A. K. Salomon. 2011. Integrating traditional and scientific knowledge through collaborative natural science field research: identifying elements for success. *Arctic* 64(4): 437–445.

Huntington, H. P., P. K. Brown-Schwalenberg, and K. J. Frost. 2002. Observations on the workshop as a means of improving communication between holders of traditional and scientific knowledge. *Environmental Management* 30(6): 778–792.

Hurrell, J. W. 1996. Influence of variations in extratropical wintertime teleconnections on Northern Hemisphere temperature. *Geophysical Research Letters* 23: 665–668.

ICC (Inuit Circumpolar Council). 2011. A circumpolar Inuit declaration on resource development principles in Inuit Nunaat. http://www.inuitcircumpolar.com/resource-development-principles-in-inuit-nunaat.html.

Imaituk Inc. 2011. *A matter of survival: Arctic communications infrastructure in the 21st century.* Arctic communications infrastructure assessment report. Prepared for the Northern Communications and Information Systems Working Group.

Johnson, N. 2016. Ilisaqsivik Society of Clyde River. In *Care, Cooperation, and Activism in Canada's Northern Social Economy.* F. Abele and C. Southcott, eds., 83–101. Edmonton: University of Alberta Press.

Johnson, N., S. Gearheard, and J. Natanine. 2016. Community actions to address seismic testing in Nunavut, Canada. *Practicing Anthropology* 38(3): 13–16.

Kay, J. E., and A. Gettleman. 2009. Cloud influence and response to seasonal Arctic sea ice loss. *Journal of Geophysical Research* 114, D18204, http://doi:10.1029/2009JD011773.

Kazár, E., and D. J. Bohaska. 2008. Toothed whale (*Mammalia: Cetacea: Odontoceti*) limb bones of the Lee Creek Mine, North Carolina, In *Geology and Paleontology of the Lee Creek Mine, North Carolina, IV.* C. E. Ray, D. J. Bohaska, I. A. Koretsky, L. W. Ward, and L. G. Barnes, eds., 271–324. Virginia Museum of Natural History Special Publication 14.

Kelley, T. C., R. E. Stewart, D. J. Yurkowski, A. Ryan, and S. H. Ferguson. 2015. Mating ecology of beluga (*Dephinapterus leucas*) and narwhal (*Monodon monoceros*) as estimated by reproductive tract metrics. *Marine Mammal Science* 31: 479–500.

Koblitz J. C., P. Stilz, M. H, Rasmussen, and K. L. Laidre. 2016. Highly directional sonar beam of narwhals (*Monodon monoceros*) measured with a Vertical 16 Hydrophone Array. PLoS ONE 11(11): e0162069. doi:10.1371/journal.pone.0162069

Kovacs, K. M., P. Lemons, J. G. MacCracken, and C. Lydersen. 2015. Walruses in a time of climate change. *Arctic Report Card: Update for 2015*, http://www.arctic.noaa.gov/Report-Card/Report-Card-2015.

Krupnik, I. 2009. 'The way we see it coming': building the legacy of indigenous observations in IPY 2007–2008. In *Smithsonian at the poles: contributions to International Polar Year Science*, 129–142.

Krupnik, I., and D. Jolly, eds. 2002. *The earth is faster now: Indigenous observations of Arctic environmental change.* Fairbanks: Arctic Research Consortium of the United States.

Krupnik, I., and G. C. Ray. 2007. Pacific walruses, indigenous hunters, and climate change: bridging scientific and indigenous knowledge. *Deep Sea Research Part II: Topical Studies in Oceanography* 54(23): 2946–2957.

Laidre, K. L., and M. P. Heide-Jørgensen. 2005a. Arctic sea ice trends and narwhal vulnerability. *Biological Conservation* 121(4): 509-517.

———— 2005b. Winter feeding intensity of narwhals (*Monodon monoceros*). *Marine Mammal Science* 21(1): 45–57.

———— 2007. Using narwhals as ocean-observing platforms in the High Arctic. *Oceanography* 20(4): 30–35.

———— 2011. Life in the lead: extreme densities of narwhals *Monodon monoceros* in the offshore pack ice. *Marine Ecology Progress Series* 423: 269–278.

Laidre, K. L., M. P. Heide-Jørgensen, R. Dietz, R. C. Hobbs, and O. A. Jørgensen. 2003. Deep-diving by narwhals *Monodon monoceros*: differences in foraging behavior between wintering areas? *Marine Ecology Progress Series* 261: 269–281.

Laidre, K. L., M. P. Heide-Jørgensen, and J. R. Orr. 2006. Reactions of narwhals, *Monodon monoceros*, to killer whale, *Orcinus orca*, attacks in the eastern Canadian Arctic. *The Canadian Field-Naturalist* 120(4): 457–465.

Laidre, K. L., I. Stirling, L. F, Lowry, Ø. Wig, M. P. Heide-Jørgensen, and S. H. Ferguson. 2008. Quantifying the sensitivity of Arctic marine mammals to climate-induced habitat change. *Ecological Applications* 18 (sp2).

Laurin, M., and J. A. Gauthier. 2012. *Amniota*. Mammals, reptiles (turtles, lizards, Sphenodon, crocodiles, birds) and their extinct relatives. Version 30 January 2012. http://tolweb.org/Amniota/1 4990/2012.01.30 in *The Tree of Life Web Project*, http://tolweb.org/

Lavers, Chris. 2009. *The Natural History of Unicorns*. New York: William Morrow.

Lee, D. S. 2004. The ecological and social dynamics of Inuit narwhal foraging at Pond Inlet, Nunavut. Ph.D. Dissertation, Department of Geography, McGill University, Montreal.

Lee, D., and G. W. Wenzel. 2004. Narwhal Hunting by Pond Inlet Inuit: an analysis of foraging mode in the floe-edge environment. *Études/Inuit/ Studies* 28(2): 133–158.

LGL and Greeneridge. 1986. Reactions of beluga whales and narwhals to ship traffic and ice-breaking along ice edges in the eastern Canadian High Arctic: 1982–1984. *Environmental Studies* 37. 301 p. Indian and Northern Affairs Canada, Ottawa Ont.

Liljedahl, A. K., J. Boike, and R. P. Daanen. 2016. Pan-Arctic ice wedge degradation in warming permafrost and its influence on tundra hydrology, *Nature Geoscience* 9: 312–318. http://doi:10.1038/ngeo2674.

Locke, M. 2008. Structure of ivory. *Journal of Morphology* 269(4): 423–450.

Macdonald, A. K. Leus, and H. Hoare. 2016. Maxillary canine tooth growth in Babirusa (genus *Babyrousa*). *Journal of Zoo and Aquarium Research* 4(1): 22–29.

Mansfield, A. W., T. G. Smith, and B. Beck. 1975. The narwhal, *Monodon monoceros*, in eastern Canadian waters. *Journal of the Fisheries Research Board of Canada* 32: 1041–1046.

Marcoux, M. 2011. Narwhal communication and grouping behaviour: a case study in social cetacean research and monitoring. PhD thesis, Department of Natural Resource Sciences. Montreal: McGill University.

Marcoux, M., M. M. Auger-Méthé, and M. M. Humphries. 2009. Encounter frequencies and grouping patterns of narwhals in Koluktoo Bay, Baffin Island. *Polar Biology* 32(12): 1705–1716.

———— 2012a. Variability and context specificity of narwhal (*Monodon monoceros*) whistles and pulsed calls. *Marine Mammal Science* 28: 649–665.

Marcoux, M, B. C. McMeans, A. T. Fisk, and S. H. Ferguson. 2012b. Composition and temporal variation in the diet of beluga whales, derived from stable isotopes. *Marine Ecology Progress Series* 471: 283-291.

Masters, P. M., J. L. Bada, and J. S. Zigler, Jr. 1977. Aspartic acid racemization in the human lens during ageing and in cataract formation. *Nature* 268: 71–73.

Mathewson, S. 2016. Narwhal nursery located in busy Canadian waters; are the elusive sea animals at risk? *Nature World News.*

McGhee, Robert. 1972. *Copper Eskimo Prehistory.* National Museum of Canada. Publications in Archaeology 2. Ottawa.

McGowen, M. R., M. Spaulding, and J. Gatesy. 2009. Divergence date estimation and a comprehensive molecular tree of extant cetaceans. *Molecular Phylogenetics and Evolution* 53(3): 891–906.

Milinkovitch, M. C., A. Meyer, and J. R. Powell. 1994. Phylogeny of all major groups of cetaceans based on DNA sequences from three mitochondrial genes. *Molecular Biology and Evolution* 11(6): 939–948.

Moore, S. E., and H. P. Huntington. 2008. Arctic marine mammals and climate change: impacts and resilience. *Ecological Applications* 18: S157–S165.

Morgan, B. 2013. Federal Agencies in U.S. and Canada allege illegal narwhal tusk smuggling. *Nunatsiaq News,* 4 January.

Mossman, H. W. 1937. Comparative morphogenesis of the fetal membranes and accessory uterine structures. *Contributions to Embryology* 26:129–246.

de Muizon, C. 1993. Walrus-like feeding adaptation in a new cetacean from the Pliocene of Peru. *Nature* 365(6448): 745.

de Muizon, C., D. P. Domning, and M. Parrish. 1999. Dimorphic tusks and adaptive strategies in a new species of walrus-like dolphin (Odobenocetopsidae) from the Pliocene of Peru. *Comptes Rendus de l'Académie des Sciences-Series IIA-Earth and Planetary Science* 329(6): 449–455.

Nadasdy, P. 1999. The politics of TEK: power and the integration of knowledge. *Arctic Anthropology* 36(1-2): 1–18.

Newsome, S. D., M. T. Clementz, and P. L. Koch. 2010. Using stable isotope biogeochemistry to study marine mammal ecology. *Marine Mammal Science* 26(3): 509–572.

Noongwook, G., The Native Village of Savoonga, The Native Village of Gambell, H. P. Huntington, and J. C. George. 2007. Traditional knowledge of the bowhead whale (*Balaena mysticetus*) around St. Lawrence Island, Alaska. *Arctic* 60(1): 47–54.

Nunavut Bureau of Statistics. 2016. 2016 Nunavut food price survey: comparison of Nunavut & Canada CPI food price basket items. http://www.stats.gov.nu.ca/en/Economic%20prices.aspx.

Nunavut Tourism. 2016. Nunavut Marine Tourism Plan: Communities Prepared for and Benefitting from Marine Tourism. Accessed online at: http://www.gov.nu.ca/sites/default/files/nunavut-marine-tourism-management-plan-final-english.pdf.

Nweeia, M. T., F. C. Eichmiller, C. Nutarak, N. Eidelman, A. A. Giuseppetti, J. Quinn, J. G. Mead, K. K'issuk, P. V. Hauschka, E. M. Tyler, C. Potter, J. R. Orr, R. Avike, P. Nielsen, D. Angnatsiak. 2009. Considerations of anatomy, morphology, evolution, and function for narwhal dentition. In *Smithsonian at the Poles*, eds. I. Krupnik, M.A. Lang, S. E. Miller, 223–240. Washington DC: Smithsonian Institution Scholarly Press.

Nweeia, M. T., F. C. Eichmiller, P. V. Hauschka, E. Tyler, J. G. Mead, C. W. Potter, D. P. Angnatsiak, P. R. Richard, J. R. Orr, and S. R. Black. 2012. Vestigial tooth anatomy and tusk nomenclature for Monodon monoceros. *The Anatomical Record* 295(6): 1006–1016.

Nweeia, M. T., F. C. Eichmiller, P. V. Hauschka, G. A. Donahue, J. R. Orr, S. H. Ferguson, C.A. Watt, J. G. Mead, C. W. Potter, R. Dietz, A. A. Guiseppetti, S. R. Black, A. J. Trachtenberg, and W. P. Kuo. 2014. Sensory ability in the narwhal teeth organ system. *The Anatomical Record* 297: 599–617.

Obed, N. 2017. Presentation for panel on "Exercising leadership in a global-izing North". Fletcher Arctic VI Conference: Exploring paths to sustainable development in the Arctic. February 17–18. Medford, MA.

Orr, J. R., R. Joe and D. Evic. 2001. Capturing and handling of white whales (*Delphinapterus leucas*) in the Canadian Arctic for instrumentation and release. *Arctic* 54: 299–304.

Owen, R. 1846. *A History of British Fossil Mammals, and Birds*. London: John Van Voorst.

Palsbøll, P. J., M. P. Heide-Jørgensen, and R. Dietz. 1997. Population structure and seasonal movements of narwhals, *Monodon monoceros*, determined from mtDNA analysis. *Heredity* 78: 284–292.

Parry, William Edward. 1821. *Journal of a voyage for the discovery of a northwest passage from the Atlantic to the Pacific; performed in the years 1819-20, in His Majesty's ships Hecla and Griper, under the orders of William Edward Parry*. London: J. Murray.

Pashley, D. H. 1986. Sensitivity of dentin to chemical stimuli. *Endodontics and Dental Traumatology* 2: 130–137.

Pearce, T., H. Wright, R. Notaina, A. Kudlak, B. Smit, J. Ford, and C. Furgal. 2011. Transmission of environmental knowledge and land skills among Inuit men in Ulukhaktok, Northwest Territories, Canada. *Human Ecology* 39(3): 271–288.

Peterson, B. J., R. M. Holmes, J. W. McClelland, C. J. Vörösmarty, R. B. Lammers, A. I. Shiklomanov, I. A. Shiklomanov, and S. Rahmstorf. 2002. Increasing river discharge to the Arctic Ocean. *Science* 298: 2171–2173.

Petersen, S. D., D. Tenkula, and S. H. Ferguson. 2011. Population genetic structure of narwhal (*Monodon monoceros*), Department of Fisheries and Ocenas, Canadian Science Advisory Secretariat Research Document 021: vi + 20 p.

Piniarneq. 2016. Data from the Greenlandic hunt from the Directorate for and Fisheries. *Greenland Home Rule Government*, 1993–2013.

Pithan, F., and T. Mauritsen. 2014. Arctic amplification dominated by temperature feedbacks in contemporary climate models. *Nature Geoscience* 7: 181-185. http://doi:10.1038/ngeo2071.

Pomet, Pierre. 1694. Histoire générale des drogues (General history of drugs). Chapter 8, no. 33. Paris: Jean-Baptiste Loyson and Augustin Pillon.

Porsild, M.P. 1918. On "Savssats": A Crowding of Arctic Animals at Holes in the Sea Ice. The Geographical Review, Vol. VI, No. 3 (September).

Price, S. A., O. R. Bininda-Edmonds, J. L. Gittleman. 2005. A complete phylogeny of the whales, dolphins and even-toed hoofed mammals (Cetartio-dactyla). *Biological Reviews* 80(3): 445–473.

Reeves, R. R. P., and E. Mitchell. 1981. The whale behind the tusk. *Natural History* 90: 50–57. American Museum of Natural History.

Reeves, R. R., P. J. Ewins, S. Agbayanic, M. P. Heide-Jørgensen, K. M. Kovacs, C. Lydersene, R. Suydamf, W. Elliott, G. Poleth, Y. van Dijki, and R. Blijleveni. 2014. Distribution of endemic cetaceans in relation to hydrocarbon development and commercial shipping in a warming Arctic. *Marine Policy* 44: 375–389.

Remnant, R. A., and M. L. Thomas. 1992. Inuit traditional knowledge of the distribution and biology of High Arctic narwhal and beluga. Unpublished report prepared by North/South Consultants Inc., Winnipeg, MB. 96 p.

Richard, P. R. 1991. Abundance and distribution of narwhals (*Monodon monoceros*) in northern Hudson Bay. *Canadian Journal of Fisheries and Aquatic Sciences* 48: 276–283.

Robbe, P. 1994. *Les Inuit d'Ammassalik, chasseurs de l'Arctique.* Mémoires du Muséum National d'Histoire Naturelle, Ethnologie Tome 159. Paris: Musée de l'Homme.

Roberge, M. M., and J. B. Dunn. 1990. Assessment of the subsistence harvest and biology of narwhal (*Monodon monoceros* L.) from Admiralty Inlet, Baffin Island, N.W.T., 1983 and 1986–89. *Canadian Technical Report of Fisheries and Aquatic Sciences.* 1747: 1–32.

Rohner, T. 2016. Nunavut Housing Corp announces distribution of new units. *Nunatsiaq News* online. October 27. http://www.nunatsiaqonline.ca/stories/article/65674nunavut_housing_corp._announces_distribution_of_new_units/

Rosing, J. 1999. *The Unicorn of the Arctic Sea: The Narwhal and its Habitat.* (Trans., N. J. Groves). Penumbra Press 81.

Rybczynski, N., J. C. Gosse, C. R. Harington, R. A. Wogelius, A. J. Hidy, and M. Buckley. 2013. Mid-Pliocene warm-period deposits in the High Arctic yield insight into camel evolution. *Nature Communications* 4: 1550. http://doi:10.1038/ ncomms2516.

Savelle, J. 1994. Prehistoric exploitation of white whales (*Delphinapterus leaucas*) and narwhals (*Monodon monocerus*) in the Eastern Canadian Arctic. In Studies of White Whales (*Delphinapterus leaucas*) and Narwhals (*Monodon monocerus*) in Greenland and adjacent waters. E. Born, R. Dietz, and R. Reeves, eds. *Meddelelser om Grønland*, (Bioscience) 39: 101–117.

Schaefer, K., T. Zhang, L. Bruhwiler, and A. P. Barrett. 2011. Amount and timing of permafrost carbon release in response to climate warming. *Tellus* 63B: 165–180. http://doi:10.1111/j.1600-0889.2011.00527.

Serreze, M. C., A. P. Barrett, J. C. Stroeve, D. N. Kindig, and M. M. Holland. 2009. The emergence of surface-based Arctic amplification, *The Cryosphere* 3: 11–19. www.the-cryosphere.net/3/11/2209/.

Serreze, M. C., A. P. Barrett, and J. Stroeve. 2012. Recent changes in tropospheric water vapor over the Arctic as assessed from radiosondes and atmospheric reanalyses, *Journal of Geophysical Research* 117, D10104, http://doi:10.1029/2011JD017421.

Serreze, M. C., B. Raup, C. Braun, D. R. Hardy, and R. S. Bradley. 2017. Rapid wastage of the Hazen Plateau ice caps, northwestern Ellesmere Island, Nunavut, Canada. *The Cryosphere* 11(1): 169-177.

Shapiro, A. D. 2006. Preliminary evidence for signature vocalizations among free-ranging narwhals (*Monodon monceros*). *Journal of the Acoustical Society of America* 120: 1695–1705.

Sharp, M. J., G. Wolken, M-L. Geai, D. Burgess, A. Arendt, B. Wouters, J. Kohler, L. M Andreassen, and M. Pelto. Glaciers and icecaps outside Greenland. In *State of the Climate in 2013*. https://dspace.library.uu.nl/ bitstream/handle/1874/347576/135.pdf?sequence=1

Shepherd, A., E. R. Ivins, G. A. Valentina, et al. 2012. A reconciled estimate of ice-sheet mass balance. *Science 338*. http://doi:10.1126/science.1228102.

Shepard, O. 1930. *The Lore of the Unicorn*. London: George Allen and Unwin.

Silverman, H. B. 1979. Social organization and behavior of the narwhal, *Monodon monoceros* L. in Lancaster Sound, Pond Inlet, and Tremblay Sound, Northwest Territories. 147pp. Montreal: McGill University.

Silverman, H. B., and M. J. Dunbar. 1980. Aggressive tusk use by the narwhal (*Monodon monocerus L.*). Nature 284: 57.

Smith, L. C., and S. R. Stephenson. 2013. New Trans-Arctic shipping routes navigable by midcentury. *Proc. National Academy of Sciences* 110: E1191–E1195.

Smith, T. G., and B. Sjare. 1990. Predation of belugas and narwhals by polar bears in nearshore areas of the Canadian High Arctic. *Arctic* 43: 99–102.

Sonne, C., P. S. Leifsson, and R. Dietz. 2013. Liver and renal lesions in mercury-contaminated narwhals (*Monodon monoceros*) from Northwest Greenland. Taylor & Frances Online. *Toxicological and Environmental Chemistry* 95(3): 515–528. http://doi/abs/10.1080/02772248.2013.783666.

Stetkevych, Jasroslav. 2002. In search of the Unicorn. *Journal of Arabic Literature* 33(2): 121.

Stewart, D. B. 2001. Inuit knowledge of belugas and narwhals in the Canadian Eastern Arctic. Report prepared for the Canadian Dept. of Fisheries and Oceans, Iqaluit, Nunavut, 32p.

Stewart, D. B., A. Akeeagok, R. Amarualik, S. Panipakutsuk, and A. Taqtu. 1995. Local knowledge of beluga and narwhal from four communities in the Arctic. *Canadian Journal of Fisheries and Aquatic Science*, 2065. 48 p.

Strimmer, K. S., and Arnt von Haeseler. 1996. Quartet Puzzling: A quartet maximum-likelihood method for reconstructing tree topologies. *Molecular Biology and Evolution* 13(7). DOI:10.1093/oxfordjournals.molbey.a025664.

Stuck, H. 1917. *A Winter Circuit of Our Arctic Coast.* New York: Scribners.

Tester, F. J. 2009. *Iglutaasaavut* (our new homes): Neither "new" nor "ours." Housing challenges of the Nunavut Territorial Government. *Journal of Canadian Studies* 43(2): 137–158.

Thewissen, J. G., and E. M. Williams. 2002. The early radiations of Cetacea (Mammalia): evolutionary pattern and developmental correlations. *Annual Review of Ecology and Systematics* 33(1): 73–90.

Thiemann, G. W., S. J. Iverson, and I. Stirling. 2008. Polar bear diets and Arctic marine food webs: insights from fatty acid analysis. *Ecological Monographs* 78: 591–613.

Thomas, T. A., S. Raborn, R. E. Elliott, and V. D. Moulton. 2016. Marine mammal aerial surveys in Eclipse Sound, Milne Inlet, and Pond Inlet, 1 August-17 September 2015. LGL Draft Report No. FA0059-2. Prepared by LGL Limited, King City, Ontario for Baffinland Iron Mines Corporation, Oakville, Ontario. 85 p. + appendices.

Thompson, D. W. J., and J. M. Wallace. 1998. The Arctic Oscillation signature in the wintertime geopotential height and temperature fields. *Geophysical Research Letters* 25: 1297–1300.

Thompson, Zadock. 1853. An account of some fossil bones found in Vermont. *American Journal of Science* 9(26): 256–263.

Tivy, A., S. E. L. Howell, B. Alt, S. McCourt, R. Chagnon, G. Crocker, T. Carrieres, and J. J. Yackel. 2011. Trends and variability in summer sea ice cover in the Canadian Arctic based on the Canadian Ice Service Digital Archive, 1960–2008 and 1968–2008. *Journal of Geophysical Research* 116 (C03007).

Tomilin, A.G., 1967. Mammals of the USSR and adjacent countries. vol. 9, Cetacea. *Israel Program for Scientific Translation* (1124).

Truth and Reconciliation Commission. 2015. *Canada's residential schools: the Inuit and northern experience.* The final report of the Truth and Reconciliation Commission of Canada, vol. 2. Montreal & Kingston: McGill-Queen's University Press.

Urata, S.M., 2014. *Evidence of positive selection in the mitochondrial cytochrome B gene of cetaceans.* University of California, San Diego.

Ursing, B. M., and U. Arnason. 1998. Analyses of mitochondrial genomes strongly support a hippopotamus-whale clade. *Proceedings of the Royal Society of London Series B: Biological Sciences* 265(1412): 2251–2255.

Vélez-Juarbe, J., and N. D. Pyenson. 2012. *Bohaskaia monodontoides*, a new monodontid (*Cetacea, Odontoceti, Delphinoidea*) from the Pliocene of the western North Atlantic Ocean. *Journal of Vertebrate Paleontology* 32(2): 476–484.

Vibe, C. 1967. *Arctic animals in relation to climatic fluctuations.* Meddelelser om Grønland 170(5). Copenhagen: C.A. Reitzels Forlag.

Watt, C. A., and S. H. Ferguson. 2011. Stable isotope and fatty acid analyses of samples from entrapped narwhals (*Monodon monoceros*). DFO, Canadian Scientific Advisory Secretariat Research Document 2010/134: iv + 12 p.

Watt, C. A., J. Orr, B. LeBlanc, P. Richard, and S. H. Ferguson. 2012. Satellite tracking of narwhals (*Monodon monoceros*) from Admiralty Inlet (2009) and Eclipse Sound (2010-2011). DFO, Canadian Scientific Advisory Secretariat Research Document 2012/046. iii + 17 p.

Watt, C. A., M. P. Heide-Jørgensen, and S. H. Ferguson. 2013. How adaptable are narwhal? A comparison of foraging patterns among the world's three narwhal populations. *Ecosphere* 4(6): 71.

Watt, C. A., and S. H. Ferguson. 2015. Fatty acids and stable isotopes (δ13C and δ15N) reveal temporal changes in narwhal *(Monodon monoceros)* diet linked to migration patterns. *Marine Mammal Science* 31: 21–44.

Watt, C. A., J. R. Orr, M. P. Heide-Jørgensen, N. H. Nielsen, and S. H. Ferguson. 2015a. Differences in dive behaviour among the world's three narwhal *(Monodon monoceros)* populations correspond with dietary differences. *Marine Ecology Progress Series* 525: 273–285.

Watt, C. A., S. D. Petersen, and S. H. Ferguson. 2015b. Genetics and fatty acids assist in deciphering narwhal (*Monodon monoceros*) social groupings. *Polar Biology* 38: 1971–1981.

Watt, C.A., J. R. Orr, and S. H. Ferguson. 2015c. A shift in foraging behaviour of beluga whales *(Delphinapterus leucas)* from the threatened Cumberland Sound population may reflect a changing Arctic food web. *Endangered Species Research* 31: 259–270. http://doi:10.3354/esr00768.

Watt, C. A., M. Marcoux., J. B. Dunn, R. Hodgson, R. Moore, and S. H. Ferguson. 2016a. Effect of the 2015 narwhal *(Monodon monoceros)* entrapment on the Eclipse Sound narwhal stock. Department of Fisheries and Oceans Canada, *Canadian Scientific Advisory Secretariat Research Document*. 2016/nnn. vi + xx p.

Watt, C. A., J. R. Orr, and S. H. Ferguson. 2016b. Spatial distribution of narwhal (*Monodon monoceros L.*) diving for Canadian populations helps identify important seasonal foraging areas. *Canadian Journal of Zoology*. (in press)

Wegmann, M., Y. Orsolini, M. Vázquez, L. Gimeno, R. Nieto, O. Bulygina, R. Jaiser, D. Handorf, A. Rinke, K. Dethloff, A. Sterin, and S. Brönnimann. 2015. Arctic moisture source for Eurasian snow cover variations in autumn, *Environmental Research Letters,* 10. http://doi:iopscience.iop.org/1748-9326/10/5/054015.

Wenzel, G. 1991. *Animal rights, human rights: ecology, economy, and ideology in the Canadian Arctic*. Toronto: University of Toronto Press.

Westdal, K. 2008. Movement and diving of northern Hudson Bay narwhals *(Monodon monoceros)*: relevance to stock assessment and hunt co-management. Masters of Science Thesis. Department of Environment and Geography, University of Manitoba, 103 p.

Westdal, K. H., J. W. Higdon, and S. H. Ferguson. 2013. Attitudes of Nunavut Inuit toward killer whales *(Orcinus orca)*. *Arctic* 66(3): 279–290.

Whitehead, H. 1998. Cultural selection and genetic diversity in matrilineal whales. *Science* 282: 1708–1711.

Winer, J. N., B. Arzi, D. M. Leale, and F. J. M. Verstraete. 2016. Dental and temporomandibular joint pathology of the walrus (*Odobenus rosmarus*). *Journal of Comparative Morphology* 155(2): 242-253.

Whitmore, F. C., Jr., and J. A. Kaltenbach. 2008. Neogene Cetacea of the Lee Creek Phosphate Mine, North Carolina. In C. E. Ray, D. J. Bohaska, I. A. Koretsky, L. W. Ward, and L. G. Barnes (eds.), *Geology and Paleontology of the Lee Creek Mine, North Carolina, IV*, pp. 181–269. Virginia Museum of Natural History Special Publication 14.

Wischnitzer, R. 1951. The Unicorn in Christian and Jewish Art. *Historia Judaica* 13: 141–156.

Yan, J., K. Zhou, and G. Yang, 2005. Molecular phylogenetics of 'river dolphins' and the baiji mitochondrial genome. *Molecular Phylogenetics and Evolution* 37: 743–750.

Zhang, X., R. Brown, L. Vincent, W. Skinner, Y. Feng, and E. Mekis. 2011. Canadian climate trends, 1950–2007. Canadian biodiversity: ecosystem status and trends 2010. Technical Thematic Report No. 5. Canadian Councils of Resource Ministers. Ottawa, ON. iv + 21 p. http://www.biodivcanada.ca/default.asp?lang=En&n=137E1147-0.

Zhang, X., J. He, J. Zhang, I. Polyakov, R. Gerdes, J. Inoue, and P. We. 2013. Enhanced poleward moisture transport and amplified northern high-latitude wetting trend. *Nature Climate Change* 3: 47–51. http://doi:10.1038/NCLIMATE1631.

Zhou, X., S. Xu, Y. Yang, K. Zhou, and G. Yang. 2011. Phylogenomic analysis and improved resolution of Cetartiodactyla. *Molecular Phylogenetics and Evolution* 61(2): 255–264.

Index

Page numbers in *italics* refer to figures.

acoustic environment, 170–72
Aelianus, Claudius, xx
air temperature, 138–40, *139*
Alaska pipeline, 143
albedo feedback, 138–39
al-Qazwini, Zakaria, 36
altruism, 173
AMAP. *See* Arctic Monitoring and
    Assessment Programme (AMAP)
amauti, 97
amphibians, 24
Amundsen, Roald, 95
ancestry tree. *See* phylogenetic tree
Angnatsiak, David, 131, *131*
angyi, 96
anthropogenic activities, 47, 50, 53, 120,
    151, 173
aquatic mammals, 78
archaeology, 106–7
Arctic Amplification, 138–39, 145
Arctic Council, 178
Arctic Monitoring and Assessment
    Programme (AMAP), 146
Arctic Oscillation, 135
aspartic acid racemization, 41
Avike, Rasmus, 128, 130–31, *130*
Baffinland Iron Mine, 120, 157–58, 161
balaenids, 8–9
balaenopterids, 9
baleen, 7, 8, 74
baleen whales. *See* mysticetes
barnacles, 14
Basilosaurus, 22, 23, *23*
beaked whales, 5, 59
beavers, 95
beluga whales, *13*, 27, 31, 59, 77, *85*, 152;
    compared to narwhals, 76–77; and
    mercury, 147
Berger Inquiry, 159

blowholes, 17–18, *17*. *See also* whales:
    respiratory system
blubber, 15–16, *15*. See also *maqtaaq*
Bohaska, Dave, *85*
Bohaskaia monodontoides, 84, *85*, 87
bowhead whales, 96, 171
breaching, 10, *10*
breathing holes. See *sapput*
Breydenbach, Bernhard, 37
Caesar, Julius, 33
callosities, 14
camels, 88
cetaceans. *See* dolphins; porpoises; whales
Cetartiodactyla, 75–76, 78
cetartiodactyl ancestor, 4, 8, 73, 78
classification: narwhals, 41, 71, 77–78; whales,
    xviii, 3–4, 5–7
climate change, xxvi–xxvii, 89, 120, 135–45,
    148–49, 154–55, 158, 173, 183
climate cycles, 89
Clyde River, 164, 167; seismic testing protest,
    157, *157*, 166–67
coastal erosion, 144
Cole, Steve, 173
contaminants. *See* pollution
cryosphere, 135
culture sharing, 28
Delphinoidea, 75–76
Denbola brachycephala, 87
dentin, 61–63, 65
diving, 21–23. *See also under* narwhals
DNA, 23, 80–81
dolphins, 6, *6*, 31; intelligence, 27–28;
    reproduction, 12
dugongs. *See* sea cows
echolocation, 19, 171; beluga whales, 77;
    narwhals, 19–20, 51, 52, 174. *See also*
    narwhals: directional beam
ecotourism. *See* tourism
entrapment, 46–47, 115, 127
Erik the Red, 135

Eskimos. See Greenland Inuit; Inuit
etymology: of "narwhal," 5, 41; of "whale," 5
evolution, 4, 23, 72, 80–81; of narwhals, 72, 74, 83, 88; preadaptation, 88; of whales, xix, 4, 18, 22, 23–24, 74–76, 74
Fable of the Ancients, 33
feeding methods: dolphins, 29; humpback whales, 29, 31; narwhals, xvii, xxii, 47–49, 51, 54, 54, 57, 150; orcas, 28; whales, 8–11, 9. *See also individual methods*
fin whales, 9
fish, 3, 24, 149, 150, 151, 165
fisheries, 109, 165, 165
fishing, 168, 169
Fleisher, Albert, 131, 131
food web, 49, 53, 150–52, 154, 174
fossils: beluga whales, 86; extinct whales, 87; marine mammals, 85, 86; narwhals, 85–86, 88
Frobisher, Martin, xx–xxi, 158
Frobisher's Mines, 159, 159
fur trade, 158
genome sequencing, 80–81. *See also* Narwhal Genome Initiative
Gesner, Conrad, 36, 37
global warming. *See* climate change
GPS tracking, 175
greenhouse gases, 135, 145, 154, 174
Greenland, 132–33, 135
Greenland Ice Sheet, 134, 135, 143, 145
Greenland Inuit, 115, 127, 146; clothing, 108; governance, 161; hunting equipment, 108, 109; and resource development, 161
grey whales, 13
grocery stores, 162–63, 163
Haruka, 23
Hildegard of Bingen, 36
hippopotamuses, 72–73
HTO. *See* Hunter and Trappers Organization (HTO)
human activities. *See* anthropogenic activities

human development. *See* anthropogenic activities
humpback whales, 10, 13, 14, 26, 31; song, 19, 19, 28; tail-prints, 26, 26
Hunter and Trappers Organization (HTO), 110
hunting strategies: floe edge, 111–13; ice leads, 114–15; open water, 113–14; sit and wait, 111
Hunt of the Unicorn, xvi
hydrodynamics, 55–57
ice: glacial, 142–43, 142; sea, 49, 136–38, 136, 137, 144, 148–49, 150, 154–55, 154, 155, 171, 174
ice ages, 89
ice wedges, 143
industrial development. *See* resource development
infrastructure, 166
intelligence, 27–31
Inughuit. *See* Greenland Inuit
Inuit, xx, xxiv–xxvi, 53; and climate change, xvii, 120, 144, 155; community, 98, 100–101; culture, 99–100, 116–18, 167, 169, 181–82; economy, 119, 161–66, 174; employment, 158, 161, 164; food, 98–100, 161–63; governance, 101, 102–3, 109, 159–60, 167; housing, 163; hunting, 95–97, 126, 144, 156, 161–63, 162, 181; life on the land, 98; modernization, xxv–xxvi, 161–62; and narwhal study, xxvi, 120, 123–31, 124, 125, 152–53, 181; navigation, 95; and resource development, 160–61, 169; and scientific study, 95–96, 99, 124, 167, 169, 171–72, 184; sharing, 116–18, 118, 162
Inuit Circumpolar Council, 155
Inuit Qaujimajatuqangiiqt (IQ), 94–97, 109, 110, 184
Inuit Tapiriit Kanatami, 166
Inuit traditional knowledge. *See* Inuit Qaujimajatuqangiiqt (IQ)
inuksuit, 93, 93
inuksuk, 176, 177, 186

Inurak, Charlie, 127, *128*
IQ. *See* Inuit Qaujimajatuqangiiqt (IQ)
Ittaq Heritage and Research Centre, 167
ivory, xx
Jakobshavn Glacier, *134*, 135
jet stream, 145
kayaks, *108*
killer whales. *See* orcas
Lady and the Unicorn, xvi, *xvi*
land claims, 159–60
land mammals, 78
Last Ice Area, 154–55
Little Ice Age, 89, 107
lunge-feeding, 9
Makeyev, V. M., 85
mammals, 3, 11, 12, 13, 24; marine
    adaptations, 14. *See also* aquatic mammals;
    land mammals; marine mammals
manatees. *See* sea cows
maqtaaq, 41, 112, 114, 116–18, *116*, *118*, 174
marine mammals, 54, 146; Arctic
    adaptations, 170
Marine Mammal Tag, 110
McInnis, Joe, 173
mercury, 146–47, *147*
molecular signals, 89
mysticetes, 7, *7*, 8; toothless, 74;
    vocalization, 18–19
narwhal (narwhals), *xv*, *38–39*, *53*, *64*, *76*, *79*,
    85; age, 41; Canadian vs. Greenlandic,
    126–27; capturing, 66–67, *66*; and climate
    change, xvii, 53, 89, 120, 150–53, 174, *178*;
    communication, 51–52; compared to beluga
    whales, 76–77; conservation, 53, 110, 153,
    155, 174–75; directional beam, 52, 120;
    distribution, 44–45, *44*, 105, 152; diving, xvi,
    49, *49*, *128*; DNA, xix, 70, 71–72, 79, 82–83,
    83; double-tusked, 42, *43*, 60–61; flukes, *55*,
    56–57; habitat, xxi–xxii, xxiii, 46, 150; in
    Inuit culture, xxiv, 41, 174; legends, xvi,
    xviii, xxiv, *xxiv*, 177; male-female
    differences, 42, 57–58, 60; and mercury,
    146; migration, *107*, 128, 136; molting, 128;

pods, 50–51; in popular culture, xv, 178, *178*;
    population, 127, 158; predators, 52; prey, 48,
    48, 120, 153; reproduction, 43; scientific
    study, xviii, *xix*, 40, 43, 45, 65, *65*, 68–69,
    68, *69*, *81*, 153, 175; sexual expression, 59;
    sexual selection, 42, 43; social behavior,
    50–51, 130–31; tracking, 45–46; tusk, xvi,
    xvii, xviii, 5–6, 20, 41, 42, *42*, 54, 58, 59–65,
    60, *62*, *63*, *69*, 78–79, *83*, *114*, 118–19, 126,
    174, 177; tusked females, 42, 60, 126, 130;
    vocalization, xvii, 51, 54, *54*
narwhal artifacts, *119*, *121*; carved tusk, 186,
    186; cup, *xxi*, xxvii; drinking tube, *109*;
    lance, *xxi*; Saqqaq container, xxiii;
    throne, xvi, *xvii*
Narwhal Genome Initiative, 82–83
narwhal hunting, xxiii–xxiv, *xxv*, 41, 90–91,
    109–18, *111*, *112*, *116*, *117*
National Museum of Natural History
    Narwhal exhibition, 177–87, *179*, *180*, *182*
natural gas, 144, 152, 157, 166
Nielsen, Pavia, 130, *130*
ningiqtuq. *See* Inuit: sharing
NIRB. *See* Nunavut Impact Review Board
    (NIRB)
NLCA. *See* Nunavut Land Claims Agreement
    (NLCA)
NMC. *See* Nunavut Marine Council (NMC)
noise pollution, 120, 170–72, *171*, 174. *See also*
    acoustic environment
non-quota limitations (NQLs), 109
North Atlantic Oscillation, 135
Northern Sea Route, 144–45
North Water Polynya, 136–37, 155
Northwest Passage, 144–45, 164–65
NPC. *See* Nunavut Planning Commission
    (NPC)
NQLs. *See* non-quota limitations (NQLs)
NTI. *See* Nunavut Tunngavik Incorporated
    (NTI)
Nunavut Coat of Arms, *101*, 103
Nunavut Impact Review Board (NIRB), 160
Nunavut Land Claims Agreement (NLCA), 160

Nunavut Mace, *101*, 102–3, *102*, *103*
Nunavut Marine Council (NMC), 160
Nunavut Planning Commission (NPC), 160
Nunavut Tunngavik Incorporated (NTI), 160
Nunavut Water Board (NWB), 160
Nunavut Wildlife Management Board
  (NWMB), 109, 160
Nutarak, Cornelius, *122*, 127, 129
NWB. *See* Nunavut Water Board (NWB)
NWMB. *See* Nunavut Wildlife Management
  Board (NWMB)
Obed, Natan, 166
Odobenocetops, xvii, 86, 87
odontocetes, 5–6, 8, 14, 59, 74; vocalization,
  19–20
oil, 120, 144, 152, 157, 158–59, 166, 174
orcas, *2*, *8*, 59, 158; in Inuit culture, 29, *29*,
  95–96; as narwhal predators, 52–53, 150,
  174
Palaeoeskimos, 106–7
Palluq, Teema, 167
passive acoustic monitoring (PAM), 54
Peeterloosie, Jayko, 129–30, *129*
permafrost, 143, 144–45
permafrost carbon feedback, 145
phylogenetics, 71–72, 75–76, 80
phylogenetic tree, 72, *72*, *73*, 75, *75*
Pikialasorsuaq Commission, 155
pilot whales, 146
pitch, 24–25
Planck effect, 140
play, 31
polar bears, 14, 52, *96*, 136, 155, *155*
polar desert, 140
pollution, 152, 165, 184. *See also* mercury
polynyas, 105, 136–37
Pomet, Pierre, 36–37
Pond Inlet, *xxv*, *92*, *93*, 167, 181–82
porpoises, 6, 12
precipitation, 140–41, 145
Qikiqtani Inuit Association (QIA), 160, 161
reindeer, 141
reptiles, 24

residential schools, 160
resource development, 158–61, 166–67,
  174–75, *175*. *See also under* Greenland Inuit;
  Inuit
Reuwich, Erhard, 37
right whales, 14
river discharge, 140–41
roll, 24–25
Ruben, Abraham, 177, 185–86, *185*
sapput, 114–15
Scandinavia, xx
sea cows, 13, 16
Sea-ice Monitoring and Real-Time
  Information for Coastal Environments
  (SmartICE), 167, 169
sea level rise, 143, 145
sea lions, 14
seals, 14
sea otters, 14
seismic testing, 120, 127, 152, 157, 166
self-awareness, 28
Shahnama (*Book of Kings*), *36*
shipping, 120, 144, 151, 157–58
sikujjausimajat. *See* entrapment
sister groups, 72, 75–76
skim-feeding, 8
skyhopping, xxii, *xxiii*; narwhals, *152*;
  orcas, *30*, *31*
SmartICE. *See* Sea-ice Monitoring and
  Real-Time Information for Coastal
  Environments (SmartICE)
Smithsonian Museum Support Center, *177*, 177
snow, 140–41
social complexity, 28
sperm whales, 31, 59
storm tracks, 140
strapped tooth whales, 59
Stuck, Hudson, 98
suction feeding, 8
TAHs. *See* total allowable harvest levels (TAHs)
taxonomy. *See* classification
temperature inversion, 139
Thule Culture people, 106–7

toothed whales. *See* odontocetes

total allowable harvest levels (TAHs), 109

tourism, 151, 164–65

tubercules, 14, *14*

Tunumiit. *See* Greenland Inuit

Unicorn at Fountain with Men and Animals,
  35, 35

Unicorn in Captivity, 32, 34

unicorns, xvi, 33–37, *34–35, 36*; in Christian
    belief, 34; in classical literature, 33–34;
    habitat, 37; health benefits, 34–37; in
    Hebrew scripture, 33

Vikings, xx

walruses, 14, 136, 144, *148*; hunting of, *94*

walrus-whales. See *Odobenocetops*

water cycle, 140–41

whale lice, 14

whales, 4; buoyancy, 21; circulatory system,
    16–17; communication, 19; digestive
    system, 8–11; DNA, 75–76, 80; fins, 25;
    flippers, 25–26, 73; flukes, 26, 55–56; hairs,
    13; hearing, 20–21, 171; intelligence, 26–31;
    metabolism, 23; migration, 15; movement,
    24–26; prey, 8; reproduction, 11–13, 15, 16;
    respiratory system, 17–18; sexing, 11;
    skeletal system, 23–25; thermoregulation,
    15–17; vocal system, 18–21. *See also*
    individual species

whale song, 19. *See also* humpback whales:
    song; whales: communication

whaling, 158

World Wildlife Fund (WWF), 154–55, 165, 174

yaw, 24–25

Credits

Adam, O., CNRS: 1.12
Bakry, Marcia: 1.6; 1.10
Berkeley-N. Pyenson: 1.6
Bradberry, W.: 1.3
British Museum, Wikipedia Commons: 0.10
Buell, Carl: 6.1
Burch, Judith Varney: 0.19
Camp Crazy Photography: 1.8
Clark, Chip: 1.13b; 1.13c
Clark, Christopher: 11.12
Cole, Dan: 0.2
Department of Fisheries and Oceans, Canada: 3.16
Di Loretto, James: 1.17; 8.4; 8.7b
Dietz, Rune: 10.7
Dorset Fine Arts: 0.0
Fish, Frank: 3.18; 3.19
Fitzhugh, William W.: 8.18; 10.1; 10.6; 11.4a,b; 11.8
Freund, Gretchen: 1.1; 1.16; 3.1; 3.14; 4.7; 4.11a; 4.11b
Gearheard, Shari: 8.15b
Getty Images: 0.16; 7.1
Gingerich et al. 2001: 5.4
Giuseppetti, A., NIST: 4.4
Greeninfo Network: 11.14
Gregory, A. John: 5.7
Groc, I.: 3.8; 4.8
Grønnow, Bjarne 1994: 232: 0.14
Hand, Kevin: 3.10; 3.13; 4.1; 4.5; 5.1; 5.10; 9.15
Hallendy, Norman: 7.2
Houston, Alice: 9.7
Johnson, Noor: 11.2; 11.3; 11.5; 11.6; 11.7
Kipling Gallery, Toronto: 12.9; 12.10
Laurin and Gauthier 2012: 5.2
Lee, David: 8.2
Loring, Eric: 8.11; 8.15a
Loring, Stephen: 0.15; 8.3; 8.5; 8.9; 10.9; 12.11

Marcoux, Marianne: 3.18
Meehan, Joseph: 0.8; 0.16; 1.20; 1.0; 3.3; 3.5; 3.15; 4.2; 4.3; 5.9; 7.6; 7.7; 7.8; 8.7a; 8.10; 8.16; 8.17; 9.1; 9.2; 9.3; 9.4; 9.6; 9.8; 9.9; 9.10; 9.11; 9.12; 9.13
Metropolitan Museum of Art: 2.1; 2.3; 2.4; 2.5; 2.6; 2.7
Milinkovitch et al. 1994: 5.6
Moeller, Kim: 0.1; 0.2; 12.6
Musée National du Moyen Âge, formerly Cluny Museum, Paris: 0.7
Nat'l Snow+Ice Data Center: 10.2; 10.3; 10.4; 10.5; 10.12
Navidim: 1.15
Nweeia, Martin: 11.13; 13.1
Nunavut Assembly: 7.9; 7.10
NY Jewish Theological Seminary: 2.2
Ohern, Robin: 8.8
Ovgaard, Bettina: 0.17
Owen, Richard: 6.4
Parrish, Mary: 1.2; 6.3
Peeters, Pamela: 9.7; 12.5; 12.7
Perkins, O.: 1.11
Pitman, R.: 1.19
Porsild, Morten 1918: 8.12
Rey, N.: 3.2
Richard, Wilfred: 0.5; 0.12; 10.0; 10.14; 11.1; 11.9; 11.10; 11.11; 13.0; 13.2
Ruben, Abraham Anghik: 12.1; 12.8
Saxgren, Henrik 7.0: 8.1; 8.14
Shooyook, Samuel: 13.1
Solhan, Christyna: 3.4; 12.2; 12.4
Smithsonian Archives: 1.13a
Smith. Nat'l. Anthr. Archive: 8.13
Smithsonian Natural History: 6.2
Strimmer, von Haeseler 1996: 5.3
Stroeve and Barrett, NSIDC: 10.12
Swank, S.: 12.12

Tundra Books: 12.3
Tunny, J.: 1.4
Velez-Juarbe: 6.2
Ward, Nathalie. NOAA: 1.14
Watt, C. et al. 2013: 3.6; 3.7; 10.10
Weather Underground: 10.13
Weiss, K.: 0.11
White, D: 3.11; 3.12
Wikipedia Commons: 1.5; 1.7; 1.9; 1.18
Williams, Glenn: 0.6; 0.13; 3.0; 3.9; 4.6; 5.8; 7.3; 7.4; 7.5; 10.8; 10.11
Wright, C.: 0.9; 4.9; 4.10

Acronyms

CNRS
Centre Nationale de la Recherche Scientifique (France)
DFO
Department of Fisheries and Oceans, Canada
IPI
International Polar Institute Press
MMA
Metropolitan Museum of Art
NMNH
National Museum of Natural History (Smithsonian Institution)
NOAA
U.S. National Oceanographic and Atmospheric Administration
NSIDC
U.S. National Snow and Ice Data Center
USNM
United States National Museum (used for catalog designation)